The Entire World of Early Developing Sounds™ Instructional Workbook

Shannon Collins, MA, CCC-SLP
Angie Sterling-Orth, MS, CCC-SLP

www.sayitright.org

Duplicating

All rights reserved. Permission is granted to the user to photocopy and make duplication masters of pages from this book in limited form for instructional or administrative use only. Reproduction of any kind is limited to the instructional or administrative use of a single user. If reproduction is needed by more than one educational instructor/user, then additional copies must be purchased. This book may not be reproduced in its entirety nor may it be reproduced or transmitted in any form or by any means, electronically, mechanically, including photocopying and recording, or by any information storage and retrieval systems, without written permission from the publisher.

ISBN 978-1-934701-05-8

© 2008 Say It Right™ All rights reserved.

Say It Right™
Tybee Island, Georgia
888-811-0759
www.sayitright.org

Printed in the United States of America

The Entire World of . . .™, The Entire World of Early Developing Sounds™ and Say It Right™ are trademarks of Say It Right™.

About the Authors

Angie Sterling-Orth, MS, CCC-SLP, received both her bachelor of science and master of science degrees in communication sciences and disorders from the University of Wisconsin—Eau Claire, in Eau Claire, Wisconsin. She has worked in the field of speech-language pathology in the public schools and then in product development at Thinking Publications. Since 2002 she has been an instructional academic staff member and clinical supervisor at UW–Eau Claire in communication sciences and disorders.

Shannon Collins, MA, CCC-SLP, received her bachelor of science in secondary education-communicative disorders from the University of Wisconsin-River Falls in River Falls, Wisconsin and master of arts degree in speech and hearing sciences from Washington State University in Spokane, Washington. She has worked in the field of speech-language pathology in the public schools in the states of Washington, Michigan, and Texas. Since 2001, she has been an instructional academic staff member and clinical supervisor at UW–Eau Claire in communication sciences and disorders.

Included
download & print

To access FREE downloadable copies of the exercises in this book
send an e-mail to:
downloads@sayitright.org

The subject line must read: **Early Developing Sounds**

Instructions will be sent on how to obtain your download.

For information on downloading the forms, copyrights and usage go to:
http://www.sayitright.org/product_downloads.html

Contents

Acknowledgments		ix
Introduction		1
Chapter 1	*Introduction to Early Developing Sounds*	3
Chapter 2	*Assessment*	9
Chapter 3	*Treatment*	13
	How to Use This Resource	16
	General Treatment Tips and Techniques	21
	"How To" Step-by-Step	30
Chapter 4	*Targeting P & B*	31
	P & B Screening Tool	32
	P & B Teaching Tips	33
	P & B Production Illustrations	34
	P & B Target Lists	35
	P & B Book Lists	39
	P & B Activities	41
	P & B Pictures	46
	P & B Patterns	54
	P & B Homework Pages	62
Chapter 5	*Targeting M & N*	69
	M & N Screening Tool	70
	M & N Teaching Tips	71
	M & N Production Illustrations	72
	M & N Target Lists	73
	M & N Book Lists	77
	M & N Activities	79
	M & N Pictures	84
	M & N Patterns	92
	M & N Homework Pages	96

Chapter 6	*Targeting K & G*	*105*
	K & G Screening Tool	106
	K & G Teaching Tips	107
	K & G Production Illustrations	108
	K & G Target Lists	109
	K & G Book Lists	113
	K & G Activities	115
	K & G Pictures	120
	K & G Patterns	128
	K & G Homework Pages	138
Chapter 7	*Targeting T & D*	*145*
	T & D Screening Tool	146
	T & D Teaching Tips	147
	T & D Production Illustrations	148
	T & D Target Lists	149
	T & D Book Lists	153
	T & D Activities	155
	T & D Pictures	160
	T & D Patterns	168
	T & D Homework Pages	176
Chapter 8	*Targeting F & V*	*185*
	F & V Screening Tool	186
	F & V Teaching Tips	187
	F & V Production Illustrations	188
	F & V Target Lists	189
	F & V Book Lists	193
	F & V Activities	195
	F & V Pictures	200
	F & V Patterns	208
	F & V Homework Pages	214

Chapter 9	*Targeting W & H*	*223*
	W & H Screening Tool	224
	W & H Teaching Tips	225
	W & H Production Illustrations	226
	W & H Target Lists	227
	W & H Book Lists	231
	W & H Activities	233
	W & H Pictures	236
	W & H Patterns	240
	W & H Homework Pages	242

Appendixes

Appendix A: General Activity Ideas	248
Appendix B: Parent Memo	250
Appendix C: Suggestions for Conversation and Carryover	251
Appendix D: Blank Card Pattern	253
Appendix E: Lesson Plan Format	254
Appendix F: Data Collection form	255

References   *257*

To Kris Retherford, our department chair and friend:
You inspire us and encourage our scholarly activity. You are our model.

To our "boys," Mike and John; and Braxton, Hutson, and Colin:
You inspire us to work hard and you reward us with your love and support.

SC & ASO

Introduction

Nothing brings a smile to a parent's face quicker than the sound of his or her infant or toddler experimenting with the production of sounds. It seems quite natural, yet miraculous at the same time, to hear a little one start to produce sounds. While the production of sound appears to be accidental, at first in the form of giggles, raspberries, and lip smacks, these random acts start to progress into intentional speech sounds very quickly as a child reaches one year of age. Soon, even very young children are stringing sounds together to form those wonderful first words. However automatic these early stages seem to be, development of early developing sounds should not be taken for granted.

Difficulty with the development of early developing sounds can result from of a wide range of situations and conditions. Speech-language pathologists (SLPs) have always identified and provided remediation to children who struggle with the development of speech sounds but much of our efforts has been on the later developing and harder to produce sounds. With advances in medicine, medical technology, and health care in general, an increasing number of infants are surviving stressful pregnancies, traumatic deliveries, and early and severe health conditions. Oftentimes, these circumstances result in side effects, one of which can be a delay or disruption in the development of speech sounds. The need now exists to emphasize early developing sounds.

The Entire World of Early Developing Sounds™ Instructional Workbook is a comprehensive and flexible tool for targeting speech sounds that typically develop for children between 12 months and four years of age. These sounds include: /k/ and /g/, /f/ and /v/, /t/ and /d/, /w/ and /h/, /p/ and /b/, and /m/ and /n/. This resource is a follow-up to the very popular *"Entire World of™..."* series which includes workbooks, games, and card sets for later developing sounds (such as variations of the /r/ phoneme and affricates /ch/ and /j/).

The first half of this resource presents an introduction to early developing sounds, discusses evaluation issues and provides suggestions for where to begin treatment, and details how to use this resource. The second half contains the early developing sounds "Treatment Guides." A unit for each of the six pairs of targeted sounds is included. Each unit contains:

- ▶ A Screening Tool
- ▶ Teaching Tips
- ▶ Production Illustrations
- ▶ Target Lists (for words, phrases, and sentences)

- ▶ Book Lists
- ▶ Activities
- ▶ Pictures (for use in preparing cards for production practice)
- ▶ Patterns (for use in the activities)
- ▶ Homework Pages (for parents or caregivers to provide extra practice in other environments)

This resource was created for SLPs in all types of work settings, including schools, home-based programs, or clinical settings. The easy-to-use tools and suggestions, along with the comprehensive focus on early developing sounds will make this a tool you reach for time and time again.

We hope you enjoy.

Shannon Collins
Angie Sterling-Orth

Chapter 1
Introduction to Early Developing Sounds

The development of speech is a complicated and intricate process. Speech development is intertwined with the development of other systems and domains such as language, cognition, motor skills, and literacy skills. While it is beyond the scope and purpose of this resource to discuss the development of speech in great detail, a basic understanding of the acquisition of early developing sounds will be helpful. Both speech perception and speech production are critical during the first years of acquisition of spoken communication.

Speech Perception

Though the production of intentional speech sounds and the use of first words can seem to develop overnight, the acquisition of speech is a gradual process. Even prior to an infant's first use of sounds, the stage of speech perception is critical. Research has shown that humans are "wired" to attend to speech sounds and, more specifically, infants can detect minimal contrasts between pairs of speech sounds (Eimas, Siqueland, Jusczyk, & Vigorito, 1971). During the first year of life, infants move through the critical stage of speech perception, learning from the environment so that when the motor-speech mechanism and cognition have reached a necessary level of development, first words can be spoken with intact early developing sounds.

Speech Production

Early development of speech is highly guided by the infant's speech production mechanism (i.e., structures of respiration, phonation,

Chapter 1–Introduction

resonation, and articulation). Vowel productions begin prior to the use of consonant sounds. Generation of vowel sounds requires little attention to specific articulatory moves. When crying, yawning, and during other pre-speech vocal play, very young children produce a wide range of vowel sounds both intentionally and accidentally. At around 12 months of age, a child's speech mechanism becomes ready for the production of consonant sounds. Table 1 summarizes Stoel-Gammon and Dunn's (1985) description of the early acquisition of speech.

Table 1: Acquisition of Speech

Stage	Age	Hallmarks
Prelinguistic Stage	1 month-18 months	• Speech-like and nonspeech productions
First Words	1 year-18 months	• Simple syllable shapes (CV, CVC, CVCV) • Production of stops (/k/ and /g/, /t/ and /d/, /p/ and /b/) • Production of nasals (/m/ and /n/) • Production of glides (/w/ and /j/)
Phonemic Development	18 months-4 years	• Consonant clusters appear • Multisyllabic shapes emerge • Substitutions for later developing sounds are common
Stabilization of the Phonological System	4 years-8 years	• Remaining sound classes develop (stridents, affricates, liquids) • Reading and writing contribute to refinement to the speech system

Source: Stoel-Gammon & Dunn (1985)

Disordered Speech

Most children progress through the early stages of speech and language acquisition. However, the development of speech sounds can be delayed or interrupted by a variety of circumstances. Parents, health care providers, and day-care providers may become aware that a child's speech sound use is atypical for the child's age, even when a child is very young. However, many errors of speech

Introduction

sound use are considered "developmental" in nature and within normal limits for a child's age. Differentiating between typical and delayed speech sound use falls within the unique scope of practice of a speech-language pathologist.

The American Speech-Language-Hearing Association (2008) provides the following distinctions:

> ***Speech sound disorder***—problems with *articulation* and/ or *phonology* that result in mistakes in a child's use of speech to produce words.
>
> ***Articulation disorder***—problems producing specific age-expected speech sounds. Sounds can be distorted, deleted, or added.
>
> ***Phonological process disorder***—patterns of sound errors in a child's speech repertoire.

A ***delay*** in speech development suggests a child is moving along in an expected sequence, but behind the typical age-expected timeline. A ***disorder*** implies deviation from typical development.

When observing a child's speech repertoire, one of two perspectives for description can be used. A phoneme-based perspective notes the speech sounds a child produces or is lacking. Table 2 shows a commonly accepted order of acquisition of speech sounds for spoken English.

Table 2: Acquisition of Speech Sounds

Age	Speech-Sound Acquisition
12 – 18 months	Vowels develop
18 – 24 months	/m, n, h, w, p, b, t, d/
2 – 3 years	/k, g, f, v, ʃ/
3 – 4 years	/s, z, dʒ, tʃ/ Consonant clusters develop
4 – 5 years+	/l, r, θ, ð/

Source: Hodson (1997)

Chapter 1–Introduction

A different model is one that looks at broad phonological patterns or processes. **Phonological processes** are those patterns of production being used by children to simplify or minimize the expected, adult-like patterns of speech. For example, the phonological process of *fronting* results in a child saying "tap" for "cap," whereby the /k/ in "cap" is a fronted velar produced as a /t/ at the front of the mouth. Individuals taking a phonological process approach look at development and disorder by indicating the ages at which specific phonological processes should be suppressed, thereby allowing accurate and adult-like forms of production of speech sound classes to be used. Table 3 shows Grunwell's (1987) suggestion of the progression of the suppression of phonological processes for spoken English.

Table 3: Suppression of Phonological Processes

Phonological Process	Example	Age of Suppression
Weak Syllable Deletion	*puter* for computer	2 to 3½ years of age
Final Consonant Deletion	*daw* for dog	2 to 3 years of age
Reduplication	*buhbuh* for bubbles	2 to 2½ years of age
Cluster Reduction	*top* for stop	2½ to 4 years of age
Stopping	*tee* for three, *do* for zoo, *two* for shoe	2½ to 4½ years of age
Fronting	*dat* for cat	2½ to 3 years of age
Gliding	*wing* for ring	3 to 6 years of age

Source: Grunwell (1987)

Developmental norms for ages of acquisition of speech sound use and ages of suppression for phonological processes help professionals better understand the presence, absence, or at-risk nature of speech.

Clearly, speech sound disorders result in compromised intelligibility of a person's spoken communication. Though different children may present similar error patterns, causes of disorder vary considerably. Some of the more common causes for speech sound disorders include, but are not limited to:

- Recurrent middle ear infection (otitis media with effusion)
- Hearing loss or deafness
- Cleft palate
- Developmental apraxia of speech
- Cerebral palsy
- Acquired traumatic brain injury
- Cognitive delay
- Developmental articulation or phonological disorder (not otherwise specified)

Regardless of cause, the need for services to remediate a speech sound disorder include a comprehensive assessment. Assessment determines the presence of a speech sound disorder and leads to a comprehensive treatment program.

Chapter 2
Assessment

The purpose of assessment should be considered as the evaluation is planned. One purpose of assessment is to determine the presence or absence of a disorder. When assessment is being conducted for this purpose, it is often linked to determination of eligibility and funding for services. When assessing children suspected of a speech sound disorder, determination of needs and priorities of treatment targets is also the focus of assessment. Not only is it important to know what is lacking or deviant in a child's speech repertoire, it is also critical to know what skills the child possesses. Strengths, needs, and challenges can be determined during a well-planned, comprehensive assessment and can guide treatment.

Assessment Procedures

Case History Information Collection

Pertinent medical, educational, and psychological information should be gathered. A customized case history form can be created and used for this process. In addition, commercially available tools that include survey and interview guides are available and can be completed with or by parents and other caregivers to collect background information. Ideally, case history information will be acquired prior to the actual testing. This way testing and further information gathering can take background information into account (for example, using toys of particular interest to a child to gather a speech sample).

Hearing Evaluation

Regardless of the child's age, appropriate procedures should be used to determine hearing status. For many children 3 to 6 years of age, this will include a pure-tone air conduction screening. For younger children, or those with delayed cognition, hearing screening meth-

Chapter 2 – Assessment

ods that do not require behavioral responding might be necessary. Tympanometry along with otoacoustic emissions testing (OMEs) can be useful. As another option, sound-field testing can make a general suggestion regarding hearing status. While speech-language pathologists can usually administer hearing screening procedures with ease, for younger or more challenging children, the assistance of an audiologist might be necessary. It is important to understand a child's hearing status prior to the start of treatment and regardless of the treatment approach being used.

Oral-Mechanism Exam

Some speech disorders are a direct result of an insufficient oral mechanism (e.g., cleft palate, velocardiofacial syndrome, etc.). Other children may not have specific or diagnosed oral mechanism insufficiency, but may lack some strength or coordination needed to support age-expected speech. Formal and commercially available tools can be used to guide an oral-mechanism exam. The speech-language pathologist should conduct an oral-mechanism examination as part of a comprehensive speech assessment.

Speech Testing

Most speech-language pathologists are quite used to using formal and standardized tests for determining the presence or absence of a disorder. Speech sound use can certainly be assessed with, at least in part, the use of a specific test. A multitude of tests exist for this purpose. For the most part, specific tests follow a particular assessment approach (e.g., phoneme-based approach versus a phonological process or pattern approach). Regardless of the approach a speech-language pathologist takes, certain variables must be considered and incorporated into the assessment process.

Single Words—Most commercially available tests use a child's production of single words to gather a speech sample for analysis. Single-word, elicited samples allow all sounds to be obtained, provide a context for comparison, and usually allow the calculation of a score that can align with eligibility, funding, and accountability purposes. Table 4 presents a sampling of commercially available tests for gathering an elicited speech sample at the single-word level. For a complete listing of articulation and phonology assessment tools, refer to Williams (2003).

Assessment

Table 4: A Sampling of Commerically Available Speech Assessment Tools

Test	Publisher Information	Appropriate Ages	Approach
PAT-3: Photo Articulation Test-3rd Edition (PAT-3) Barbara Lippke, Stanley Dickey, John Selmar and Anton Soder.	Pro-Ed	3–9 years	Phoneme-based
Goldman-Fristoe Test of Articulation 2nd Edition (GFTA-2)—Ronald Goldman and Maclayne Fristoe	Pearson	2–21 years	Phoneme-based
Hodson Assessment of Phonological Patterns 3rd Edition (HAPP-3)—Barbara Hodson	Pro-Ed	2–8 years	Phonological process-based
Kahn-Lewis Phonological Analysis 2nd Edition (KLPT-2)—Linda Kahn and Nancy Lewis	Pro-Ed	2–21 years	Phonological process-based

Conversational Speech—Not only should a single-word level of responding be analyzed, but a sampling of a child's conversational speech should be obtained. Since children are faced with connected speech in communicative contexts on a daily basis, that level of responding must be reviewed in a comprehensive assessment. A speech sample should be gathered using developmentally appropriate materials and methods. Ideally, a child will be engaged in communication with a parent or caregiver, or observed communicating in an actual classroom situation. Gathering the most natural and representative sample of a child's connected speech is desired. The speech sample can be analyzed for errors and error patterns and compared to the elicited single-word sample for consistencies and discrepancies. Furthermore, the conversational speech can be used to calculate percent of intelligibility.

Chapter 2 – Assessment

Intelligibility—*Intelligibility* refers to the degree to which (usually in the form of a percentage) a child is understood by others in connected speech. Some formal speech assessment tools include procedures to measure and judge intelligibility. Informal procedures can also be used (see Watson, Murthy, and Wadhwa, 2003). A variety of guides for intelligibility exist. One such general guide of typical expectations of rates of intelligibility by age is displayed in Table 5.

Table 5: Rates of Speech Intelligibility

Age	Degree of Intelligibility to Strangers
1 year	25%
2 years	50%
3 years	75%
4 years	100%

Source: Coplan & Gleason (1988)

Keep in mind the familiarity of the listener, the context, and many other factors feed into the degree of intelligibility.

Stimulability—*Stimulability* refers to the degree to which accurate productions from a child can be facilitated, or "stimulated" (Hodson, 2007). Stimulability testing is sometimes included as a part of a commercially available formal assessment. However, clinician-directed procedures can be easily generated and conducted. To judge stimulability, increase or decrease the amount of support as the child is directed to produce a sound. Figure 1 is a continuum of support to consider.

Phoneme or pattern selection is often based upon the degree of stimulability of a phoneme. Furthermore, treatment techniques that are well-matched to a particular child (e.g., such as use of a direct model) can be discovered during stimulability testing or probing.

Figure 1

Least Challenging
Direct Model—Sound in Isolation
No Model—Sound in Isolation
Direct Model—Word
No Model—Word
Direct Model—Sentence
No Model—Sentence
Connected Speech
Most Challenging

Chapter 3
Treatment

For many of the children evaluated, a clear need will be present. Certain settings, such as the school setting, will have established eligibility criteria that need to be met in order for services to be provided. This will vary from agency-to-agency, state-to-state, and district-to-district. For children requiring intervention, an intervention plan is developed and selection of treatment targets begins. It is imperative that a purposeful and intentional process be followed as treatment planning is conducted. The treatment program should be comprehensive, well-documented, and include evidence-based practices (Hodson, 2007). There are several approaches to treatment that can be considered.

Treatment Approaches Compared

The profession of speech-language pathology has evolved for decades. Through the years, a multitude of treatment strategies and approaches have been used to target speech sound use. Table 6 on pages 14-15, graphically provides a comparison of several treatment approaches.

Chapter 3 – Treatment

Table 6 : Comparison of Treatment Approaches

Approach	Target Selection	Instructional Strategies	Production Practice
Phoneme-Based Approaches (Fairbanks, 1960; Van Riper, 1939)	• Choose specific phonemes in error • Consider "readiness" or stimulability • Target sound-by-sound • Consider word positions for target sounds • Reach mastery (90% success) for each sound in each position in words in conversation before moving to next sound	• Placement cues • Models and diagrams of the speech mechanism used to show placement • Direct clinician model for demonstration purposes • Overt and explicit discussion of sounds in error and use/misuse of the targets • Negative model used to compare to desired production	• Mass practice of targets is key to treatment • Hierarchy of responding is used to increase level of challenge when desired percentage of accuracy is achieved (e.g., sound in isolation; then in single words, phrases, sentences, and connected speech) • Specific and direct feedback given after practice attempts
Contrast Approaches (Williams, 2003; Gierut, 1989)	• Minimal contrast pairs for errors (i.e., word pairs that differ by just one phoneme are targeted simultaneously) • Maximal oppositions are selected for treatment (i.e., sound in error along with a sound that is maximally different from the sound in error are targeted in pairs) • Multiple oppositions (i.e., several words are targeted that differ by just one phoneme from a word containing an error)	• Direct clinician model for demonstration purposes • Discrimination work when stimulability is reduced	• Mass practice of word pairs or sets • Practice includes the target word plus the comparison word(s) (i.e., minimal, maximal, and multiple opposition work)

Comparison of Treatment Approaches

Approach	Target Selection	Instructional Strategies	Production Practice
Phonological Process Approach (Hodson, 2007)	• "Cycles" are created based on omissions and deficiencies of speech patterns • Exemplar phonemes from each selected pattern are targeted • "Readiness" or stimulability considered when targets are selected	• Focused auditory stimulation and bombardment of the target pattern • Direct models to draw child's attention to targets • Experiential play activities designed to create context that naturally bombards with targets	• Minimization of negative practice is key • Confrontational naming activities designed to create context that naturally elicit accurate use of targets • Phonological awareness work pairing speech perception with speech production
Hybrid Approach	• Target phonemes based on developmental appropriateness in addition to stimulability • Establish "cycles" based on all needed targets	• Focused auditory stimulation via bombardment • Direct models and explicit placement instruction to draw awareness and attention to targeted skills • Experiential play activities designed to bombard with targets • Discrimination work when stimulability is lacking • Specific, direct, and immediate feedback provided in a developmentally appropriate manner	• Confrontational naming activities designed to facilitate accurate mass practice of targets • Minimal pairs practice to connect discrimination work with speech practice • Phonological awareness development

Chapter 3 – Treatment

More recently, three major approaches have been described (Hodson, 2007). Table 6 highlights each of these approaches in addition to a "hybrid" approach that is suggested for use in this resource.

Co-occurring Conditions

It should come as no surprise that children who exhibit articulation and phonological disorders will often have co-occurring conditions that exacerbate and/or parallel difficulty with speech sound use. Some children with disordered phonology present with a fluency disorder. Many children with reduced intelligibility also demonstrate expressive and receptive language challenges. Children with all types of cognitive delays may also demonstrate challenges with speech. Regardless of the combination of factors, attention to co-occurring conditions should be carefully considered during intervention planning.

Choices made during treatment planning should consider the perspective of teachers, parents, and other service providers. Level of motivation and attention of the child should also play a significant role when deciding what to target and how to handle coexisting factors. The accommodating and flexible nature of phonological intervention makes it easy to address in intervention other areas of communication (e.g., fluency, expressive and receptive language). For example, for a child who stutters, phrase-level responding that encourages fluency can be used during production practice of speech sounds. As another example, for a child with a receptive language disorder, attention to word meanings and category names and members can be selected based on phonological patterns being targeted.

How to Use This Resource

Regardless of one's treatment approach, *The Entire World of Early Developing Sounds*™ provides a framework and materials for remediating early developing sounds. Six units provide Treatment Guides for each of these early developing sounds:

- Initial and final /p/ and /b/ (beginning on page 31)
- Initial and final /m/ and /n/ (beginning on page 69)
- Initial and final /k/ and /g/ (beginning on page 105)
- Initial and final /t/ and /d/ (beginning on page 145)

How to Use This Resource

▸ Initial and final /f/ and /v/ (beginning on page 185)

▸ Initial /w/ and /h/ (beginning on page 223)

Not only are twelve specific sounds addressed in this resource, the following tools are provided within each unit.

Screening Tool

A one-page Screening Tool is provided in each unit. Although screening is typically used to determine whether further assessment is required, in this resource the screening tool serves as a probe for determining if the child is stimulable for the sound at the following levels: isolation, single-word, phrase, and sentence. Use this form to check for stimulability, to experiment with elicitation techniques, to determine level of practice for treatment activities, and to monitor progress. Present the target sound by modeling it and having the child imitate it or by using picture cards as prompts. The pictures for use with the screening tool are also provided for duplication within the unit. Here are the specific steps for administering the Screening Tool.

1. Using assessment information from a formal assessment measure, choose the Screening Tool based on the specific sounds the child had in error.

2. Determine if the child can produce the sound in isolation. Have the child imitate your production of the speech sound in isolation (e.g., "say mmmmm" to facilitate the /m/ sound). You may need to encourage the child to watch your mouth or use a mirror as he or she imitates the sound in isolation.

3. Duplicate the pictures provided in the unit (onto heavy stock paper if desired) and cut them apart. To determine if the child can produce the sound in words, phrases, and sentences, have the child name the pictures and/or use them in a phrase or sentence. If the child is unfamiliar with the picture, use a delayed imitation format to encourage production. For example, say, "This is a mouse. It eats cheese. What is this? It's a _____." If the child still is unsure of the item, ask the child to say it after you say it and indicate on the screening form that this was done in direct imitation.

Note: Depending on the child's level of success with the target

Chapter 3 – Treatment

sound at the single-word level, administer the phrase- and sentence-level productions. Most children working on early developing sounds are not readers and will need to imitate your productions in these contexts. However, children with a structural deficit due to cleft lip and/or palate may be readers and, if so, can simply read the phrases and sentences provided in the screening form.

4. Determine where to start based on the child's ability to produce the sound at these various levels. Write goals and objectives based on the child's productions, which will serve as benchmarks to measure progress.

There may be occasions when a child's behavior may interfere with this probing procedure. When this occurs, use the picture cards you have created (or use real objects) and place them in a bucket filled with beans or rice or tape them on the wall. The probes can be play-based as the child discovers the items/pictures in the bucket or on the wall and names them.

Teaching Tips

Once a target is determined appropriate for treatment, suggestions are offered on the Teaching Tips page. Basic developmental information is provided, followed by notes related to the production process for the phoneme. In addition, suggestions for stimulating accurate production of the phoneme are described.

Production Illustrations

Each unit includes a mouth diagram with placement cues. This illustration can be duplicated and used during treatment activities, especially with older children (ages 4 and up), to show placement of the articulators.

Target Lists

For each pair of phonemes in this resource, target lists are provided. Lists for single words, phrases, and sentences are included. Care has been taken to choose those words that have facilitative contexts for correct production of the target phonemes. For example, when initial /k/ is the target, words that provide a challenge such as *cookie* and *cake* are not included since they include an initial /k/ and a final /k/. Furthermore, multisyllabic words are avoided, as longer words tend to provide unnecessary challenge when working on early developing sounds. When a more challenging context is needed

How to Use This Resource

to facilitate generalization of new phonological skills, phrase and sentence levels should be used.

Since only single-syllable words are provided in this resource, the medial position is not targeted. This decision is based on the premise that children, regardless of age, who need remediation for early developing sounds, have complicated and significantly compromised phonological systems and/or clear structural deficits. The medial position is not a facilitating context for early work on a target sound. Furthermore, once the initial and final positions emerge and are mastered, the medial word position may be facilitated (Elbert, Dinnsen, & Powell, 1984; Elbert, Powell, & Swartzlander, 1991; Kent, 1982). However, if attention to medial position is needed, use word-initial and word-final targets in phrase or sentence contexts (e.g., "*The cup is broken,*" which creates a medial /p/ context; "*See the funny bear,*" which creates a medial /b/ context). When planning activities for younger children, refer to these lists of to get ideas for target words. When working with older children (ages 4 and up), the word, phrase, and sentence lists may be useful as stimulus items to elicit mass production practice. If using the phrases and sentences with nonreaders, direct imitation (i.e., saying the phrase or sentence as a model and then having the child repeat it) or delayed imitation (i.e., having a short delay inserted) will be necessary. Ideally, you will want to elicit production of phrases and sentences naturally from children during structured and unstructured treatment activities. This would prevent the phrase and sentence lists provided from needing to be used. The activities provided within each unit were specifically designed with this goal in mind.

Title	Publication Info
Peek-A-Boo!	Janet & Allan Ahlberg (1981) Puffin Books
Pete's a Pizza	William Steig (1998) Joanna Colter
If You Give a Pig a Pancake	Laura Numeroff (1998) Harper Collins
Pig in the Pond	Martin Waddell (1996) Candlewick
Do Pigs Have Stripes?	Melanie Walsh (1996) Houghton Mifflin
Pickin' Peas	Margaret Read MacDonald (1998) HarperCollins
Pig Goes to Camp	David McPhail (1985) Scholastic

Book Lists

Suggested children's books that are filled with words containing the target phonemes are provided. Publisher information, suggested age range, and target words that can be found within each book are outlined. Refer to these Book Lists when looking for a book to include during a treatment session. Books can be useful when working with young children as they provide a natural and motivating context for focused auditory input (bombardment). Books can also be useful when working with older children at the conversational level of practice. Older students who can read can work on accurate use of target sounds in connected speech as they read a book selected from the Book Lists. The use of children's literature is critical when

Chapter 3 – Treatment

targeting literacy, language development, and increased intelligibility (Hoffman, 1992; Montgomery, 1992; Norris & Hoffman, 1993).

Activities

The activities provided are of two types. Within the units, activities are phoneme-specific. These activities describe experiential play activities, usually centered around a theme, based on a target phoneme in either the initial or final position. The activities are motivating and purposeful for children 2 to 4 years of age and include snack ideas, craft activities, motor activities, and song or finger plays. In addition, **Appendix A: General Activity Ideas** describes quick and fun activities that are not phoneme-specific. They are great for children of all ages, but are especially useful for mass practice of phonemes for children ages 4 and up.

Pictures

For each unit, 12 reproducible pictures, based on the target word list, are provided. The pictures can be reproduced, cut part, and then laminated to create picture cards for use in production practice and with the activities.

Patterns

Some activities require the use of patterns to complete the activities. All patterns are provided for duplication.

Homework Pages

Homework pages that can be duplicated and sent home to encourage additional practice in alternate settings are included. The homework pages provide families and other care providers (e.g., daycare teachers, early childhood teachers, preschool teachers, grandparents, etc.) with information regarding the skill being targeted and progress being made in treatment. Research suggests that increased successful practice opportunities

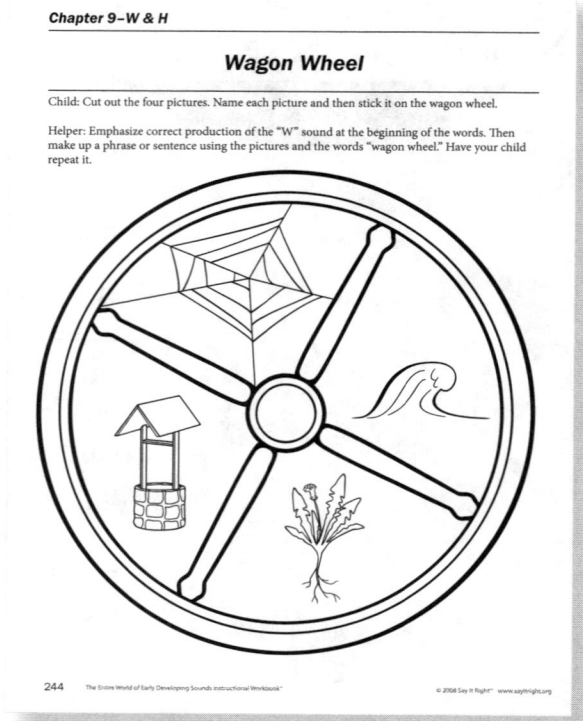

How to Use This Resource

and structured exposure to targets can facilitate the development and generalization of skills (Broen, Doyle, & Bacon, 1993; Shelton, Johnson, & Arndt, 1972). A reproducible memo is included in **Appendix B: Parent Memo**. It provides friendly and clear directions and general guidance for use of the homework pages that are selected and sent home with students. Duplicate, add comments, and include the memo with the homework activities.

Other Resources

The desired goal of treatment is correct production of all sounds in conversational speech. So many children reach a high degree of success during production-practice activities at the word, phrase, and sentence levels, but then struggle with generalization of newly acquired skills into conversation (Bankson & Byrne, 1972; Shriberg & Kwiatkowski, 1990). McReynolds (1987) determined that two important factors greatly influence generalization to conversation—external environmental factors and internal within-child factors. Specifically, McReynolds' (1987) and Ertmer and Ertmer's (1998) recommendations for facilitating generalization of phonology have been incorporated within *Appendix C: Suggestions for Conversation and Carryover*.

Another useful resource provided is Appendix D. *Appendix D: Blank Card Pattern* provides a template for creating cards with other words you would like to customize for the child.

General Treatment Tips and Techniques

It is true that when developing a child's phonology, SLPs should have a clear, logical plan. However, when working with young children, the best-made plans can be challenging to implement. The following suggestions and ideas provide guidance:

1. Use **direct imitation** as a primary treatment technique. To help children avoid negative practice (i.e., practicing target words repeatedly with errored production attempts), pair the direct verbal model, as often as needed, to elicit accurate production. The direct model can be used for any level of intervention and is sometimes necessary to set the pattern for phrase and sentence productions from children. To use the direct imitation technique, provide a model and have the child repeat it. For example, the clinician would say, "The glass is blue," and the student would respond, "The glass is blue."

"Tell me cup. Your turn now."

"Cup."

Chapter 3 – Treatment

Using direct imitation before the child's practice attempt can be powerful. However, be sure to fade the direct model, as soon as possible.

2. ***Placement cuing*** can be powerful for some children. Use the mouth diagrams provided in each unit to help children visualize where the tongue and lips are during production of a target sound. This is often most successful with children over 4 years of age, but can be tried with children between 3 and 4. Give the mouth parts fun names and use age-appropriate direction. For example: "When we make our /ssssss/, think of a snake. Your tongue is the snake and your mouth is the cage. Hiss the air from on top of your tongue but don't let the snake sneak out of the cage."

3. Once a child is stimulable for a target, mass practice can solidify the accurate production pattern. **Mass practice** refers to having a child produce numerous productions of a target. For children between 3 and 4 years of age, elicit at least 6 successful practice moments during a minute of a treatment session. For older children, aim to elicit a dozen or more practice items per minute of activity. Of course, there will be moments of each session that will be spent on different tasks, but during a strategic speech practice activity, keep mass practice as high as possible without frustrating or tiring the child.

4. When working on ***voicing contrasts***, take advantage of tactile feedback by having children feel the neck region (yours or their own). Help them pair voiced and voiceless sound combinations as they feel the difference between "voice on" and "voice off."

5. ***Play-based therapy*** is often the most developmentally appropriate approach, even for speech sound development, and especially for children under the age of 3 or 4 years. Refer to the Activities included within each unit for play-based ideas. An excessive amount of accurate production models of the targets should be inserted throughout the play. These productions are referred to as bombardment. Bombardment of the target phoneme allows the younger child to hear many successful productions and saturates the activity with a phonological focus. Respond to the development level of each child when determining the need for a play-based approach. Accurate production from the child

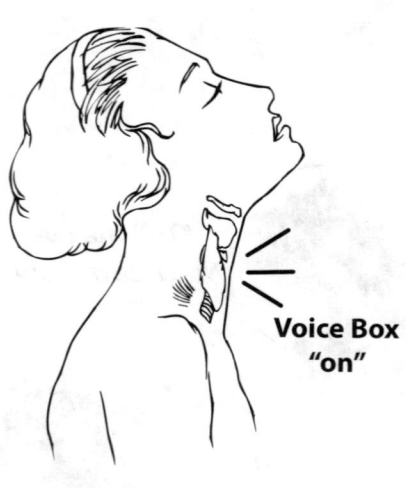

Voice Box "on"

How to Use This Resource

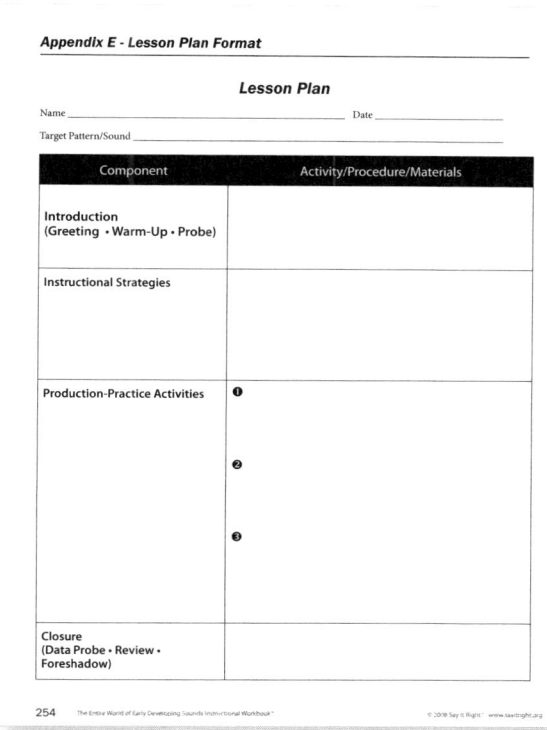

can be elicited naturally during this carefully planned playtime.

6. ***Lesson planning*** should not be dismissed, even for an experienced clinician. A blank format is provided for your use in **Appendix E: Lesson Plan Format.** This guide will help you shape your lesson planning. Keep in mind that every session, even a brief, 20-minute session, can and should include the following four components.

✓ **Introduction**—The Introduction to a treatment session should include one or more (possibly all) of the following:

- Greeting
- Review—Talk about the last session's targets and/or activities and any homework the client completed during the time between sessions.
- Preparatory Set—Help the child understand the current session's target(s). This is a direct instruction principle that enables the child to be aware of his or her goals so that treatment activities have more meaning. This might be a part of the review phase and/or it might include providing new information. This element may be extremely subtle, or even absent, for children who are very young (i.e., discussing the goals may have little or no meaning to the child). The preparatory set may include discussing the schedule for the session and discussing the importance of each activity scheduled.
- Warm Up—A warm-up exercise may be useful for children of all ages. This is the final phase of the Introduction and can be thought of as a quick exercise for the brain. A warm-up activity is designed merely to get the child listening and thinking carefully, and ready to work.

✓ **Instruction**—For many children, instruction is the key component of the lesson plan since they might need exposure to the skill that is lacking. Instruction may take various forms depending on the child, the stage of treatment, and a host of other variables. Be certain to fill your sessions with plenty of instruction, rather than simply drilling or testing the child continuously. The following ideas provide just a sampling of types of instruction:

Chapter 3 – Treatment

- Direct Instruction—This is the most overt way to provide instruction to a child. Typically direct instruction is used with older students and adults, but it's also effective with elementary-age students. Direct instruction is exactly what the term implies—directly teaching the client the skill being targeted.

- Bombardment—A wonderful way to target communication skills, especially with young children. Bombardment of the target means to fill an activity (e.g., a craft, baking, reading a book, etc.) with many examples of the target skill.

- Play-Based Language Intervention—A play-based session is structured to include bombardment of specific targets, exposure to rich language models, and opportunities for a child to use language. This type of instruction is most appropriate for children whose cognitive levels are between 6 months and 6 years.

✓ **Production-Practice**—Every session must include production-practice opportunities for the child. Production-practice sometimes occurs during an instructional activity. For example, during a phonology game, the child may receive articulatory placement instruction and instruction via bombardment of the target phoneme, but is also asked to produce the target sound before each turn. However, sometimes production practice is its own phase of the lesson plan. So for a child who is working on increased use of /k/ while reading, the instruction phase may include a reminder of the /k/ sound, then the production-practice phase would entail having the child read short passages while attempting to use the /k/ accurately. Be certain to include sufficient production practice in every session.

✓ **Closure**—Every session should have an obvious closure. This makes the ending of the session more natural. There are many items to include in a closure, but a closure need not consume more than 2 to 5 minutes of a session. Consider these ideas for closing a session:
  - Review—Talk about the target that was practiced and the importance of the skill.

Lesson Planning

Introduction

Instruction

Production-Practice

Closure

How to Use This Resource

- Encourage Homework—Explain any homework that is assigned and its importance.
- Foreshadow—Hint about the next session's target or activity. Get the child excited to return.

7. *Data collection* provides a feedback loop for all well-thought remediation plans. **Appendix F: Data Collection Form** presents a sample, generic guide to consider for use when collecting session data. Use session data to plan for follow-up sessions, provide summative data to parents, and make continuation of services decisions.

8. *Behavior management* can make provision of services challenging at times. During remediation sessions, a child is often asked to practice to his or her weakness and this can be frustrating, embarrassing, and difficult. Fortunately, improving one's communication skills is intrinsically motivating for most children and adults. In addition, many forms of speech intervention include play and other developmentally appropriate practices that children of all ages find enjoyable and motivating. However, specific thought must be given to helping clients get and stay motivated, and to preventing and addressing challenging behaviors. Consider the following ideas.

✓ **Facilitating Motivation**
- With most children you will be able to talk openly and honestly about remediation goals and how improving their communication skills is a terrific and important activity.
- Help children see their progress on a regular basis (i.e., every session). Even if only at a very basic level (e.g., saying something like "We talked about a lot of new words today! Way to go!"), it is important to give children feedback on their progress. With some children, you can be more specific and direct with your statements of progress (e.g., saying "You practiced the /g/ sound today and you repeated the sound perfectly 10 different times. That's awesome!"). Sometimes, especially when marked improvement is shown, comparing a child's performance to past performances makes a big impact (e.g., saying, "Last

Chapter 3 – Treatment

time you practiced your sound 30 times with success. This time you did 100 practice words. Wonderful!"). Use this technique cautiously so that it does not seem like you are suggesting a past performance was unacceptable.

- Have the child help choose activities and materials for the sessions whenever possible, even if this means simply having the child choose whether to use crayons versus markers or making a choice of paper color to use. Having choices makes a powerful impact on keeping a child motivated and involved. When possible, have the child help choose the order of events for the session and/or the specific activities to use.

- Talk with the child's parent(s) on a regular basis. Providing the parent with feedback at each session helps the child see that the parent is interested in his or her progress. Seek input from parents for objectives and activities in order to keep intervention focused on functional outcomes.

✓ **Planning for Successful Interactions**

- Set limits and establish rules from the start. Be certain the child understands your expectations. Have him or her help set the rules. Write the rules down and have them visible for every session. Review rules and expectations as needed.

- Before stating that a particular behavior is "forbidden," determine whether the rule is necessary. For example, consider how important it may or may not be to sit at the table when working with a child. If the "work" can also be done effectively on the floor, a rule that the child must sit in a chair at all times may not be necessary. Furthermore, be cautious about setting rules that require judgment calls, since your judgment and the child's judgment will be very different at times. Be certain to include a rule that makes it clear that behaviors that harm materials or people are not allowed. The ultimate rule should be that the child listen carefully and follow your directions.

Rules:
1.
2.
3.

How to Use This Resource

> **Praise:**
> *Catch'em Being Good!*

- Prior to giving a directive, carefully consider whether you need to use a command or a request. Be cautious about requesting a child do something (e.g., "Would you like to come sit at the table?"). Instead, you'll frequently want to use declarative statements to direct child behavior (e.g., "Now you need to put the ball down and sit at the table"). Requests provide children with a choice to make, even when you didn't intend for there to be a choice. There may be times when you actually want the child to make a choice, in which case using a request is perfectly fine.

- Be consistent with your words and actions. This means you should handle similar situations in similar fashions. This helps the child come to understand expectations and consequences. In addition, it shows fairness and helps you earn respect with the child.

- Praise the child frequently. Keep the saying "Catch'em being good!" in mind at all times. Use positive feedback for accurate responses and desirable behaviors. Once you feel you are praising a child enough, praise him or her again.

- Keep activities fun and interesting. Activities that are fun and functional are bound to keep children engaged and learning. Don't hesitate to add humor whenever possible.

- Structure the schedule and tasks so to avoid struggle and frustration. If you know that a challenging skill is going to be targeted, break up an activity with a tension-relieving game. Keep variety high without causing too much commotion.

- Alert the child with sufficient notice before changing activities. This amount of notice will vary depending on the activity and the child.

- Avoid the negative. Couch directions in positive terms whenever possible (e.g., saying, "Here is your juice box Billy" as you redirect the child away from your juice box, rather than saying "Billy, that is not your juice. This is your juice).

- Use reminders rather than questions. For example, if the child throws his napkin on the floor rather than in the garbage can as directed, say "Oops. You

Chapter 3 – Treatment

still need to throw your napkin away" rather than saying, "Did you throw your napkin in the garbage can?" Don't ask a question you obviously know the answer to, since this sets the child up to potentially tell an untruth when responding.

✓ **Dealing with Negative Behaviors**

- Work hard to avoid use of the word "No" and saying, "Don't…" when negative or undesirable behaviors arise. For many of the children we work with, this only exacerbates the behavior. This does not mean you can't address the behavior—quite the opposite. There are many strategies, much more powerful and positive than "No" that will get behavior back on track. Ignore negative behaviors whenever possible. However, if you suspect the child does not realize that the behavior is inappropriate, a positive and direct response is often necessary (e.g., saying "The door needs to stay closed"). In addition, negative behaviors that violate pre-established rules and those that infringe on the safety of others must be addressed.

- Tell the child what you want them to do, rather than what they shouldn't be doing. Instead of saying "No. Don't tilt back on your chair" say something like, "Be safe. Keep four on the floor. Time to sit quietly". Or, instead of saying "No, we're not doing trains now" say something like "Trains are for later. Time to look at books." Stay positive and avoid getting frustrated. Remember, the key is to keep kids communicating, learning, and practicing their communication skills.

- Restate the rule that is being violated. This procedure is especially helpful when working with children who have attention and/or memory challenges and when just starting out with a child. At first, children may break a rule unintentionally and a gentle reminder is often sufficient.

- Substitute a toy or activity when one is taken away. For example, if a child is tearing picture cards you are using for a remediation activity, give the child a pencil, ball, or other item to hold on to while you

How to Use This Resource

control the cards.

- Adjust the environment. Move closer to the child and/or otherwise adjust your proximity in an attempt to reduce distracting behaviors. Simply resting your hand on a shoulder or sliding your chair a tad closer may eliminate certain behaviors. On the other hand, distancing yourself a bit might have a positive reaction in other children. Consider moving from the table to the floor or taking an activity to the hallway. These adjustments can also make a huge, positive difference.

- Take a break. Change the activity and/or announce a "pit stop" so that you and the child can get rejuvenated. Be careful that the child does not sense that his or her negative behavior dictated the stopping of the action. This can be a careful balance and should be used cautiously. For example, if you were hoping to get through six more pages in a book and the child starts talking negatively and rocking back in the chair, announce a break to get a drink of water and then go back to finishing the book.

- Rehearse the desired behavior. Some children may understand that they are making inappropriate choices, but do not know an appropriate choice to make. If you suspect this is the case, model an appropriate response and direct the child to perform the same behavior.

- Extreme behaviors may arise from time to time. These must be dealt with promptly and directly. There are many techniques for dealing with children who present extreme behavior challenges. For some children, a specific behavior plan (like one they may be using at home or at school) may need to be implemented during intervention.

Conclusion

Use this resource in its entirety or pick and choose just those activities or tools that fill a need in your service delivery. Refer to the Appendices for more handy items. The following table summarizes the steps to implementing this resource. The Treatment Guide units follow.

Chapter 3 – Treatment

"How To" Step-by-Step

1. **Evaluate**
   a. Case History
   b. Hearing Evaluation
   c. Oral-Mechanism Exam
   d. Speech Testing

2. **Interpret Results**
   a. Determine Eligibility
   b. Make Recommendations
   c. Make Follow-Up Referrals

3. **Create a Treatment Plan**
   a. Select Target Phonemes
   b. Probe for Starting Point
   c. Determine Techniques to Facilitate Success
   d. Plan for Generalization

4. **Implement Treatment Plan**
   a. Bombard the Child with Models
   b. Facilitate Successful Practice of Target Phonemes
   c. Probe for Accuracy
   d. Assign Homework

5. **Re-Evaluate/Recommend**
   a. Probe
   b. Review
   c. Test
   d. Refer/Dismiss/Continue

Chapter 4
Targeting P & B

- Screening Tool
- Teaching Tips
- Production Illustrations
- Target Lists
- Book Lists
- Activities
- Pictures
- Patterns
- Homework Pages

P & B Screening

Student Name_____ Date of Birth_____

Screening Date_____ Examiner_____

Use "+" or "—" to indicate the child's production of the phoneme at each level (in isolation, in a word, in a phrase, and in a sentence). Use imitation, delayed imitation, or pictures to elicit the child's productions.

Target–Initial	Target–Final /p/	Target–Initial /b	Target–Final /b
SOUND IN ISOLATION: /p/		**SOUND IN ISOLATION:** /b/	
pan	cup	bed	cub
it's a pan	it's a cup	in a bed	it's a cub
The pan is black.	I need a cup of milk.	It is under the bed.	The bear has a cub.
pie	soap	bee	web
it's a pie	use soap	flying bee	it's a web
The apple pie is hot.	Wash your hands with soap.	I was stung by a bee.	The spider web was very large.
pool	map	bus	robe
a deep pool	it's a map	school bus	warm robe
The pool was busy on a hot day.	Use a map to find your way.	We will take a bus to town.	Put on a robe after your shower.

DATA COLLECTION/SCREENING NOTES:

P & B Teaching Tips

Development Information

The consonant pair of /p/ and /b/ begins to develop as early as infancy. Typically developing children will start to experiment with /p/ and /b/ through babble and through early first-words such as "papa" and "ball." Mastery of the /p/ and /b/ sound pair occurs for most children between 18 months and 3 years of age (Sander, 1972). The visual nature and plosive energy that combine to create these two sounds makes them salient, thus early development is possible.

Production of /p/ and /b/

This sound pair is bilabial (i.e., made with contact between both lips) and plosive (i.e., produced with a burst of air). The /p/ is unvoiced, thus the vocal folds are not set into vibration, while the /b/ is voiced. The tongue lies flat in the mouth, but an accurate /p/ and /b/ can be produced with a variety of tongue placements. The teeth are held slightly apart and the velum is lifted to block air from escaping through the nasal cavity, thus allowing air pressure to build in the mouth and explode through the lips. Use an age-appropriate description of the processes for producing these sounds, in conjunction with the illustrations on page 34 as you assist children with their first attempts to produce these sounds.

Stimulating Production of /p/ and /b/

For children who struggle to produce the /p/ and /b/ sounds, some work with the sound in isolation may be warranted. Due to the visual and powerful nature of these sounds, the following strategies may be useful when encouraging accurate production during treatment activities:

- Use the illustrations on page 34 to provide additional instruction for placement of /p/ and /b/. As needed, keep these images displayed during practice with these target sounds.
- Use an age-appropriate description of the processes for producing these sounds.
- Sit side-by-side with the child in front of a mirror. Encourage the child to watch as you press your lips together. Cue the child to match your model. Direct the child to imitate your productions of /p/ and /b/.
- Consider allowing the child to apply a small amount of flavored lip balm as a reinforcer to encourage pressing of the lips together.
- Use a tissue, cottonball, or small cracker placed on a flat surface. Have the child watch you press your lips together and then release a burst of air to produce /p/ or /b/ as you make the item move across the surface. Encourage the child to match your model.
- To encourage the voicing contrast, direct the child to apply light fingertip pressure to his/her throat or your throat as the /b/ and /p/ contrasts are produced. Talking about "turning on" the voice to make the buzzing associated with /b/.

Chapter 4 – P & B

P & B Production Illustrations

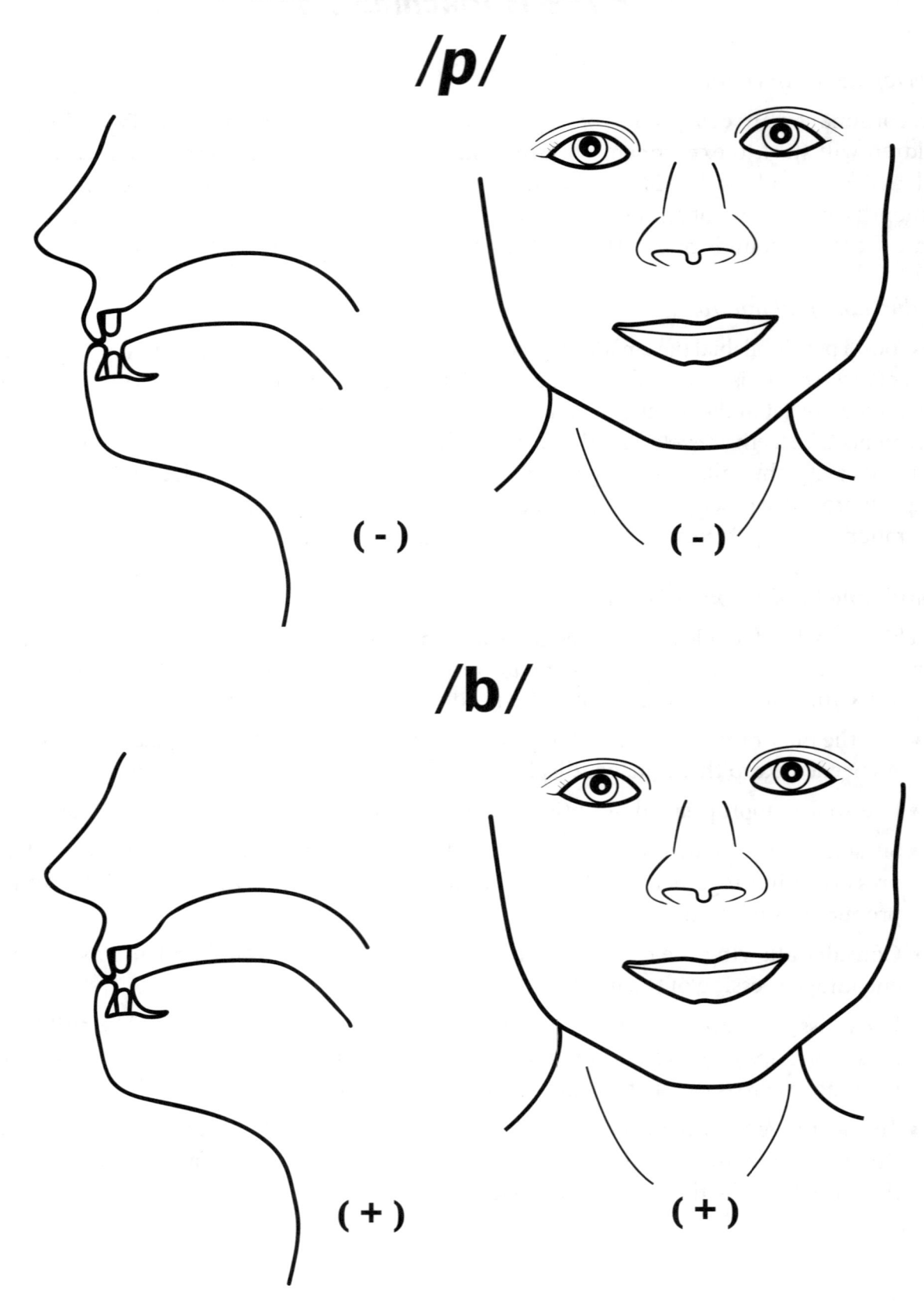

/p/

(-)   (-)

/b/

(+)   (+)

34 The Entire World of Early Developing Sounds Instructional Workbook™   © 2008 Say It Right™ www.sayitright.org

P & B Target Lists

Especially during early stages of practice, single-syllable words are most facilitative for accurate productions of target sounds. Consider the surrounding consonant and vowel sounds in a target word to control for other sounds the child may be lacking. For example, when first targeting initial /p/ with a child, avoid words that also contain medial and/or final /p/. Gradually, as a child becomes more successful with practice of a selected target sound, words of increasing length and complexity can be added to the production-practice activities.

The Entire World of Early Developing Sounds™ suggests using the target words listed for the early stages of practice with young children working on /p/ and /b/. Pages 46-53 provide representations of these words in picture form for use with production practice activities. Suggested target phrases and sentences are also provided. Phrases and sentences are most useful with older children who can read. *The Entire World of P & B Articulation Flip Book* (Ristuccia, 2007) is an excellent source for illustrated, interactive phrase and sentence practice.

When working with older children, the word, phrase, and sentence lists may be useful as stimulus items in mass production practice. If using the phrases and sentences with nonreaders, direct or delayed imitation will be necessary (i.e., saying the phrase or sentence as a model and then having the child repeat it with or without a delay). Ideally, production of phrases and sentences will be elicited naturally during structured and unstructured activities, thus it is possible that the phrase and sentence lists would not need to be used with younger children.

To target medial /p/ and /b/, use the target words in combination with another word (e.g., "my pet" to elicit medial /p/ or "tube slide" for medial /b/). Medial /p/ and /b/ target words can be added once a child is ready for practice with multisyllabic words. As medial /p/ and /b/ words are selected, continue to control for facilitative contexts to ensure children successfully produce the new sound. In addition, use multisyllabic words that are meaningful to the child (e.g., baby, cabin, etc.).

Chapter 4 – P & B

P & B Single Word Practice

Word-Initial /p/	Word-Final /p/	Word-Initial /b/	Word-Final /b/
pail	ape	ball	cub
pan	cap	bat	cob
park	cape	bath	crib
paw	chip	bee	globe
pea	cup	bear	knob
peach	hoop	bed	rib
pear	lip	bike	robe
peg	map	bell	shrub
pen	mop	bug	sub
pet	soap	bus	tub
pie	soup	book	tube
pool	up	box	web

P & B Phrase-Level Practice

Word-Initial /p/	Word-Final /p/	Word-Initial /b/	Word-Final /b/
it's a **pail**	large **ape**	play **ball**	a bear **cub**
a frying **pan**	the brown **cap**	swing the **bat**	the baby's **crib**
city **park**	batman's **cape**	take a **bath**	corn on the **cob**
the dog's **paw**	potato **chip**	a **bee** sting	spin the **globe**
green **pea**	a coffee **cup**	a grizzly **bear**	turn the **knob**
juicy **peach**	basketball **hoop**	go to **bed**	his **rib**
ripe **pear**	**lip** gloss	ride a **bike**	her **robe**
round **peg**	a road **map**	ring the **bell**	green **shrub**
write with a **pen**	a dirty **mop**	a flying **bug**	**sub** sandwich
pet the dog	use dish **soap**	a school **bus**	wash **tub**
pie and ice cream	chicken noodle **soup**	read a **book**	the small **tube**
swimming **pool**	climb **up**	**box** of cards	a spider **web**

Chapter 4 – P & B

P & B Sentence-Level Practice

Word-Initial /p/	Word-Final /p/	Word-Initial /b/	Word-Final /b/
It's a **pail** of water.	I want a potato **chip.**	She will throw the **ball.**	The bear **cub** is lost.
I cook eggs in a **pan.**	The **ape** climbed a tree.	He needs to swing the **bat.**	He sleeps in a **crib.**
Let's go to the **park.**	The boy wore a **cape.**	It's time to take a **bath.**	I like corn on the **cob.**
His **paw** is hurt.	The coffee **cup** broke.	The **bee** stung him.	He has a small **globe.**
She will eat a **pea.**	She wore a red **cap.**	The grizzly **bear** is big.	The door has a **knob.**
He cut the **peach.**	The **hoop** was too high.	It is time to go to **bed.**	He broke his **rib** during the game.
The **pear** tasted good.	She used **lip** gloss.	He has a small **bike.**	Her **robe** is blue.
He put the **pen** in his pocket.	He used a road **map.**	I heard the school **bell.**	The **shrub** is in front of the house.
Use the round **peg.**	Use a **mop** to clean.	The **bug** crawled fast.	He ate a **sub** sandwich.
I **pet** the dog.	The **soap** was new.	I ride a **bus** to school.	It's time to get in the **tub.**
I like lemon **pie.**	I love chicken noodle **soup.**	The library **book** is new.	He has a **tube** of toothpaste.
They have a swimming **pool.**	She went **up** the stairs.	Put the toys in the **box.**	The spider spun a **web.**

P & B Book List

Reading a story is a natural and motivating activity for children. Children's stories are filled with opportunities to bombard the child with words containing the target sound and to elicit productions of the target. Consult the following list to select books that contain multiple opportunities for words that contain /p/ or /b/.

	INITIAL /p/		
Title	**Publication Information**	**Interest Level**	**Target Words**
Peek-A-Boo!	Janet & Allan Ahlberg (1981) Puffin Books	2-4 years	peek
Pete's a Pizza	William Steig (1998) Joanna Colter	1-5 years	Pete, pizza, pepperoni,
If You Give a Pig a Pancake	Laura Numeroff (1998) Harper Collins	3-6 years	pig, pancake
Pig in the Pond	Martin Waddell (1996) Candlewick	1-5 years	pig, pond
Do Pigs Have Stripes?	Melanie Walsh (1996) Houghton Mifflin	4-8 years	pig
Pickin' Peas	Margaret Read MacDonald (1998) HarperCollins	4-8 years	Pickin', peas
Pig, Pig Goes to Camp	David McPhail (1985) Scholastic	2-6 years	Pig Pig, perfect, postcards, purple

	FINAL /p/		
Tie Your Socks and Clap Your Feet	Lenny Hort (2000) Atheneum/Anne Schwartz Books	4-8 years	clap
The Hippo Hop	Christine Loomis (1997) Scholastic	3-6 years	hop
Monkey Soup	Louis Sachar (1992) Knopf Books	3-6 years	soup
Sheep in a Jeep	Nancy Shaw (1991) Houghton Mifflin	2-5 years	sheep, shop, jeep
The Enormous Turnip	Kathy Parkinson (1986) Albert Whitman & Co.	4-8 years	turnip, up

Chapter 4 – P & B

INITIAL /b/			
TITLE	PUBLICATION INFORMATION	INTEREST LEVEL	TARGET WORDS
Big Red Barn	Margaret Wise Brown (1994) HarperFestival	1-5 years	big, barn
Bubble Trouble	Mary Packard (1995) Scholastic	3-6 years	bubbles, bath, big
Buzzy the Bumblebee	Denise Brennan-Nelson (1999) Gale Group	4-8 years	Buzzy, bumblebee, buzz, book
How Many Bugs in a Box?	David Carter (1988) Little Simon	2-6 years	bugs, box, beetle, boo
Chicka Chicka Boom Boom	Bill Martin, Jr. & John Archambault (2000) Aladdin	3-7 years	boom, beat
Duck on a Bike	David Shannon (2002) Blue Sky Press	1-5 years	bike
Peek-A-Boo!	Janet & Allan Ahlberg (1981) Puffin Books	2-4 years	boo, baby
Who is the Beast?	Keith Baker (1994) Voyager Books	4-8 years	beast
Where is Baby Bear?	Jane Belk Moncure (1988) The Child's World Books	2-6 years	Bear, baby, bunny, behind, belong, barn, birds, beach, boat
The Wheels on the Bus	Paul Zelinsky (1990) Dutton Children's Books	2-7 years	bus, back, bumpty, bump, babies

FINAL /b/			
Mrs. Wishy Washy	Joy Cowley (1999) Philomel Books	1-6 years	tub, scrub
Tub Toys	Terry Miller Shannon (2002) Tricycle Books	3-8 years	Tub, rub, scrub
King Bidgood's in the Bathtub	Audrey Wood (1993) Scholastic	4-8 years	Bidgood, bathtub
Rub a Dub Dub	Kin Eagle (2002) Charlesbridge Publishing	Baby-preschool	tub, rub, dub
The Tub People	Pam Conrad (1995) HarperTrophy	4-8 years	tub

P & B Activity Pages

Regardless of your approach to treatment, a variety of activities should be used to bombard children with correct productions of the target sound and to elicit production practice. The activities in this unit include a range of sound-specific options for /p/ and /b/. They are designed to appeal to children between the ages of 2 and 7.

In addition, the following are available to support your teaching of the /p/ and /b/ sounds:

- **More Activity Ideas** that can be used to target any sound are included in Appendix A.

- Sound-specific **Pictures** to be used with activities are found on pages 46-53.

- A **Blank Card Pattern**, to include your own words, is found in Appendix D.

- **Book Lists** for selecting stories are included on page 39-40.

- **Word, Phrase, and Sentence Lists** are provided on pages 36-38, to use with activities or with more traditional boards games (e.g., Sorry! Uno, and Kerplunk). To earn a turn, have the older student read or repeat words, phrases, or sentences containing the selected target phoneme. The goal is to encourage as many repetitions of the target sound as possible—be creative!

- **Homework Pages** (pages 62-67) provide activities that can be easily used by parents or other care providers to encourage successful practice in other settings. Be certain to direct children to return completed Homework Pages so you can encourage self-evaluation and monitoring of their practice. Consider having students carry a "speech folder" to store these materials and facilitate communication with others on a regular basis.

- Appendix B provides a **Parent Memo** that can be used along with selected homework activity pages.

- Appendix E includes a blank **Lesson Plan**. Use the form to ensure that all essential lesson plan components are accounted for within each session. Be certain to probe for accuracy, provide instruction/bombardment for the target sounds, and plan for a sufficient amount of successful mass production practice.

- Appendix F provides a blank **Data Collection Form** to monitor progress and adjust treatment.

- Don't forget that **Suggestions for Conversation and Carryover** are provided in Appendix B. Plan for generalization from the start and incorporate these suggestions along the way.

Chapter 4–P & B

Initial P Activities

Snack Ideas
- Pudding, popcorn, peaches, pears
- Purple juice (e.g., grape juice or Kool-Aid)

Craft
- Pudding Paint—Prepare chocolate instant pudding to represent mud. Have the child finger paint blank patterns of the Pig Pattern using the chocolate pudding.
- Puffy Paints—Purchase puffy fabric paints and let children decorate paper.

Motor and Movement
- Puddle Jump—Place a Hula Hoop on the floor and have the children jump in and out of the Hula Hoop as though they are jumping in puddles.

Songs and Finger Play

Pigs

"It's time for my pink pigs to go to sleep,"
 the great mother pig did say.
"I will count them first to see
If all my pigs come back to me.
One little pig, two little pigs, three little pigs, my dear.
Four little pigs, five little pigs—yes! All are here!"

Pigs in a Pail

Materials
- Initial /p/ book
- Pig Pattern, page 54
- Word-initial /p/ pictures, page 46
- Paper clips
- Ice cream pail
- Glue or tape

Procedure

1. Bombard the child with word-initial /p/ by introducing the sound with a story selected from the book list.

2. Duplicate 4 to 12 copies of the Pig Pattern. Duplicate the set of word-initial /p/ pictures. Attach one picture to each pig.

3. Attach a large paper clip to each pig for weight.

4. Have children stand around a large pail. Tell children to take turns "putting pigs into the pail." Have them name the pictures on the pigs.

5. Bombard the children with the word-initial /p/ sentences and phrases such as "Whoa! The pail is full of pigs!" and "Put, put, put. Put pigs into the pail!"

6. Consider variations such as Pigs in a Pan or Pigs in a Purse.

P Activity Pages

Final P Activities

Ape in a Cape

Materials
- Final /p/ book
- Ape and Cape Pattern, page 55
- Word-final /p/ pictures, page 48
- Glue or tape

Procedure
1. Bombard the child with word-final /p/ by introducing the sound with a story selected from the book list.
2. Duplicate one Ape Pattern for each child. Duplicate the set of word-final /p/ pictures. Glue or tape one picture to each Cape Pattern.
3. Have children listen as you bombard them with final /p/ words and tell them to "pick a cape for your ape." Elicit productions if appropriate.
4. Elicit productions of sentences and phrases such as, "Great! I have an ape with a grape cape."

Snack Ideas
- Grapes, soup, flap jacks
- Grape juice

Craft
- Design Your Own Cape—Cut the sides from brown paper grocery bags and decorate with paint, markers, or scraps of paper. Attach to the back of shirts with safety pins or tape.

Motor and Movement
- Jump Over the Rope—Stretch a rope across the floor and have the children jump over the rope. Add a challenge for those who are ready by having two people hold both ends of the stretched rope and raise it one to two inches for the children to jump over.

Songs and Finger Play

Up and Down

Up, up to the top
(march fingers up from chest level to eye level)

Down, down to the ground
(march fingers downward)

Up, down. Up, down. Turn around.

Chapter 4–P & B

Initial B Activities

Snack Ideas
- "Bug Juice" (Kool Aid).
- Create a bug with round crackers and peanut butter or cheese spread. Add raisins for eyes.

Craft
- Balloon Bugs—Blow up ten small balloons. Attach spots and eyes to each balloon to create bugs. Place the "bugs" in a bucket or on the floor. Have the children scoop balloon bugs with a large food strainer or butterfly net.

Motor and Movement
- Balloon Jump—Blow up ten small balloons. Attach spots and eyes to each balloon to create bugs. Using yarn or string, hang the "bugs" from the ceiling so they dangle at the child's eye level. Have the child say (or bombard them with the words) "bug," "bop," and "bat" as they bat at the bug balloons.

Songs and Finger Plays

*Bugs are Crawling**

Bugs are crawling on the ground.
Onto my shoe without a sound.
Up my shin and to my knee.
Creepy bugs all over me!
Tickle, tickle. Oooh, that itches.
Oh no! Bugs in my britches!

*From: http://www.wcls.org/kids/kidspdf/Activity%20Sheets/bugsactivitysheet.pdf

---

Bed Bugs

Materials
- Initial /b/ book
- Bed Pattern, page 56
- Bug Pattern, page 57
- Word-initial /b/ pictures, page 50
- Glue or tape
- Crayons or markers

Procedure

1. Bombard the child with word-initial /b/ by introducing the sound with a story selected from the book list.

2. Duplicate one Bed Pattern and multiple Bug Patterns for each child.

3. Have the child color the bugs and glue or tape them to the bed.

4. Have children listen as you bombard them with initial /b/ words like "bed" and "bug." Elicit productions if appropriate for each child's skill level.

5. Consider variations like Bugs in a Box, Bugs on a Bus, or Bugs in a Boat.

B Activity Pages

Final B Activities

Cub in a Tub

Materials
- Final /b/ book
- Cub Pattern, page 58
- Tub Pattern, page 59
- Word-final /b/ pictures, page 52
- Glue or tape
- Crayons or markers

Procedure

1. Bombard the child with word-final /b/ by introducing the sound with a story selected from the book list.

2. Duplicate one Cub Pattern and one Tub Pattern for each child. Duplicate the word-final /b/ pictures.

3. Have the children color the cub and glue or tape it to the tub.

4. Have children listen as you name the final /b/ pictures. Elicit productions of the words "cub" and "tub." Have children name the final /b/ pictures If appropriate for each child's skill.

Snack Ideas
- Animal crackers
- Teddy Grahams
- Mini sub sandwiches.

Craft
- Bear Cub—Create bear cubs. Duplicate a Cub Puppet Pattern (p.128) for each child. Attach all to toilet paper roll. Add paws, tail, and a head.

Motor and Movement
- Water Play—Fill a small plastic tub with water and add tub toys. Use plastic butter dishes or empty cream cheese containers to represent a tub. Add Play Mobile people and have the children recite the Rub a Dub Dub nursery rhyme as they play with the "men" in the tub..

Songs and Finger Plays

Rub a Dub Dub

Rub a dub dub,

Three men in a tub,

And who do you think they be?

The butcher, the baker,

The candlestick maker.

Turn them out, knaves all three!

Initial P Picture Cards

pail	pan
park	paw
pea	peach

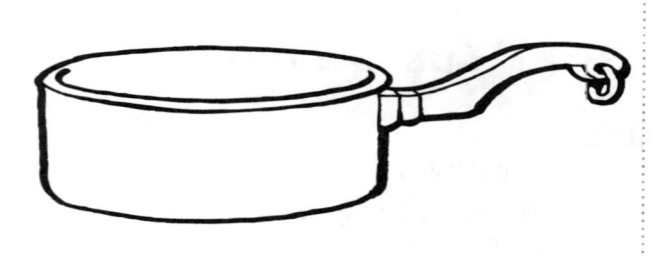

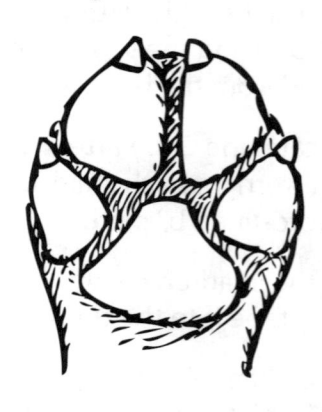

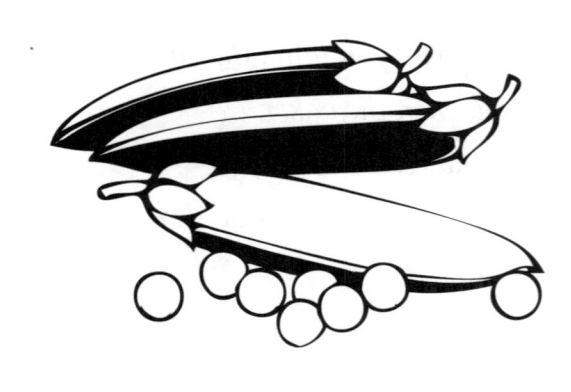

46 The Entire World of Early Developing Sounds Instructional Workbook™   © 2008 Say It Right™   www.sayitright.org

Initial P Picture Cards

peg

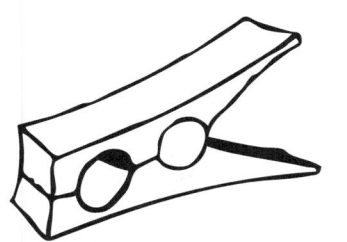

pool

pet

pie

pen

pear

47

Final P **Picture Cards**

chip	ape
cape	cup
cap	hoop

Final P Picture Cards

lip	map
mop	soap
soup	up

Initial B Picture Cards

ball	bat
bath	bee
bear	bed

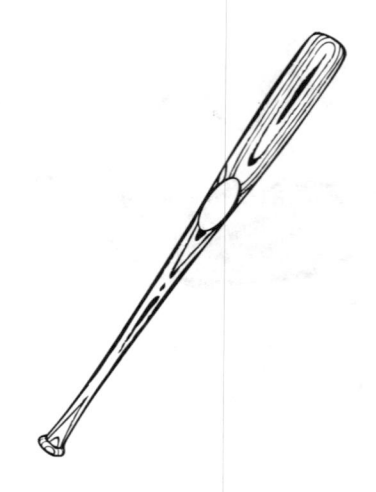

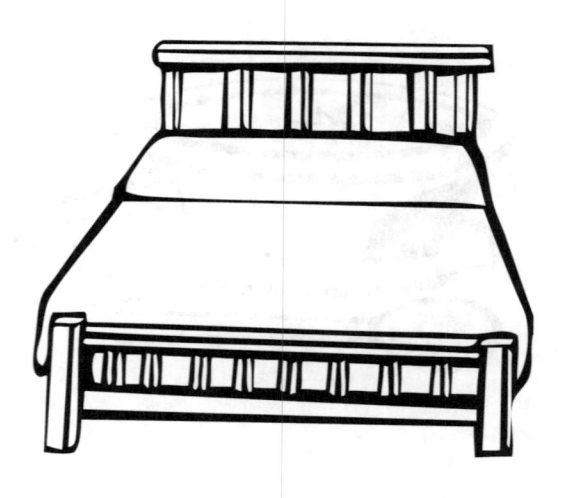

Initial B Picture Cards

bike

bell

bug

bus

book

box

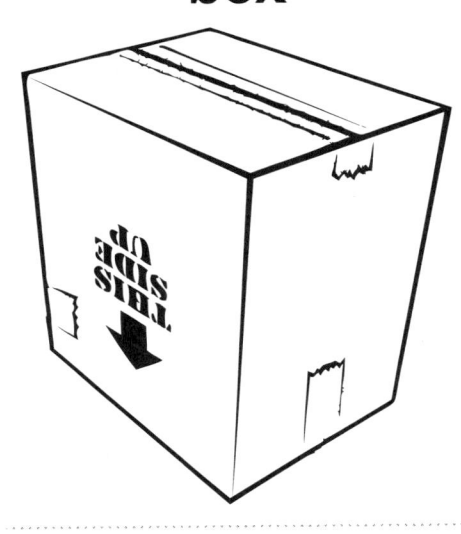

Final B Picture Cards

cub	crib
cob	globe
knob	robe

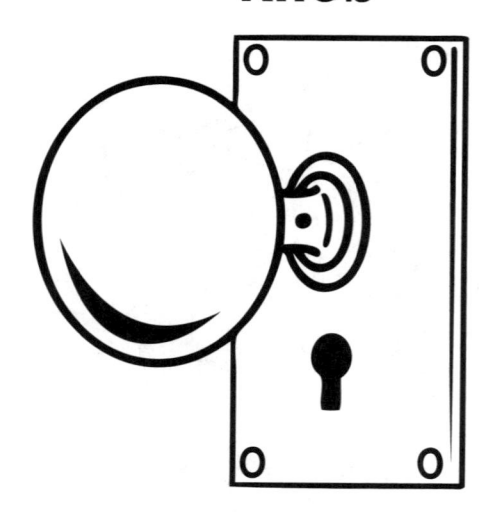

52 The Entire World of Early Developing Sounds Instructional Workbook™ © 2008 Say It Right™ www.sayitright.org

Final B Picture Cards

sub	tub
tube	web
shrub	rib

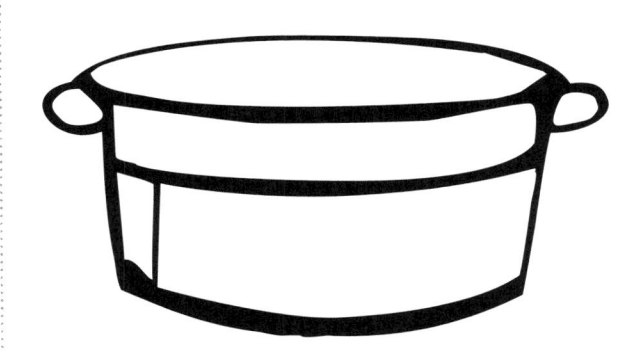

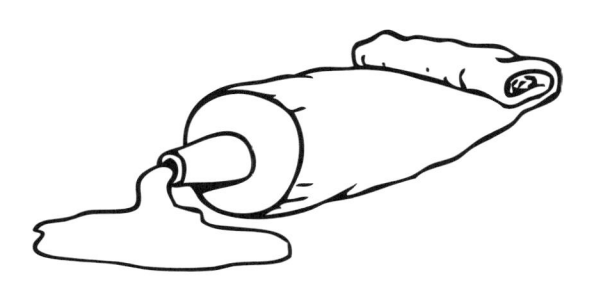

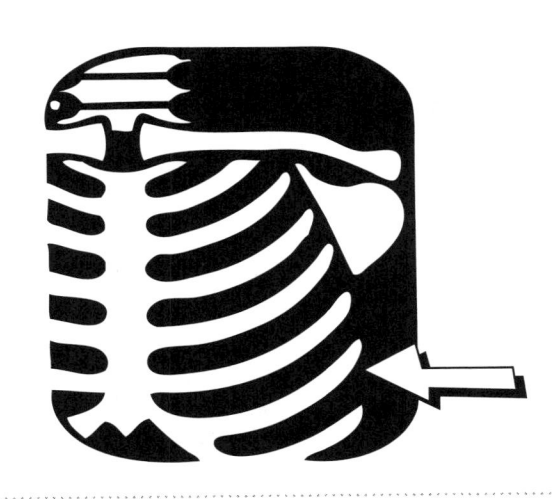

Chapter 4 – P & B

Pig Pattern

P Activity Patterns

Ape in Cape Pattern

Chapter 4 – P & B

Bed Pattern

B Activity Patterns

Bugs Pattern

57

Chapter 4 – P & B

Cub Pattern

B Activity Patterns

Tub Pattern

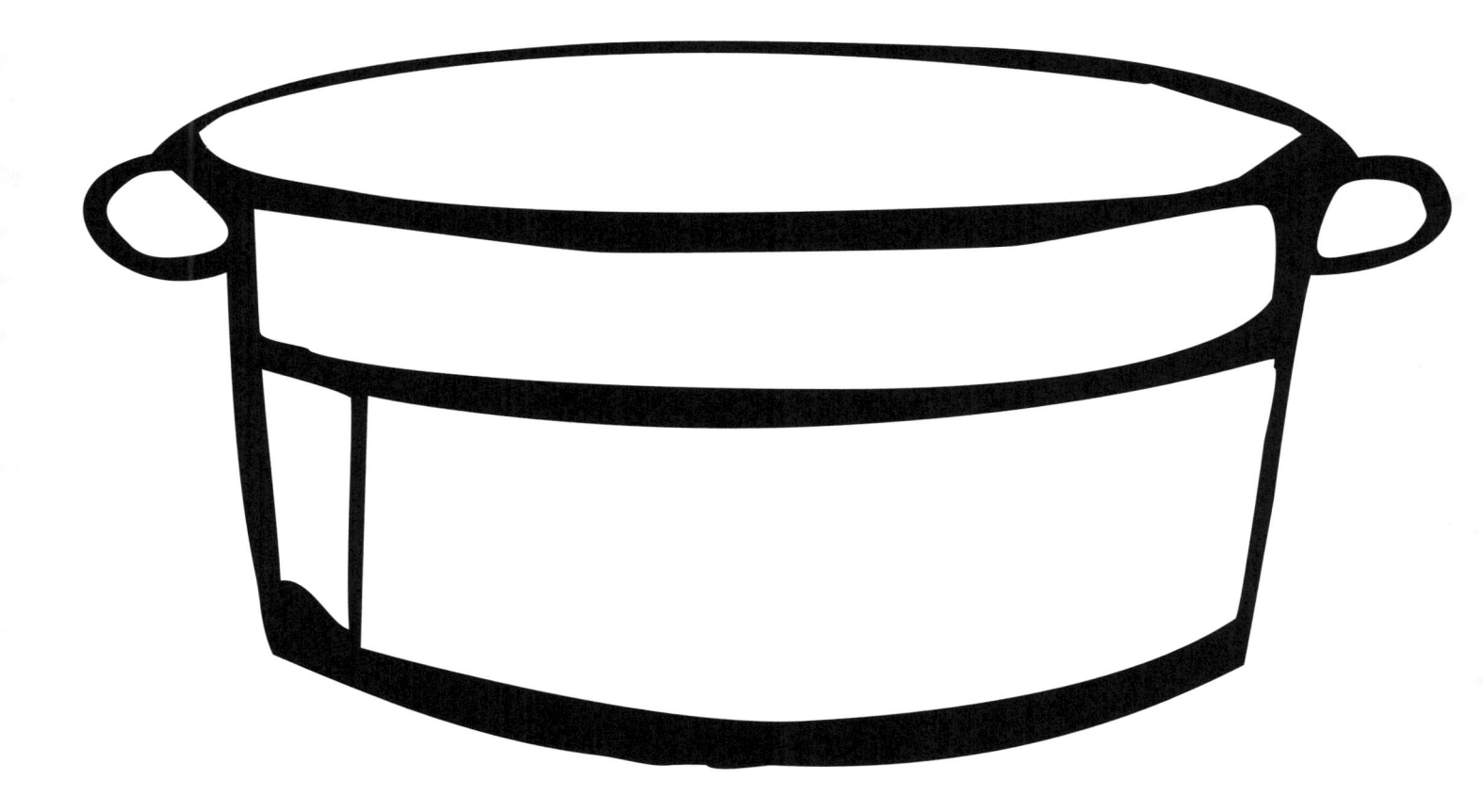

The Entire World of Early Developing Sounds Instructional Workbook™

Chapter 4 – P & B

What do You Find at the Park?

Child: Circle all the items that are found at a park. Tell about going to a park.

Helper: While you interact with your child, bombard him or her with the questions, "What do you find at the park?" Emphasize the word "park" and the sound "P" as you ask the question.

P Homework

Color the Pie

Child: Color in the pies. Tell the name of each pie.

Helper: Emphasize correct production of the word "pie." Help your child name the pies based on the color (e.g., "peach pie, apple pie") while emphasizing the sound for "P."

Chapter 4–P & B

Stop!

Child: Count the stop signs. Then color them.

Helper: As your child colors the stop signs, say "stop" and encourage your child to also say "stop," emphasizing the "P" sound at the end of the word.

P Homework

Map Fun

Child: Name the pictures on the map. Color all the pictures that rhyme with the word "map."

Helper: Name the pictures for your child then have your child say it. Emphasize the "P" sound at the end of each word.

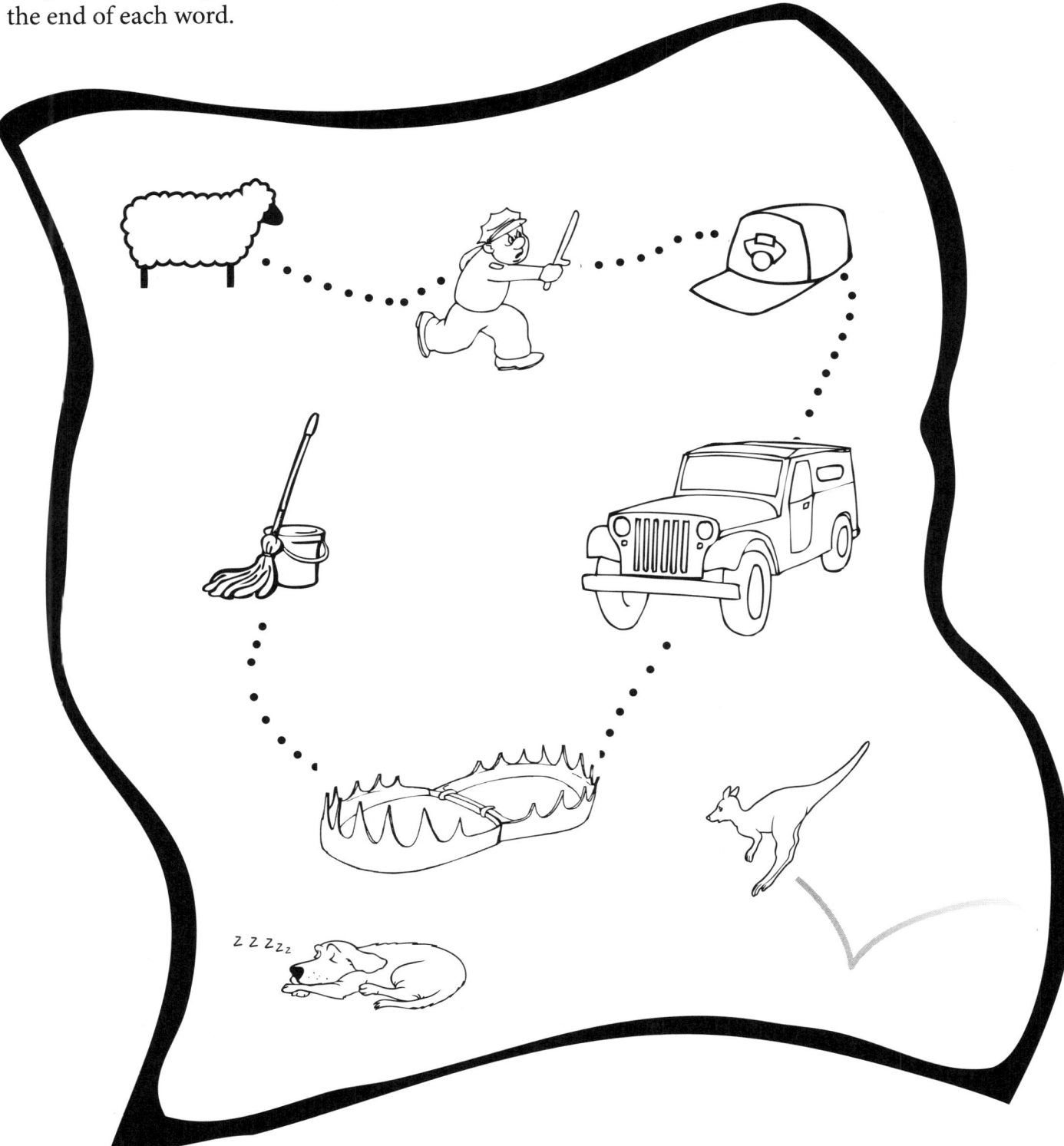

Chapter 4–P & B

Boys on the Bus

Child: Cut out the boys at the bottom of the page and glue them in the windows on the bus. As you glue each boy, say his name.

Helper: Name each picture for your child as it is added to the bus. Then have your child say it. Emphasize the "B" sound at the beginning of each word.

Ben    **Bart**    **Bill**   **Bob**    **Bud**

B Homework

Batter Up!

Child: Name all the pictures you see on the baseballs. Color the ones that start with the "B" sound.

Helper: Name each picture for your child and help him or her decide if it starts with the "B" sound. If it does, have your child say it. Emphasize the "B" sound at the beginning of each "B" word.

Chapter 4 – P & B

Web of Pictures

Child: The spider caught many items in its web. Name all the items the spider caught that use the "B" sound at the end.

Helper: Help your child name the pictures. Emphasize the "B" sound when it occurs at the end of the word.

B Homework

Gabe Tells a Fib

Child: Gabe tells fibs in this story. Retell the story after you hear it.

Helper: Read the story aloud. Emphasize a correct "B" sound when it occurs. Encourage your child to retell the story using the correct production of "B." For more practice, cut out the pictures and have your child put them in the correct order.

Gabe was playing baseball in the yard.	Gabe hit the ball and broke a window.
Gabe didn't want to tell his parents.	**Gabe told them it was Abe.**
Gabe felt bad for telling a fib.	**He told his parents. He had to scrub the tub to pay for the new window.**

Chapter 5
Targeting M & N

- Screening Tool
- Teaching Tips
- Production Illustrations
- Target Lists
- Book Lists
- Activities
- Pictures
- Patterns
- Homework Pages

M & N Screening

Student Name_____ Date of Birth_____

Screening Date_____ Examiner_____

Use "+" or "—" to indicate the child's production of the phoneme at each level (in isolation, in a word, in a phrase, and in a sentence). Use imitation, delayed imitation, or pictures to elicit the child's productions.

Target–Initial /m/	Target–Final /m/	Target–Initial /n/	Target–Final /n/
SOUND IN ISOLATION: /m/		**SOUND IN ISOLATION:** /n/	
mouse	broom	nail	fan
big mouse	use a broom	sharp nail	blowing fan
The mouse was eating cheese.	I used the broom to sweep the floor.	The hammer pounded the nail.	Turn off the fan please.
milk	home	nose	rain
milk jug	going home	clown nose	falling rain
Cold milk tastes good with cookies.	Our home is just down the road.	I need a tissue for my nose.	The rain fell all night long.
map	lamb	nest	ten
road map	little lamb	bird's nest	the number ten
Get the road map.	The lamb will grow fast.	The nest had four little blue eggs.	When I am ten I will get a new bike.

DATA COLLECTION/SCREENING NOTES:

M & N Teaching Tips

Development Information

The consonant pair of /m/ and /n/ begins to develop early. Children will start to use /m/ and /n/ as early as 6 months of age. Mastery of the /m/ and /n/ sound pair occurs for most children between 2 and 3 years of age (Sander, 1972). The visibility and continuous nature that combine to create these two sounds makes them salient and easy to produce, thus early development is possible.

Production of /m/ and /n/

Both /m/ and /n/ are nasals (i.e., made with a lowered velum and airway with no velopharyngeal closure) and continuants (i.e., produced with a continuous airstream). However, the place of production is different between the two sounds. The /m/ is a bilabial (i.e., made with contact of the two lips), while the /n/ is an alveolar or lingua-alveolar (i.e., made with contact between the tongue and alveolar ridge). The /m/ and /n/ are both voiced consonants, thus the vocal folds are in motion for both.

Stimulating Production of /m/ and /n/

For children who struggle to produce /m/ and /n/, some work with the sound in isolation may be warranted. The following strategies may be useful when encouraging accurate production during treatment activities:

- Use the illustrations on page 72 to provide additional instruction for placement of /m/ and /n/. As needed, keep these images displayed during practice with these target sounds.

- Use an age-appropriate description of the processes for producing these sounds.

- Sit side-by-side with the child in front of a mirror. Encourage the child to watch as you produce each sound. Cue the child to match your model. Direct the child to imitate your productions of /m/ or /n/.

- For /n/, consider having the child apply a small amount of peanut butter or other flavored substance on the alveolar ridge. Cue movement of the tongue to touch the peanut butter. Encourage production of /n/ during this process.

- For /m/, have the child apply a small amount of flavored lip balm as a reinforcer to encourage pressing of the lips together.

- To encourage voicing, tell the child to apply light fingertip pressure to his/her throat or your throat as the /m/ and /n/ are produced. Talk about "turning on" the voice to make the buzzing associated with /m/ and /n/.

Chapter 5 – M & N

M & N Production Illustrations

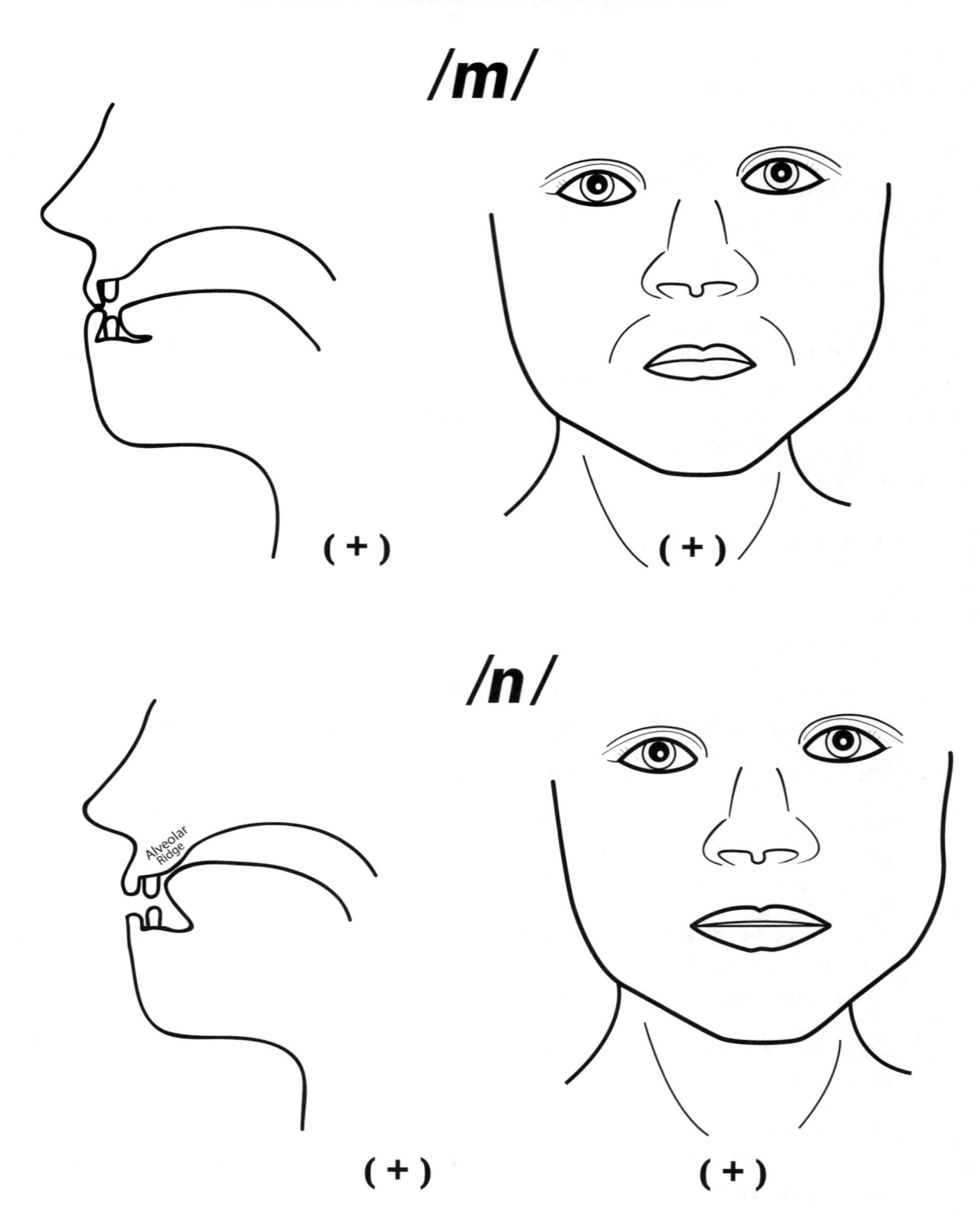

/m/

(+)   (+)

/n/

Alveolar Ridge

(+)   (+)

M & N Target Lists

Especially during early stages of practice, single-syllable words are most facilitative for accurate productions of target sounds. Consider the surrounding consonant and vowel sounds in a target word to control for other sounds the child may be lacking. For example, when first targeting initial /m/ with a child, avoid words that also contain medial and/or final /m/. Gradually, as a child becomes more successful with practice of a target sound, words of increasing length and complexity can be added to the production-practice activities.

The Entire World of Early Developing Sounds™ suggests using the target words listed for the early stages of practice with young children working on /m/ and /n/. Pages 84-91 provide representations of these words in picture form for use with production practice activities. Suggested target phrases and sentences are also provided. Phrases and sentences are most useful with older children who can read. *The Entire World of M & N Articulation Flip Book* (Ristuccia, 2007) is an excellent source for illustrated, interactive phrase and sentence practice.

When working with older children, the word, phrase, and sentence lists may be useful as stimulus items in mass production practice. If using the phrases and sentences with nonreaders, direct or delayed imitation will be necessary (i.e., saying the phrase or sentence as a model and then having the child repeat it with or without a delay). Ideally, production of phrases and sentences will be elicited naturally during structured and unstructured activities, thus it is possible that the phrase and sentence lists would not need to be used with younger children.

To target medial /m/ and /n/, use the target words in combination with another word (e.g., "her map" to elicit medial /m/ or "sunshine" for medial /n/). Medial /m/ and /n/ words can be added once a child is ready for practice with multisyllabic words. As medial /m/ and /n/ words are selected, continue to control for facilitative contexts to ensure children successfully produce the new sound. In addition, use multisyllabic words that are meaningful to the child (e.g., *monkey, cabin,* etc.).

Chapter 5 – M & N

M & N Single Word Practice

Word–Initial /m/	Word–Final /m/	Word–Initial /n/	Word–Final /n/
mail	broom	knee	bean
man	comb	nail	can
map	drum	name	chin
mat	game	nap	clown
me	ham	neck	fan
meal	home	nest	fin
milk	jam	net	man
moon	lamb	nice	pan
mop	ram	night	one
moth	room	no	sun
mouse	swim	nose	ten
mud	thumb	nut	van

M & N Phrase-Level Practice

Word–Initial /m/	Word–Final /m/	Word–Initial /n/	Word–Final /n/
the **mail**	**broom** clean	bend my **knee**	eat the **bean**
a **man**	**comb** hair	pound the **nail**	**can** do it
map reading	beat a **drum**	my **name**	my **chin**
his **mat**	**game** play	**nap** time	**clown** laughs
help **me**	eat the **ham**	tickle on **neck**	**fan** spins
a big **meal**	go **home**	the bird's **nest**	big **fin**
what a **mess**	**jam** on toast	a fishing **net**	the tall **man**
drink **milk**	little **lamb**	so **nice**	cooking **pan**
a full **moon**	**ram** runs	it's **night**	**one** book
pet the dog	big **room**	**no** means **no**	**sun** spot
swimming **pool**	**swim** fast	by a **nose**	**ten** balls
round **peg**	**thumb** tack	**nut** and bolt	tan **van**

Chapter 5 – M & N

M & N Sentence-Level Practice

Word–Initial /m/	Word–Final /m/	Word–Initial /n/	Word–Final /n/
I can get the **mail**.	The floor is **broom** clean.	He hurt his **knee**.	She will plant the **bean**.
I see the tall **man**.	Please **comb** my hair.	He uses a **nail** to build.	She **can** open the door.
This is a **map** of Wisconsin.	The **drum** is loud.	Her **name** is Katie.	He bumped his **chin**.
Wipe your feet on the **mat**.	I like to play this **game**.	It is time to take a **nap**.	The silly **clown** is happy.
Can you help **me** pour the cereal?	She will eat the **ham**.	The scarf is on her **neck**.	The **fan** keeps her cool.
His favorite **meal** is breakfast.	It is time to go **home**.	The bird built a **nest**.	The fish has a long **fin**.
I like chocolate **milk**.	Put **jam** on your toast.	The fish is in the **net**.	The **man** is playing ball.
It is a full **moon** tonight.	She found the **lamb**.	The girl is **nice** to me.	I need a **pan** to fry eggs.
Use a **mop** to clean up.	The **ram** runs fast.	I sleep at **night**.	The **one** bin is full.
The **moth** is flying.	The **room** is big.	The boy said, "**No**."	The **sun** is yellow.
The **mouse** is eating cheese.	I like to **swim**.	She can touch her **nose**.	There are **ten** tan balls.
The **mud** is dirty.	His **thumb** hurts.	The squirrel ate the **nut**.	My mom's **van** is red.

M & N Book List

Reading a story is a natural and motivating activity for children. Children's stories are filled with opportunities to bombard the child with words containing the target sound and to elicit productions of the target. Consult the following list to select books that contain multiple opportunities for words that contain /m/ or /n/.

	INITIAL /m/		
Title	Publication Information	Interest Level	Target Words
Mouse Mess	Linnea Riley (1997) Blue Sky Press	1-5 years	mouse, mess
Is Your Mama a Lama?	Deborah Guarino (1997) Scholastic	Baby-preschool	Mama
Monkey Soup	Louis Sachar (1992) Knoff Books	4-8 years	Monkey
Five Little Monkeys Jumping on the Bed	Eileen Christelow (1998) Clarion Books	2-5 years	monkeys, mama, more
Goodnight Moon	Margaret Wise Brown (2001) HarperFestival	4-8 years	moon, mouse, mush, mittens
If You Give a Moose a Muffin	Laura Joffe Numeroff (1994) HarperTrophy	4-8 years	moose, muffin, mix, make, more, mess
Pigs in the Mud in the Middle of the Rud	Lynn Plourde (2006) Down East Books	4-8 years	mud, middle
The Mitten	Jan Brett (1989) Putnam Publishing	4-8 years	mitten, mole, mouse, my, made, move
	FINAL /m/		
The Gum on the Drum	Barbara Gregorich (1993) School Zone Publishing	4-8 years	gum, drum
Mary Had a Little Lamb	Iza Trapani (2001) Charlesbridge	2-4 years	lamb
An Octopus Followed Me Home	Dan Yaccarino (2000) Puffin	Baby-preschool	home
Each Peach Pear Plum	Janet Ahlberg (1986) Puffin	Baby-preschool	plum

Chapter 5 – M & N

Final / m /

Title	Publication Information	Interest Level	Target Words
Mary Had a Little Lamb	Iza Trapani (2001) Charlesbridge	2-4 years	lamb
A Farm's Not a Farm	Brenda Parkes (1989) Rigby	4-8 years	farm

Initial /n/

Title	Publication Information	Interest Level	Target Words
Know Your Nose	June A. English (2000) Golden Books	2-5 years	nose, know
What's That Noise?	William Carman (2002) Random House	4-8 years	night, noise, knob
No, David!	David Shannon (1998) Scholastic	4-8 years	no, not
The Napping House	Audrey Wood (1984) Harcourt Brace Co.	4-8 years	napping
A Perfect Name	Charlene Costanzo (2002) Dial	4-8 years	name
Good Night, Gorilla	Peggy Rathman (1996) Putnam Juvenile	Baby-preschool	night

Final / n /

Title	Publication Information	Interest Level	Target Words
Nine Men Chase a Hen	Barbara Gregorich (1993) School Zone Publishing	4-8 years	nine, men, hen, run
One Bean	Anne Rockwell (1999) Walker & Co.	4-8 years	one, bean
The Jellybean Fun Book	Karen Capucilli (2003) Little Simon	4-8 years	bean, brown, green
The Gingerbread Man	Catherine McCafferty (2001) Brighter Child	4-8 years	man, run, can
It's Pumpkin Time	Zoe Hall (1999) Scholastic	4-8 years	pumpkin, Halloween, green

M & N Activity Pages

Regardless of your approach to treatment, a variety of activities should be used to bombard children with correct productions of the target sound and to elicit production practice. The activities in this unit include a range of sound-specific options for /m/ and /n/. They are designed to appeal to children between the ages of 2 and 7.

In addition, remember the following are available to support your teaching of the /m/ and /n/ sounds:

- **More Activity Ideas** that can be used to target any sound are included in Appendix A.

- Sound-specific **Pictures** to be used with activities are found on pages 84-91.

- A **Blank Card Pattern**, to include your own words, is found in Appendix D.

- **Book Lists** for selecting stories are included on pages 77-78.

- **Word, Phrase, and Sentence Lists** are provided on pages 74-76, to use with activities or with more traditional boards games (e.g., Sorry! Uno, and Kerplunk). To earn a turn, have the older student read or repeat words, phrases, or sentences containing the selected target phoneme. The goal is to encourage as many repetitions of the target sound as possible—be creative!

- **Homework Pages** (pages 96-103) provide activities that can be easily used by parents or other care providers to encourage successful practice in other settings. Be certain to direct children to return completed Homework Pages so that you can encourage self-evaluation and monitoring of their practice. Consider having students carry a "speech folder" to store these materials and facilitate communication with others on a regular basis.

- Appendix B provides a **Parent Memo** that can be used along with selected homework activity pages.

- Appendix E includes a blank **Lesson Plan**. Use the form to ensure that all essential lesson plan components are accounted for within each session. Be certain to probe for accuracy, provide instruction/bombardment for the target sounds, and plan for a sufficient amount of successful mass production practice.

- Appendix F provides a blank **Data Collection Form** to monitor progress and adjust treatment.

- Don't forget that **Suggestions for Conversation and Carryover** are provided in Appendix B. Plan for generalization from the start and incorporate these suggestions along the way.

Chapter 5 – M & N

Initial M Activities

Snack Ideas
- Mini-muffins, marshmallows, M&Ms, melon, mini-bagels
- Milk, milkshake

Craft
- Marble Paint—Place a piece of paper into a shoebox top and drop various paint colors on the paper. Place a few marbles on top of the paper and instruct the child to hold the box top and tip each end of the top to make the marbles roll around spreading the paint.

Motor and Movement
- Musical Chairs
- March to Music

Songs and Finger Play

Do You Know the Muffin Man

Oh, do you know the muffin man,
The muffin man, the muffin man,
Oh, do you know the muffin man,
That lives on Drury Lane?
Oh, yes, I know the muffin man,
The muffin man, the muffin man,
Oh, yes, I know the muffin man,
That lives on Drury Lane.

Muffin Match

Materials
- Initial /m/ book
- Muffin Pattern, page 92
- Word-initial /m/ pictures, page 84
- Glue or tape

Procedure

1. Bombard the child with word-initial /m/ by introducing the sound with a story selected from the book list.

2. Duplicate a copy of the muffin pattern. Duplicate two sets of the initial /m/ pictures. Attach one picture to each muffin.

3. Choose six to eight muffins to make three to four pairs for the activity. You may want to attach them to cardstock or construction paper and laminate for future use. Place the muffins face down on a table. Have children pick two muffins in an attempt to find a match. Continue playing until all matches are found.

4. Have children listen as you bombard them with initial /m/ words. Elicit productions if appropriate, as children turn over the cards.

5. Variations can include pulling muffins from a bucket or basket to find a match. Pass out a muffin to each child and instruct him or her to find the match by finding a classmate who has the same muffin

M Activity Pages

Final M Activities

Same Home

Materials
- Final /m/ book
- House Pattern, page 93
- Hula-Hoop, or yarn or string
- Word-final /m/ pictures, page 86
- Glue or tape
- Crayons or markers (optional)

Procedure

1. Bombard the child with word-final /m/ by introducing the sound with a story selected from the book list.
2. Duplicate the house pattern. Color the houses (optional). Duplicate two sets of the final /m/ pictures. Adhere one picture to each house.
3. Have children sit in a circle. Place a Hula-Hoop or make a circle out of yarn and place it in the center of the children. Place six houses in the circle. Make sure there are three pairs. Let the children take turns finding the houses that are the same.
4. Bombard the children with the target words (e.g., *same, home*), or elicit production of each target, as the home pairs are selected. Bombard with and elicit productions of sentences and phrases such as, "You found the same home!"
5. Consider variations such as bombarding them with final /m/ words from the target list for additional listening practice.

Snack Ideas
- Lime, plum
- Lime or plum juice

Craft
- Cookie Home—Use graham crackers, frosting, and candies to create a mini-gingerbread house. Use the frosting to "glue" four squares together. Add two more crackers and shape into a roof. Decorate with small candies such as, M&Ms, Dots, chocolate chips, and sprinkles.

Motor and Movement
- Get Home—Create and obstacle course for the children to go through. The mission is to get to "home" at the end.

Songs and Finger Play

Baby Bumblebee

*I'm bringing **home** my baby bumblebee*

Won't my mommy be so proud of me?

*I'm bringing **home** my baby bumblebee*

Ouch……it stung me!

Chapter 5 – M & N

Initial N Activities

Snack Ideas
- Rice Krispie nests. Make a Rice Krispie treat recipe, add food coloring, and shape the treat into a nest. Add jelly beans or M&Ms for bird eggs.
- Nectar (juice or Kool-aid).

Craft
- Play Dough Nests—Use a standard play dough recipe. When completed, form the dough into nests, let dry to harden. Use additional play dough to create bird eggs to put in the nest.

Motor and Movement
- Net Ball—Arrange the children in groups of two. Give each child a net (lacrosse sticks work well too) and toss a ball or balloon back and forth to try to catch it in the net.

Songs and Finger Plays

Home Sweet Home

A nest is a home for a bluebird
[cup hands to form a nest],

A hive is a home for a bee
[turn cupped hands over],

A hole is a home for a chipmunk
[make a hole with hands],

And a house is a home for me
[make roof with peaked hands].

Net or Nest?

Materials
- Initial /n/ book
- Net and Nest Patterns, page 94
- Word-initial /n/ pictures, page 88
- Glue or tape

Procedure

1. Bombard the child with word-initial /n/ by introducing the sound with a story selected from the book list.

2. Duplicate multiple copies of the Net and Nest Patterns. Duplicate the set of initial /n/ pictures. Attach one picture to each net or nest pattern with glue or tape.

3. Attached the nets and nests around the room and instruct the children to take a turn finding a net or nest, return to the group, and report what they found.

4. Bombard the children with the words "net" and "nest" and, as appropriate, elicit productions based on each child's skill level. Encourage the children to correctly label the /n/ word on their nest or net or say "It's a net," or "it's a nest."

5. Variations can include just labeling net or nest and not the /n/ words.

N Activity Pages

Final N Activities

Build a Cone

Materials
- Final /n/ book
- Cone
- Cone and Scoop Patterns, page 95
- Word-final /n/ pictures, page 90
- Scissors
- Glue or tape

Procedure

1. Bombard the child with word-final /n/ by introducing the sound with a story selected from the book list.

2. Duplicate one Cone Pattern for each child and up to 10 Scoop Patterns per child. Duplicate word-final /n/ pictures and attach one to each scoop with glue or tape.

3. Instruct the children to pick a scoop and add it to their cone. Encourage the children to add 10 scoops.

4. Bombard with the words "ten" and "cone" and, as appropriate, elicit productions based on each child's skill level. Encourage the children to correctly label the /n/ words on the scoops as they add them to their cone.

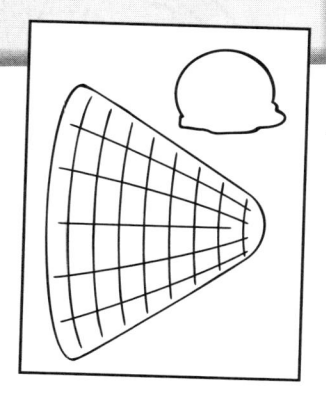

Snack Ideas
- Bran muffin, ice-cream cone
- Green juice (Kool-Aid or Gatorade type drinks)
- Green Jell-O

Craft
- Hand Print Ice Cream Cones—Trace three handprints in various colors to represent ice cream flavors (e.g., pink, white, brown). Cut out and attach them upside down and sideways to the cone pattern.

Motor and Movement
- Ice-Cream Cone Race—Use a bowl full of cottonballs and a cup to represent a cone. Put the children together in pairs, lining them up on either side of the room. One child holds the "cone" and the other child scoops the ice cream "cottonballs" out of the bowl with a large spoon or ice cream scoop and walks across the room, balancing the cottonballs on the spoon. Once they get to their partners, they put the ice cream into the cone. They continue until the cone is full.

Songs and Finger Plays

Ice-Cream Cone

One scoop, two scoops, three scoops, four.

Ice cream in a cone-we want MORE!

Initial M Picture Cards

mail	man
map	mat
me	meal

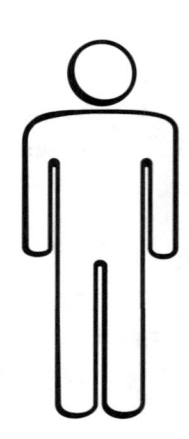

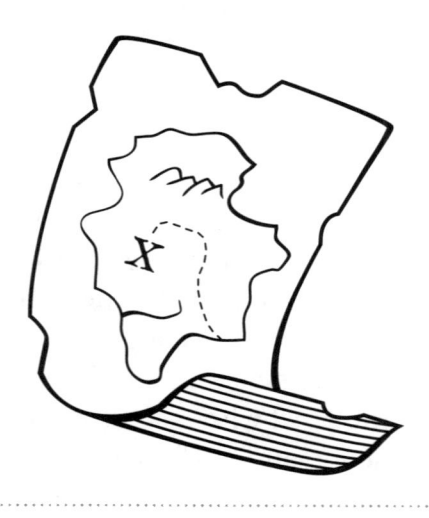

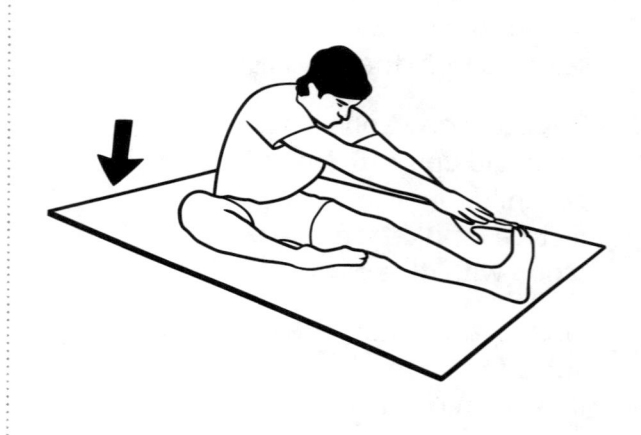

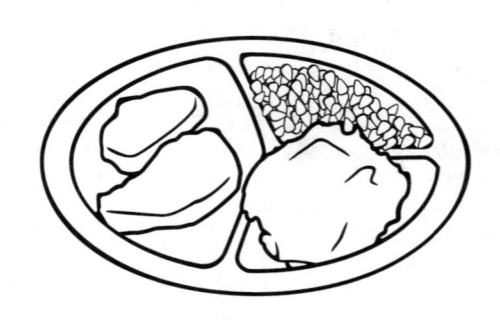

84 The Entire World of Early Developing Sounds Instructional Workbook™

© 2008 Say It Right™   www.sayitright.org

Initial M Picture Cards

mud

milk

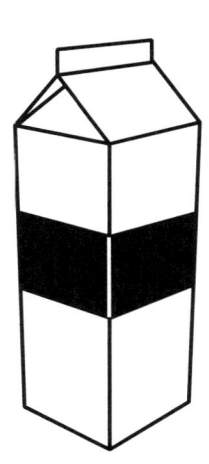

moon

mop

mouse

moth

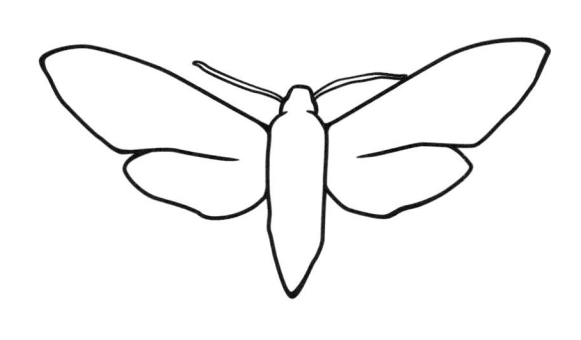

Final M Picture Cards

broom	comb
drum	game
ham	home

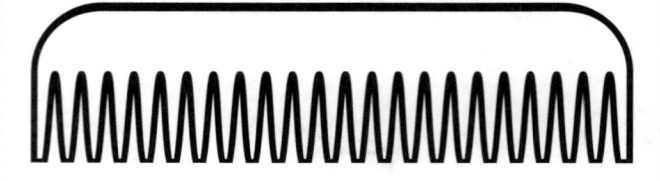

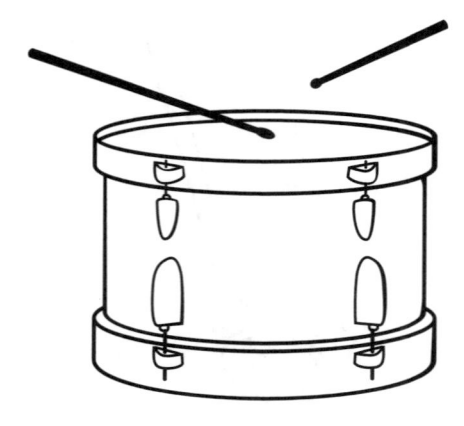

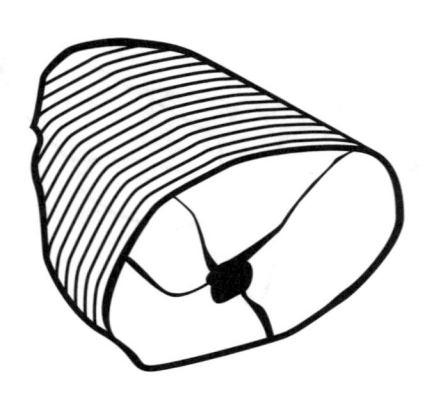

86 The Entire World of Early Developing Sounds Instructional Workbook™ © 2008 Say It Right™ www.sayitright.org

Final M Picture Cards

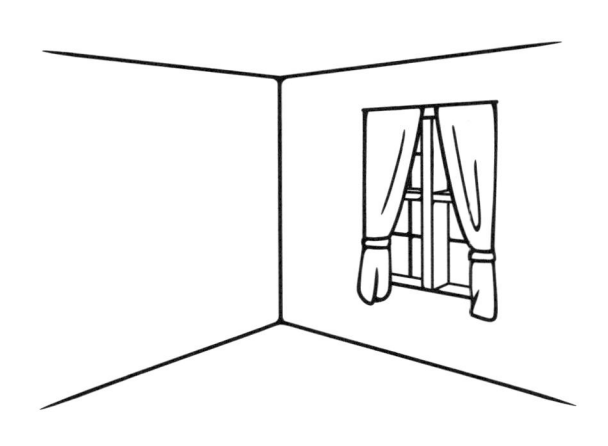

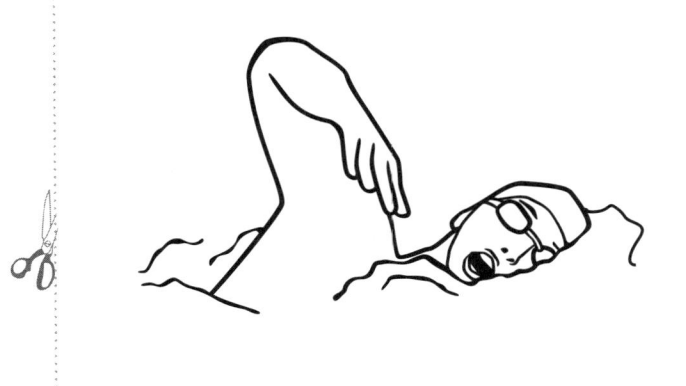

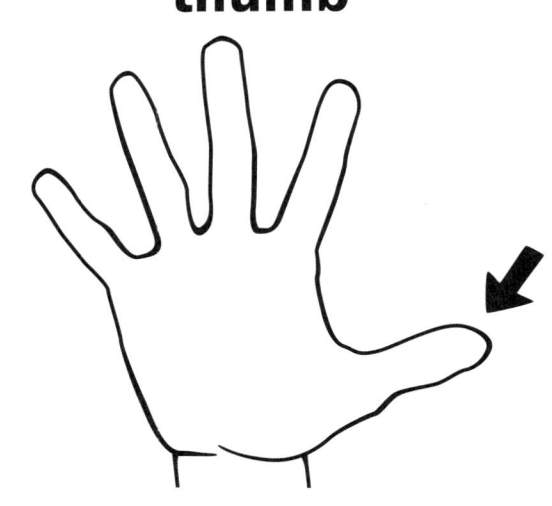

jam	lamb
ram	room
swim	thumb

Initial N Picture Cards

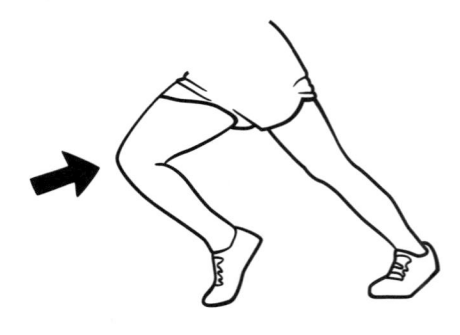

knee	nail
name	nap
neck	nest

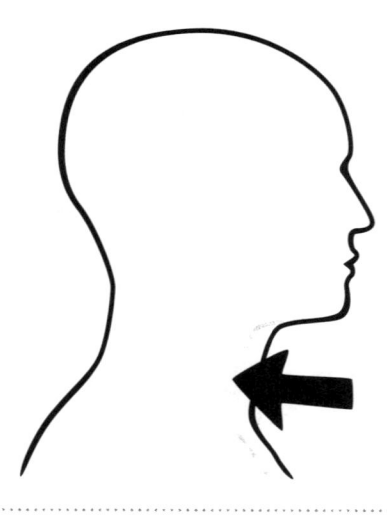

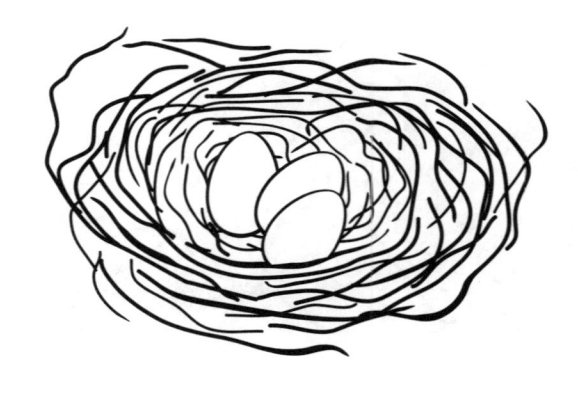

88 The Entire World of Early Developing Sounds Instructional Workbook™ © 2008 Say It Right™ www.sayitright.org

Initial N Picture Cards

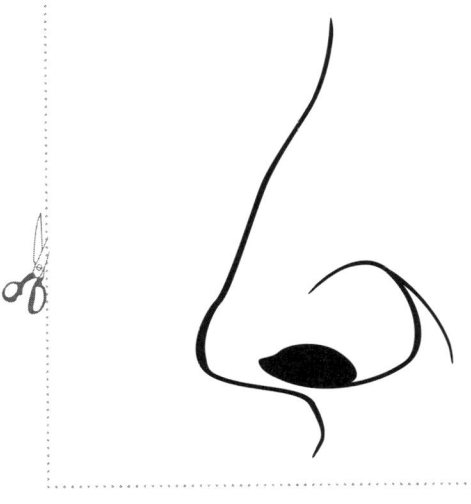

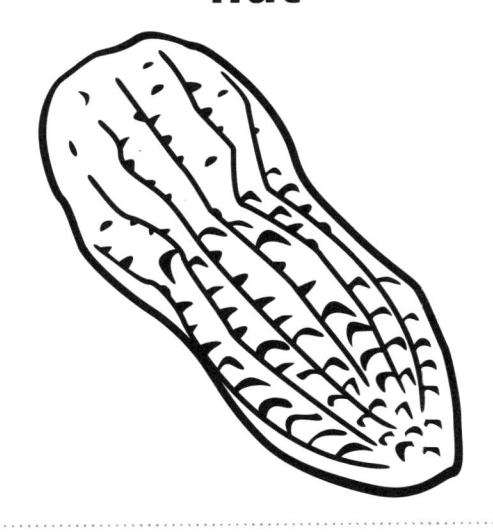

net	nice
night	no
nose	nut

Final N Picture Cards

one	ten
1	**10**

can	bean

clown	fan

90 The Entire World of Early Developing Sounds Instructional Workbook™   © 2008 Say It Right™ www.sayitright.org

Final N Picture Cards

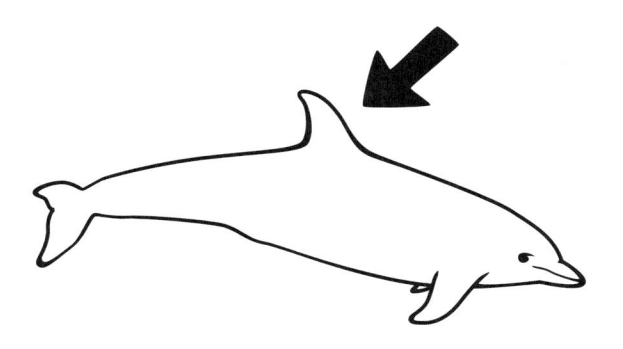

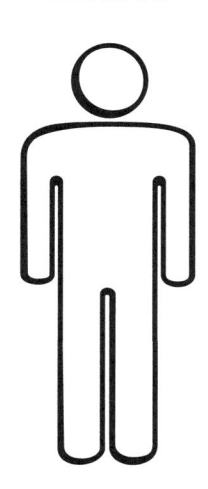

fin	man
chin	pan
van	sun

Chapter 5 – M & N

Muffin Pattern

M Activity Patterns

House Pattern

93

Chapter 5 – M & N

Net and Nest Patterns

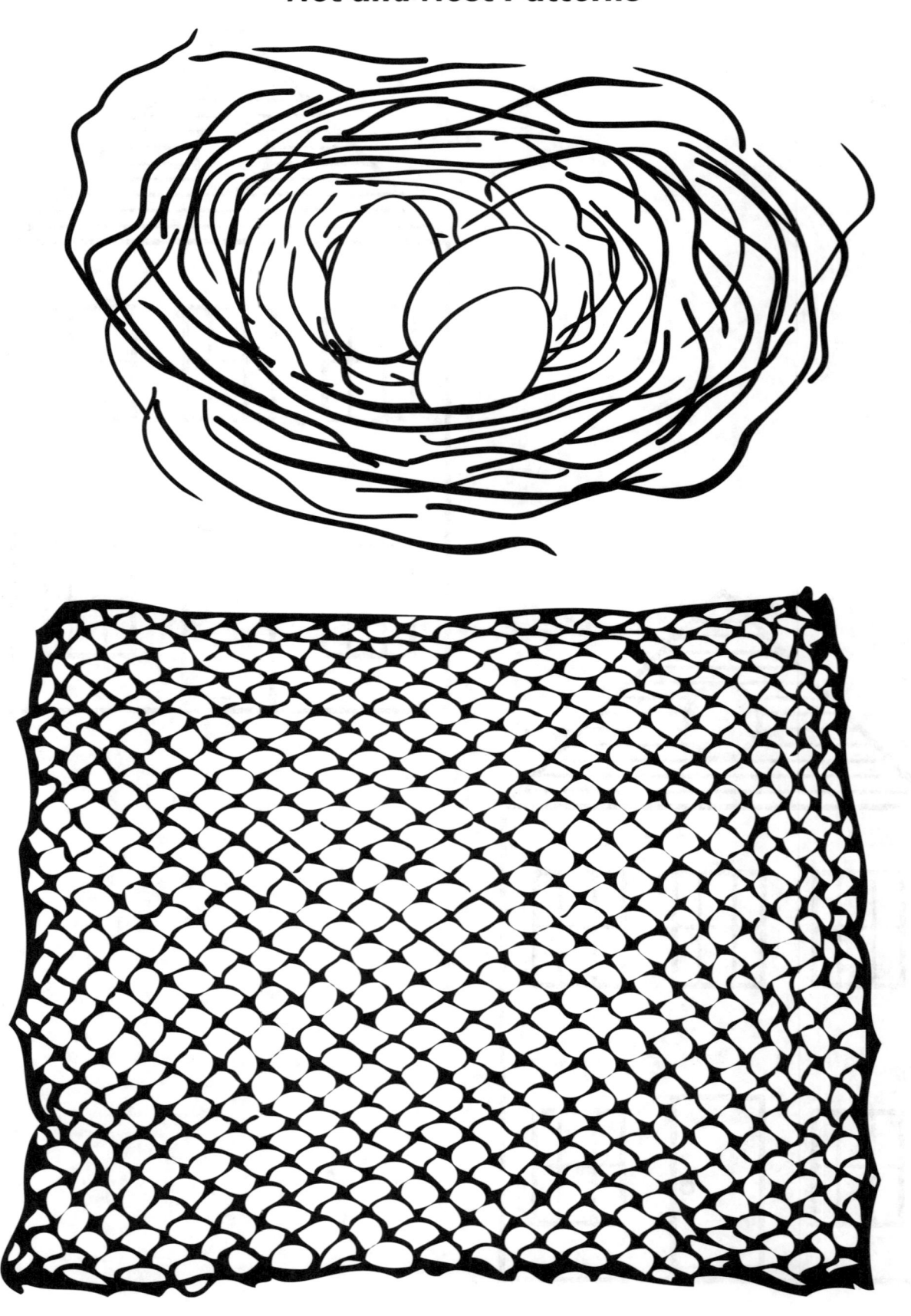

N Activity Patterns

Cone and Scoop Patterns

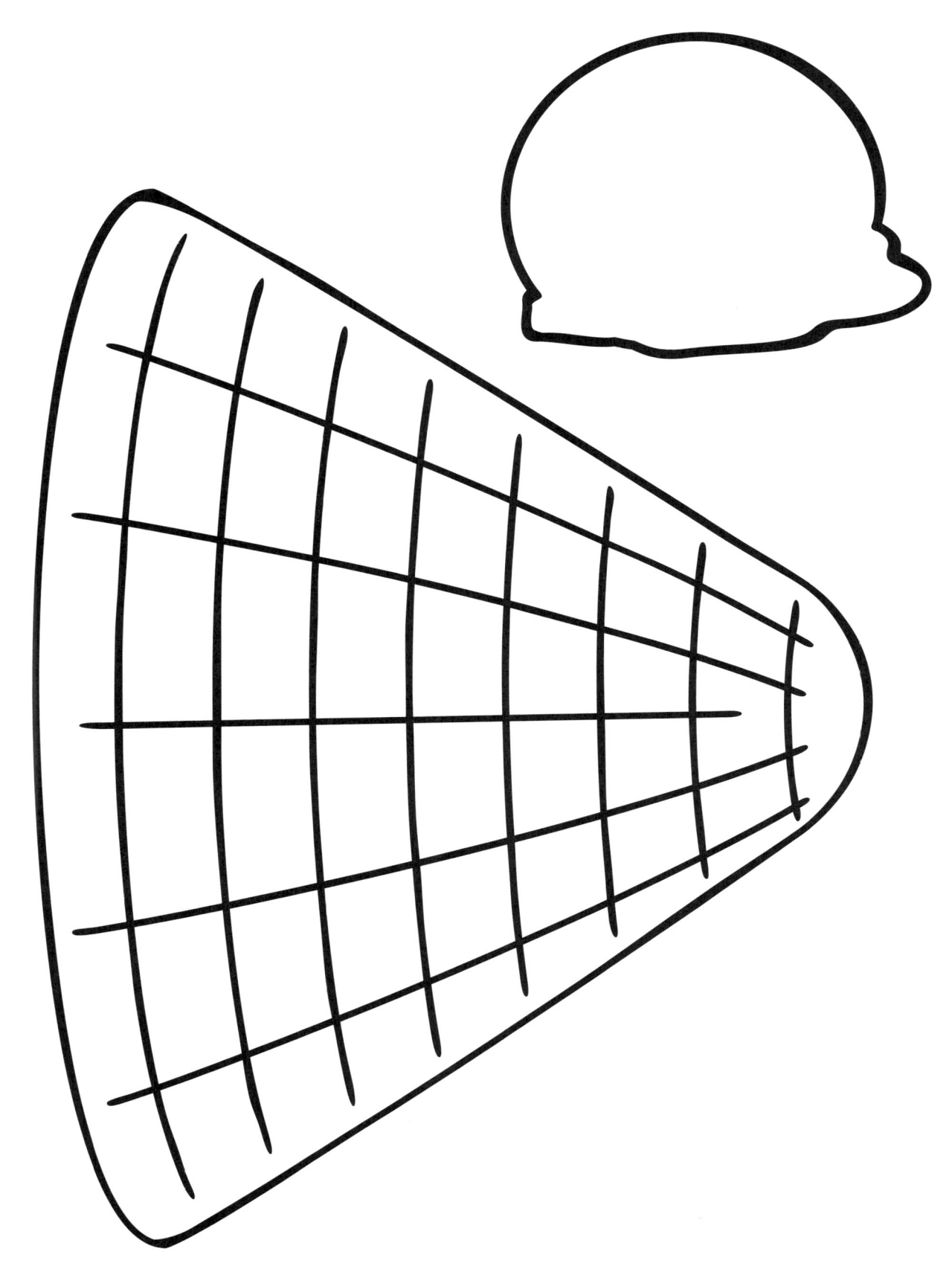

Chapter 5–M & N

Mom's Mop

Child: Mom needs to find her mop. She is holding one that looks like hers. Try to find the one that matches. When you find the matching mop, circle it and say, "I found Mom's mop."

Helper: Emphasize good pronunciation of the "M" sound.

M Homework

Moon Match

Child: Find the moon that matches each scene. Draw a line from each moon to the correct scene. Say the word "moon" each time you make a match.

Helper: Emphasize correct production of the "M" sound as the child searches for the matching moon.

Chapter 5 – M & N

Climb the Ladder

Child: Walk your fingers up the ladder, stop at each rung and name the picture. Make sure you use a correct "M" sound or you will need to go back down the ladder and start again.

Helper: Emphasize correct production of "M."

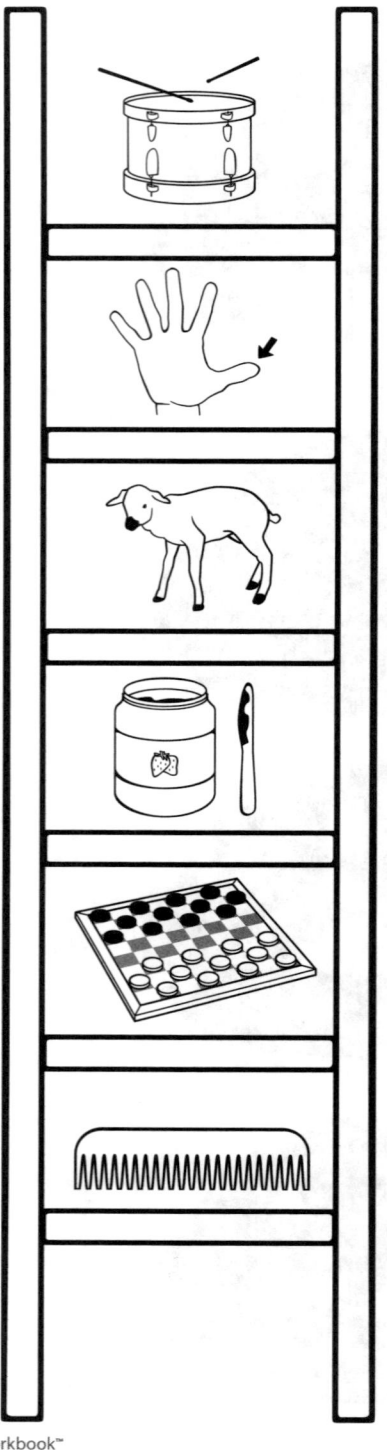

M Homework

Rhyme Time

Child: Draw a line to all the pictures that rhyme with the word time. Say each word.

Helper: Model the names of the pictures. Have the child repeat after you. Emphasize correct production of the "M" sound at the end of the words.

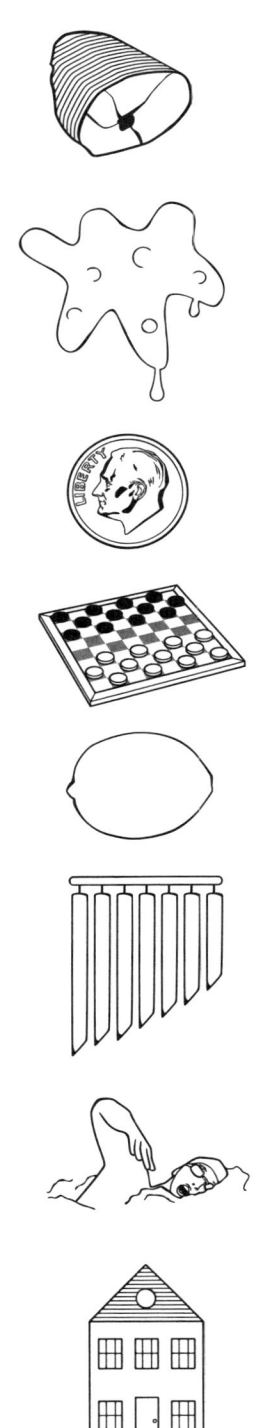

Chapter 5 – M & N

Nick's News

Child: Nick has good news. Retell the story after you hear it.

Helper: Read the story aloud. Emphasize the "N" sound as you read. Encourage the child to retell the story using the correct production of the "N" sound. For more practice, cut out the pictures and have the child put them in the correct order.

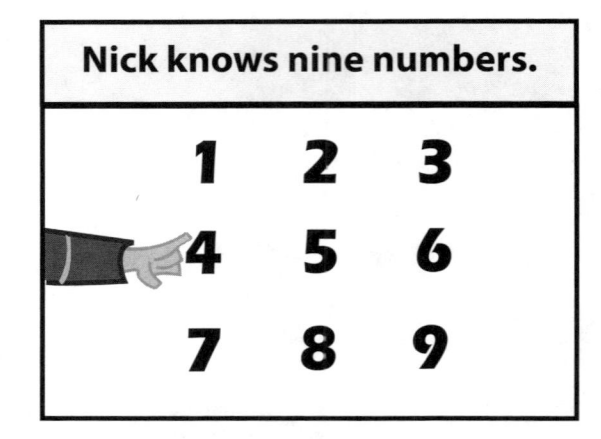

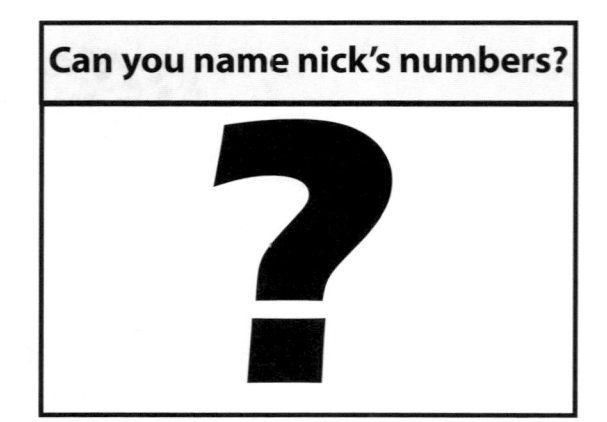

Nick has good news.	Nick knows nine numbers.
Can you name nick's numbers?	Nick can count up.
Nick can count down.	Nice counting nick!

N Homework

Ten Men

Child: There are 10 men hidden in the forest. Find the men and circle them. When you find them, say, "I found a man."

Helper: Model saying the words "man" and "men." Have the child repeat the words after you if needed.

Chapter 5 – M & N

Van Rhyme

Child: Draw a line from the van to each picture that rhymes with the word van. Say each word.

Helper: Model saying each picture and emphasize the final "N" sound. Have the child repeat after you.

N Homework

Last Sound is N

Child: Name all the pictures below. Then color the pictures that end with the "N" sound.

Helper: Help the child find the words ending in "N." Say it for the child and have the child repeat it.

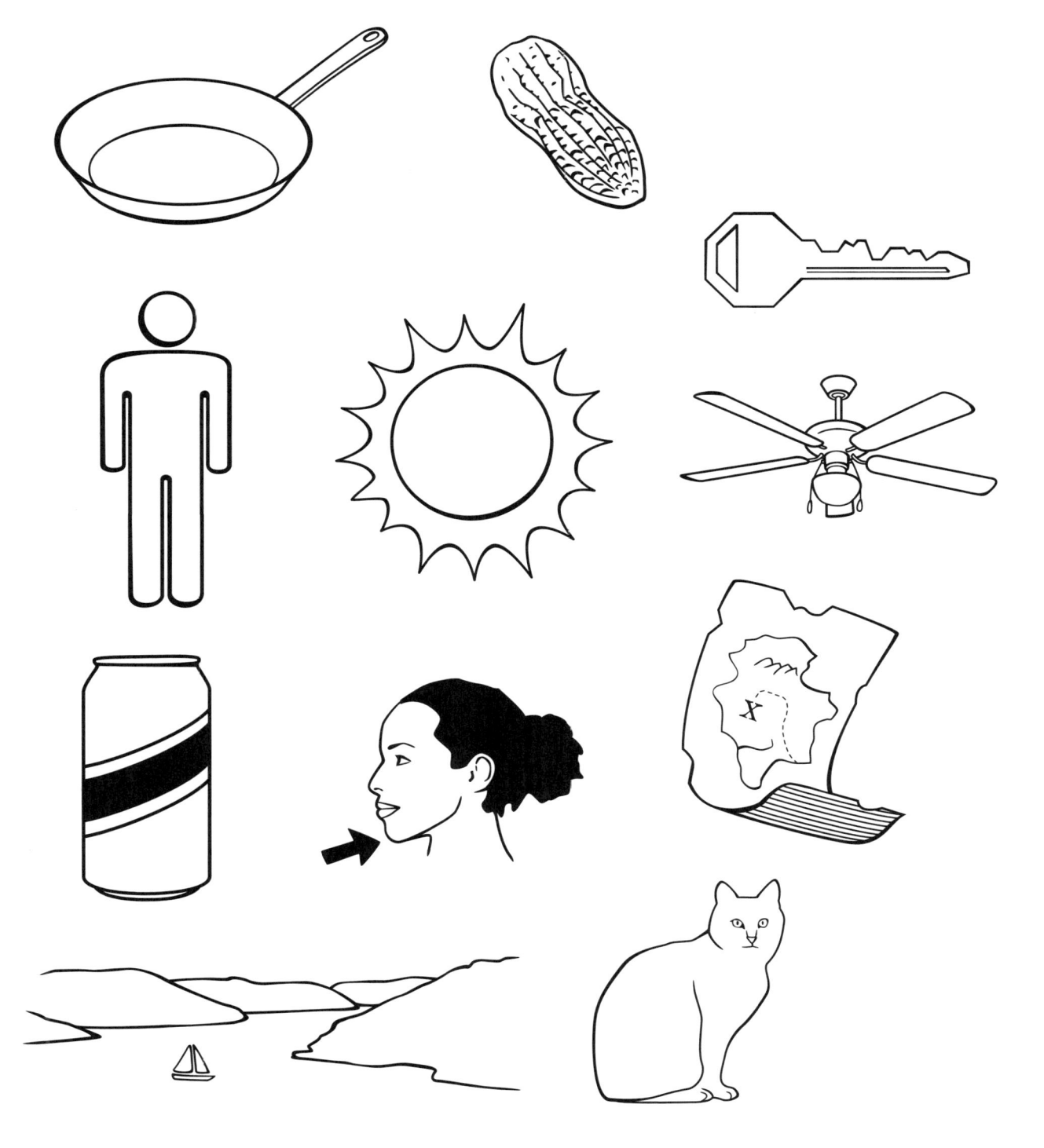

Chapter 6
Targeting K & G

- Screening Tool
- Teaching Tips
- Production Illustrations
- Target Lists
- Book Lists
- Activities
- Pictures
- Patterns
- Homework Pages

K & G Screening

Student Name_____ Date of Birth_____

Screening Date_____ Examiner_____

Use "+" or "—" to indicate the child's production of the phoneme at each level (in isolation, in a word, in a phrase, and in a sentence). Use imitation, delayed imitation, or pictures to elicit the child's productions.

Target–Initial /k/	Target–Final /k/	Target–Initial /g/	Target–Final /g/
SOUND IN ISOLATION: /k/		**SOUND IN ISOLATION:** /g/	
cap	lake	go	bag
yellow cap	in a lake	to go	blowing fan
I want to wear a baseball cap.	Let's go swim in the lake.	It's time to go to bed now.	Put the groceries in a paper bag.
cup	bike	game	pig
juice cup	a new bike	game played	muddy pig
Fill the cup with juice.	I won a new bike at the fair.	Let's play a card game tonight.	The pig won first prize.
cave	sick	gum	jog
creepy cave	very sick	chew gum	time to jog
The cave was the bear's home.	I am sick with a very bad cold.	Sam bought gum at the store.	I like to jog every morning.

DATA COLLECTION/SCREENING NOTES:

K & G Teaching Tips

Development Information

The consonant pair /k/ and /g/ begins to develop early for some children. Children will start to use /k/ and /g/ as early as 18 months of age. Mastery of the /k/ and /g/ sound pair occurs for most children between 3 and 4 years of age (Sander, 1972). The plosive energy and unique placement at the velum that combine to create these two sounds makes them salient, thus early development often occurs. For many children, /t/ and /d/ is substituted for /k/ and /g/ between 2 and 4 years of age (Grunwell, 1987). This phonological process is referred to a fronting and serves to simplify the production of the two velar sounds. For most children, velar fronting is suppressed by 4 years of age (Grunwell).

Production of /k/ and /g/

This sound pair is velar (i.e., made with contact between the velum and the pharynx) and plosive (i.e., produced with a burst of air). The /k/ is unvoiced, thus the vocal folds are not set into vibration, while the /g/ is voiced. The teeth are held slightly apart and the velum is lifted quickly, allowing air pressure to explode through the oral cavity.

Stimulating Production of /k/ and /g/

For children who struggle to produce /k/ and /g/, some work with the sound in isolation may be warranted. The following strategies may be useful when stimulating production of the sounds in isolation.

- Use the illustrations on page 108 to provide additional instruction for placement of /k/ and /g/. As needed, keep these images displayed during practice with these target sounds.

- Use an age-appropriate description of the processes for producing these sounds.

- Sit side-by-side with the child in front of a mirror. Encourage the child to watch as you part your lips slightly to demonstrate /k/ and /g/. Cue the child by tapping the throat area. Direct the child to imitate your productions of /k/ and /g/.

- To encourage the voicing feature, direct the child to apply light fingertip pressure to his/her throat or your throat as the /k/ and /g/ contrasts are produced. Talking about "turning on" your voice to make the vibration or buzzing associated with voiced /g/.

- Direct the child to cough or gently clear his/her throat. Draw attention to the velar movement. Pair the throat cough/clear with simple /k/ or /g/ words such as *go* or *key*.

Chapter 6 – K & G

K & G Production Illustrations

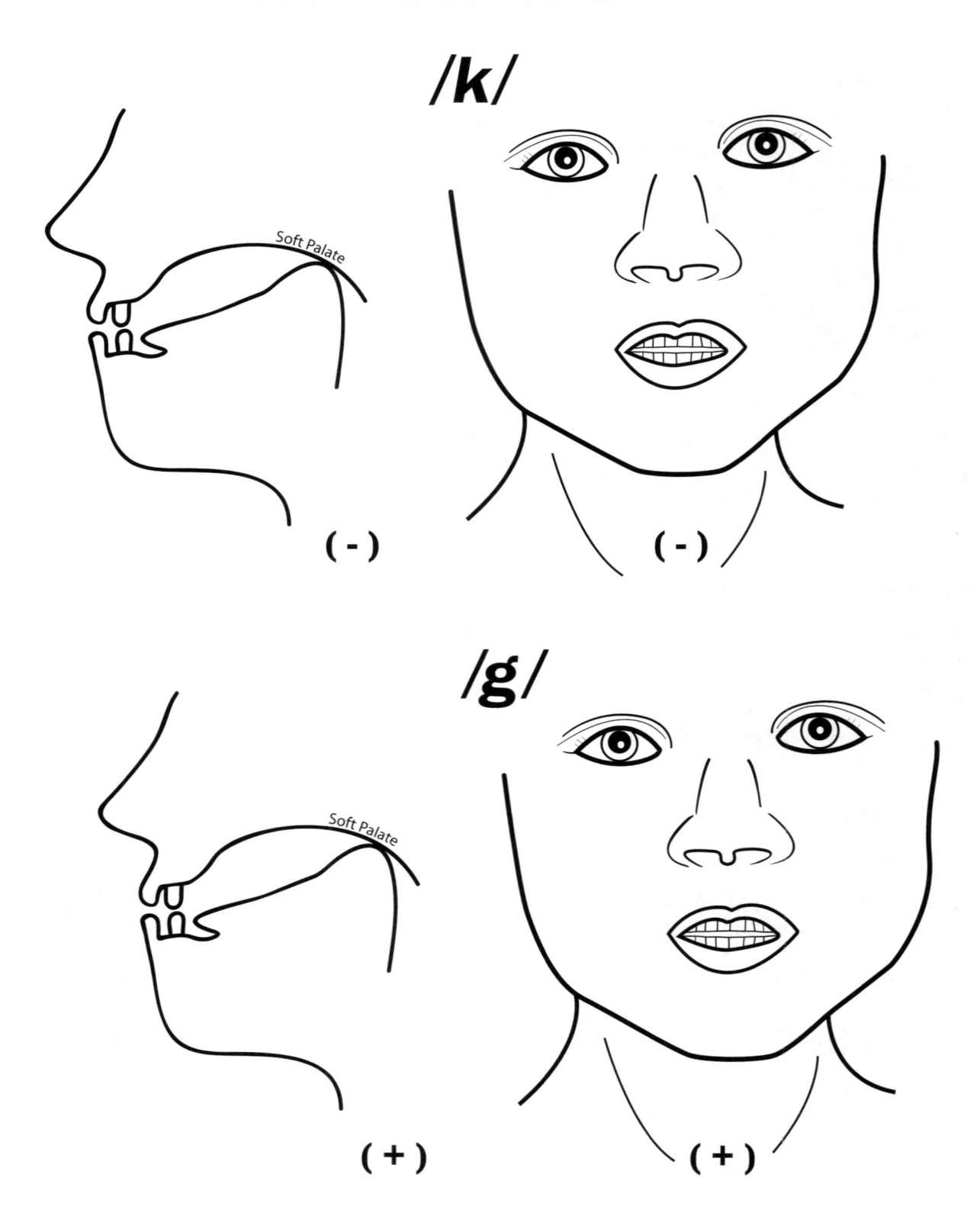

/k/

Soft Palate

(-)   (-)

/g/

Soft Palate

(+)   (+)

K & G Target Lists

Especially during early stages of practice, single-syllable words are most facilitative for accurate productions of target sounds. Consider the surrounding consonant and vowel sounds in a target word to control for other sounds the child may be lacking. For example, when first targeting initial /k/ with a child, avoid words that also contain medial and/or final /k/. Gradually, as a child becomes more successful with practice of a selected target, words of increasing length and complexity can be added to the production-practice activities.

The Entire World of Early Developing Sounds suggests using the target words listed for the early stages of practice with young children working on /k/ and /g/. Pages 120-127 provide representations of these words in picture form for use with production practice activities. Suggested target phrases and sentences are also provided. Phrases and sentences are most useful with older children who can read. *The Entire World of K & G Articulation Flip Book* (Ristuccia, 2004) is an excellent source for illustrated, interactive phrase and sentence practice.

When working with older children, the word, phrase, and sentence lists may be useful as stimulus items in mass production practice. If using the phrases and sentences with nonreaders, direct or delayed imitation will be necessary (i.e., saying the phrase or sentence as a model and then having the child repeat it with or without a delay). Ideally, production of phrases and sentences will be elicited naturally during structured and unstructured activities, thus it is possible that the phrase and sentence lists would not need to be used with younger children.

To target medial /k/ and /g/, use of the target words in combination with another word (e.g., "my cup" to elicit medial /k/ or "bubble gum" for medial /g/). Medial /k/ and /g/ target words can be added once a child is ready for practice with multisyllabic words. As medial /k/ and /g/ words are selected, continue to control for facilitative contexts to ensure children successfully produce the new sound. In addition, use multisyllabic words that are meaningful to the child (e.g., *goosebumps*, *cabin*, etc.).

Chapter 6–K & G

K & G Single Word Practice

Word–Initial /k/	Word–Final /k/	Word–Initial /g/	Word–Final /g/
calf	back	game	bag
can	bike	gas	bug
cape	block	goose	egg
cave	book	gear	frog
car	chick	ghost	hug
corn	lake	girl	jog
cow	neck	golf	jug
cub	pick	go	leg
cup	rake	good	log
cap	sack	gown	mug
key	sick	gull	pig
king	snack	gum	rug

K & G Phrase-Level Practice

Word–Initial /k/	Word–Final /k/	Word–Initial /g/	Word–Final /g/
little **calf**	in the **back**	playing a **game**	open the **bag**
can opener	new **bike**	**gas** tank	small **bug**
Batman's **cape**	yellow **block**	**goose** in the lake	crack the **egg**
a large **cave**	**book** to read	put it in **gear**	tree **frog**
drive a **car**	yellow **chick**	friendly **ghost**	giant **hug**
yellow **corn**	jump in the **lake**	a baby **girl**	**jog** uphill
the brown **cow**	around her **neck**	a **golf** course	fill the **jug**
a bear **cub**	**pick** it	**go** away	**leg** up
use the **cup**	old **rake**	**good** show	ants on a **log**
cap on	old **sack**	a wedding **gown**	a large **mug**
room **key**	**sick** of it	the **gull** flies	a messy **pig**
new **king**	yummy **snack**	bubble **gum**	use the **rug**

Chapter 6 – K & G

K & G Sentence-Level Practice

Word–Initial /k/	Word–Final /k/	Word–Initial /g/	Word–Final /g/
The **calf** ate grass.	Scratch her **back**.	I played the new **game**.	The lunch **bag** is empty.
The **can** is full of garbage.	She rode her new **bike**.	The car ran out of **gas**.	The tiny **bug** flies fast.
He wore a blue **cape**.	He will use the **block** to build.	The **goose** ate the feed.	The bird laid an **egg**.
The bear lives in the **cave**.	She read a good **book**.	Put the bike in **gear**.	The small **frog** jumped high.
The red **car** is fast.	The yellow **chick** is small.	She saw a friendly **ghost** in her dream.	The baby will **hug** his mom.
She ate **corn** for dinner.	The **lake** is deep.	The **girl** ran in the field.	He went for a long **jog**.
The **cow** mooed.	She wore a scarf around her **neck**.	The **golf** balls were in the pond.	He bought a **jug** of juice.
The bear **cub** wanted his mother.	**Pick** up the toys.	**Go** home now!	His **leg** hurt after he played soccer.
She needs a **cup**.	**Rake** the leaves in the yard.	The boy was **good** today.	The **log** cabin is in the woods.
He wore a **cap** to show team spirit.	The **sack** is heavy.	Her wedding **gown** is beautiful.	She broke the white **mug**.
The **key** is under the mat.	She felt **sick** last night.	The **gull** flew over the lake.	The **pig** played in the mud.
The **king** sat on his throne.	They had a **snack** after nap time.	The **gum** is on the shelf.	She slipped on the **rug**.

K & G Book List

Reading a story is a natural and motivating activity for children. Children's stories are filled with opportunities to bombard the child with words containing the target sound and to elicit productions of the target. Consult the following list to select books that contain multiple opportunities for words that contain /k/ or /g/.

	INITIAL /k/		
Title	**Publication Information**	**Interest Level**	**Target Words**
Curious George Flies a Kite	Margret Rey (1997) Houghton Mifflin	4-8 years	curious
Click, Clack, Moo: Cows That Type	Doreen Cronin (2001) Scholastic	4-8 years	click, clack, cow
Something's Coming	Richard Edward (1995) Candlewick	Baby-preschool	coming, cupboards
Kiss, Kiss	Margaret Wild (2003) Simon & Schuster	Baby-preschool	kiss, cub
The Giant Carrot	Jan Peck (1998) Dial	Baby-preschool	carrot, cornflower
Watch Out! Big Bro's Coming	Jez Alborough (1998) Candlewick	4-8 years	coming
The Caboose Who Got Loose	Bill Peet (1980) Houghton Mifflin	4-8 years	caboose
The Mitten	Jan Brett (1989) Putnam Publishing	4-8 years	mitten, mole, mouse, my, made, move
	FINAL /k/		
The Unicorn and the Lake	Marianna Mayer (1992) Puffin	4-8 years	lake
If You Give a Pig a Pancake	Laura Numeroff (1998) Scholastic	4-8 years	pancake
Bark, George	Jules Feiffer (1999) Laura Geringer	4-8 years	bark, quack
One Duck Stuck	Phyllis Root (2003) Candlewick	Baby-preschool	stuck, splack

Chapter 6 – K & G

Final /k/

Title	Publication Information	Interest Level	Target Words
Duck on a Bike	David Shannon (2002) Blue Sky	4-8 years	*bike, squeak, back, cluck, chick*

Initial /g/

Title	Publication Information	Interest Level	Target Words
Giggle, Giggle, Quack	Doreen Cronin (2002) Simon and Schuster	4-8 years	*giggle*
My Gum is Gone	Richard Yurcheshen (2000) Magnum Imprint	4-8 years	*gum, gone, goo, go, guess*
Go!	Daniel Kirk (2001) Random House	4-8 years	*go*
The Golden Egg Book	Margaret Wise Brown ((2004) Golden Books	Baby-preschool	*egg*
Boo to a Goose	Mem Fox (2001) Puffin	4-8 years	*goose*
Good Night, Gorilla	Peggy Rathman (1996) Putnam Juvenile	Baby-preschool	*night*

Final /n/

Title	Publication Information	Interest Level	Target Words
Big Pig on a Dig	Jenny Tyler (1999) Sagebrush	1-4 years	*big, pig, hog*
Pig Gets Stuck	Heather Amery (1989) Usborne Publishing	4-8 years	*pig*
An Extraordinary Egg	Leo Lionni (1998) Dragonfly Books	4-8 years	*egg, frog*
Little Grunt and the Big Egg	Tomie dePaola (1990) Holiday House	4-8 years	*egg*
Too Big	Claire Masurel (1999) Chronicle Books	Baby-preschool	*big*

K & G Activity Pages

Regardless of your approach to treatment, a variety of activities should be used to bombard children with correct productions of the target sound and to elicit production practice. The activities in this unit include a range of sound-specific options for /k/ and /g/. They are designed to appeal to children between the ages of 2 and 7.

In addition, remember the following are available to support your teaching of the /k/ and /g/ sounds:

- **More Activity Ideas** that can be used to target any sound are included in Appendix A.

- Sound-specific **Pictures** to be used with activities are found on pages 120-127.

- A **Blank Card Pattern**, to include your own words, is found in Appendix D.

- **Book Lists** for selecting stories are included on pages 113-114.

- **Word, Phrase, and Sentence Lists** are provided on pages 110-112, to use with activities or with more traditional boards games (e.g., Sorry! Uno, and Kerplunk). To earn a turn, have the older student read or repeat words, phrases, or sentences containing the selected target phoneme. The goal is to encourage as many repetitions of the target sound as possible—be creative!

- **Homework Pages** (pages 138-145) provide activities that can be easily used by parents or other care providers to encourage successful practice in other settings. Be certain to direct children to return completed Homework Pages so that you can encourage self-evaluation and monitoring of their practice. Consider having students carry a "speech folder" to store these materials and facilitate communication with others on a regular basis.

- Appendix B provides a **Parent Memo** that can be used along with selected homework activity pages.

- Appendix E includes a blank **Lesson Plan**. Use the form to ensure that all essential lesson plan components are accounted for within each session. Be certain to probe for accuracy, provide instruction/bombardment for the target sounds, and plan for a sufficient amount of successful mass production practice.

- Appendix F provides a blank **Data Collection Form** to monitor progress and adjust treatment.

- Don't forget that **Suggestions for Conversation and Carryover** are provided in Appendix B. Plan for generalization from the start and incorporate these suggestions along the way.

Chapter 6 – K & G

Initial K Activities

Snack Ideas
- Cookies, crackers, carrots, teddy grahams (cubs)
- Cocoa, Kool-Aid (cub juice)

Craft
- Cub Puppet—Create a cub puppet. Duplicate the Cub Puppet Pattern (page 128). Cut out the head, the paws, and the tail. Attach them to a paper lunch bag. Bombard the children with phrases and sentences that include the word "cub."

Motor and Movement
- Create a Cave—Place a blanket over a small table for a "cave." Have the children pretend they are cubs and wander the room until their "mother" calls them back to the cave. During the activity bombard the children with the phrase, "Cubs come to the cave."

Songs and Finger Play
Use hand motions as you chant.

Bear Cubs*

Five bear cubs were peeking from their cave.
The first one said, "Let's be brave."
The second one said, "Let's see what's outside."
The third one said, "I'd rather stay in and hide."
The fourth one said, "Mother will be mad."
The fifth one said, "Now, she'll be proud and glad."
Then "Grrrrr" went mother bear,
seeing her cubs outside,
And the five bear cubs scrambled back inside.

Cubs in a Cave

Materials
- Initial /k/ story
- Cub Pattern, page 129
- Cave Pattern, page 130
- Word-initial /k/ pictures, page 120
- Glue or tape

Procedure

1. Bombard the children with word-initial /k/ by introducing the sound with a story selected from the book list.

2. Duplicate six Cub Patterns and one Cave Pattern. Duplicate the set of word-initial /k/ pictures. Tape one picture to each cub.

3. Let the children know they will take turns "putting cubs in the cave" as you bombard them with initial /k/ words.

4. Have the children listen as you bombard them with the initial /k/ words. Elicit production of each target word as the children select cubs and put them in the cave. Elicit productions of sentences and phrases such as, "Count the cubs in your cave!" and "Can one more cub come in?"

5. Consider variations like "King in a cave" or "Car in a cave").

*From: http://www.geocities.com/soogal99/bearssongs.html

K Activity Pages

Final K Activities

Bike on a Track

Materials
- Track pattern on page 131
- Bike pattern on page 132
- Word-final /k/ pictures, page 122
- Glue or tape

Procedure

1. Bombard the child with word-final /k/ by introducing the sound with a story from the selected book list.

2. Duplicate copies of the bike pattern and the track pattern for each child. Duplicate the set of word-final /k/ picture cards found on pages 122-123. Along with the child, adhere the word-final /k/ pictures to the track.

3. Let the children know they will take turns "racing their bike on the track" remind them that there are items on the track that may get in their way and they need to name the item as they pass it.

4. Bombard with the target words, or elicit production of each target, as the bike is racing around the track. Bombard with and elicit productions of sentences and phrases such as "Your bike is fast!" and "Wow! Your bike went around the snake."

5. Consider variations to include use of a large track created on the floor using tape. Tape the word-final /k/ pictures on the track. Take turns racing bikes around the track.

Snack Ideas
- Snack crackers, cake
- (Kool-aid or juice) in water bottles that are used for a bike

Craft
- Bike Helmet—choose a bike helmet pattern on page 130. Draw a face to match the helmet. Encourage the children to make the face look like them (hair and eye color) and then talk about how important it is to wear a helmet while riding their bike. Help them decorate their helmet, cut it out and glue it on the face they created.

Motor and Movement
- Around the Track—create a simple obstacle course (e.g, go under a table, walk around a chair, jump through the hoola hoop) on a "track" and place items on the track that the children will need to avoid as they move through the course.

Songs and Finger Play

The Wheels on the Bike

The wheels on the bike go round and round, round and round, round and round
The wheels on the bike go round and round, all through the town.

[Continue with these verses]

The horn on the bike goes "honk, honk, honk."
The brakes on the bike go "squeak, squeak, squeak."
The rider on the bike goes "up and down."

Chapter 6–K & G

Initial G Activities

Snack Ideas
- Gumdrops, grapes
- Grape juice

Craft
- Goose pattern on page 133 color if desired.
- Feather patterns on page 134.
- Cut out the goose and feathers. Add each feather to the goose naming the picture on each feather as it is added.

Motor and Movement
- Go Goose Go—Have the children pretend they are geese. Instruct them that when you play music the geese can "GO" and they can wander around in a designated space. When the music stops, the geese must stop.
- Duck, Duck, Goose—Have the children sit in a circle. One child circles the group lightly tapping each child's head saying "Duck, duck, duck" until he choose one to be "Goose." The "goose" chases the child around the circle.

Songs and Finger Plays

Five Little Geese

Five little geese, went out to play (hold up five fingers)
Over the hills, and far away, (hold hand to eyebrows)
Mother goose said "Honk, Honk, Honk"
Four little geese came flying back. (flap arms as if flying)
[Continue to count down until there are no little geese, then sing:]
No little geese went out to play,
Over the hills and far away,
Father goose said "HONK, HONK, HONK",
And five little geese came flying back.

Go Goose Go

Materials
- Goose Pattern on page 133
- Word-initial /g/ pictures, page 124
- Crayons or markers
- Scissors
- Die

Procedure

1. Bombard the child with word-initial /g/ by introducing the sound with a story from the selected book list.

2. Duplicate copies of the goose pattern (page 133). Give each child in your group a goose.

3. Place 5 (or more depending the child's age and ability) 8 x 8 squares together in a line on the floor using tape, yarn or paper. Have the children place their geese on one end. Each child will take turns rolling a die and moving their goose the number of squares shown on the die to the other end of the grid.

4. Bombard with the words "go" and "goose" as appropriate, elicit productions based on each child's skill level as their goose moves across the squares.

5. Variations can include placing one word-initial /g/ picture on each square and encouraging the child to name the picture or adhere a word-initial /g/ one to each goose pattern and encourage the children to name the pictures on their geese.

G Activity Pages

Final G Activities

Egg Puzzle

Materials
- Final /g/ book
- Egg Patterns, page 135
- Word-final /g/ pictures, page 126
- Glue or tape
- Crayons or markers

Procedure

1. Bombard the children with word-final /g/ by introducing the sound with a story selected from the book list.

2. Duplicate Egg Patterns and cut the eggs out. Cut each egg in half.

3. Lay the egg halves in front of the children. Encourage each child to find two halves that go together to create a word-final /g/ picture.

4. Have children listen as you bombard them with the word "egg" and name the word-final /g/ words on each egg. Elicit productions, if appropriate for each child's skill level as children find egg halves that go together.

5. Consider variations like "Egg Half," where you pass out the egg halves to the children. Encourage the children to find their other half by walking around the room to compare pieces with their classmates. Once the halves are matched, have children sit in pairs and share their findings with the class.

Snack Ideas
- Eggs, ants on a log (spread cream cheese or peanut butter on celery and add raisins or chocolate chips)
- Juice in a mug

Craft
- Egg Fun—Decorate hard boiled eggs or paper eggs. Place paper eggs in a big paper basket on the wall.

Motor and Movement
- Egg Roll—Place a Hula-Hoop on the floor. Have the children gather around the Hula-Hoop. Have the children roll plastic eggs across the Hula-Hoop to a classmate. Encourage the child to announce to the receiving classmate that the egg is on its way (e.g., "Sam, here comes the egg"). Elicit productions based on each child's skill level.
- Fill plastic eggs with word-final /g/ pictures or objects. Hide them around the room and have the children find them. Elicit productions based on each child's skill level.

Songs and Finger Plays

Eggs Come in All Sizes

An egg can come in many sizes.
An egg can hold some big surprises,
Speckled, brown, white, or blue.
An egg can hold babies that are new.
Chicks from an egg are fluffy yellow,
Chicks from an egg are funny fellows!

Initial K Picture Cards

calf	can
cape	cave
car	corn

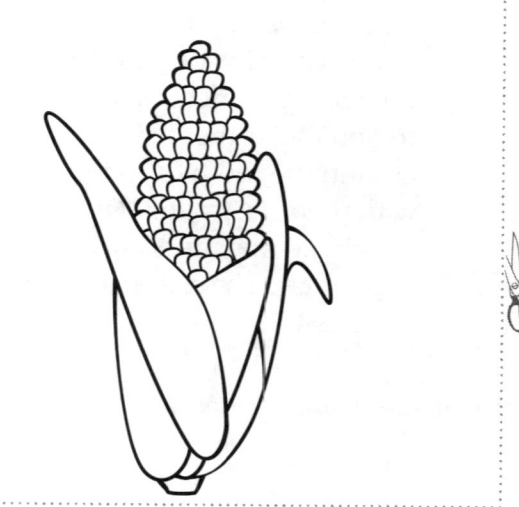

Initial K Picture Cards

cow	cub
cup	cap
key	king

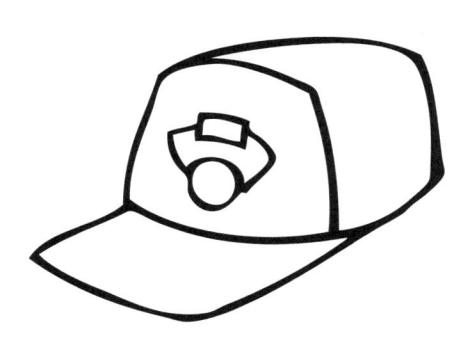

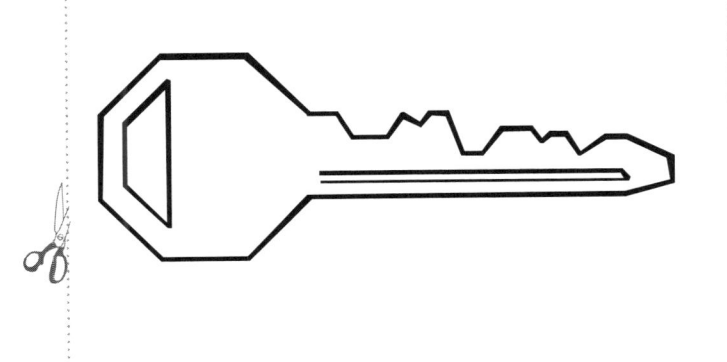

Final K Picture Cards

back	bike
block	book
chick	sick

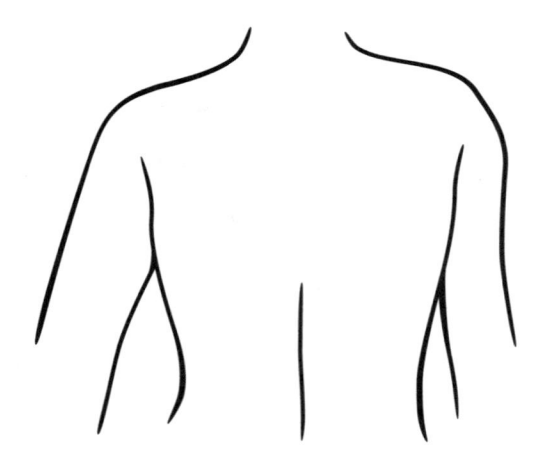

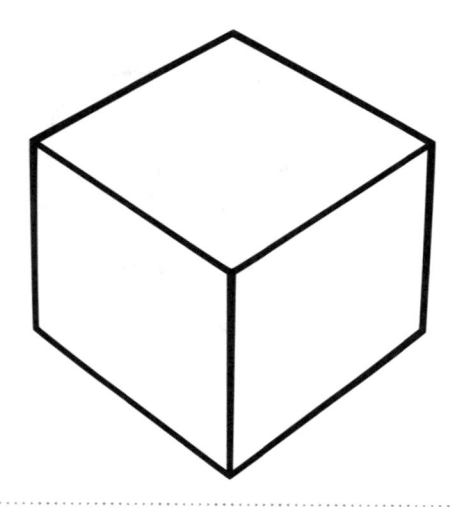

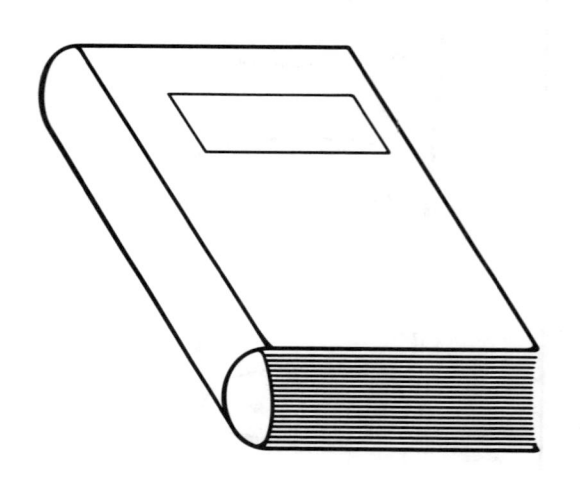

Final K Picture Cards

lake	neck
pick	rake
sack	snack

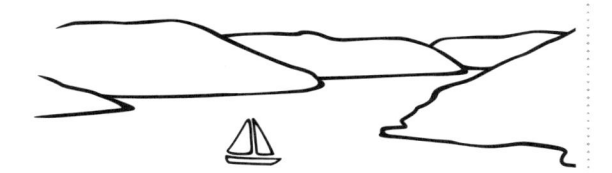

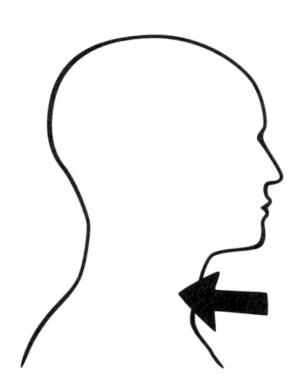

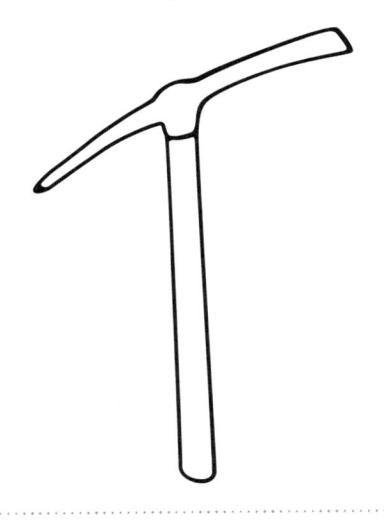

Initial G Picture Cards

game

gas

good

goose

ghost

go

Initial G Picture Cards

girl	golf
gear	gown
gull	gum

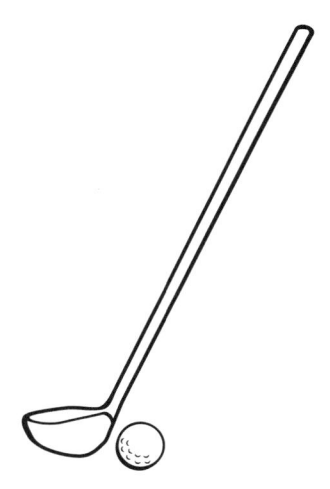

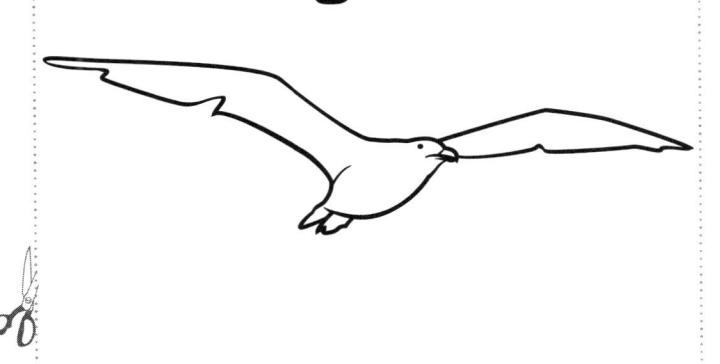

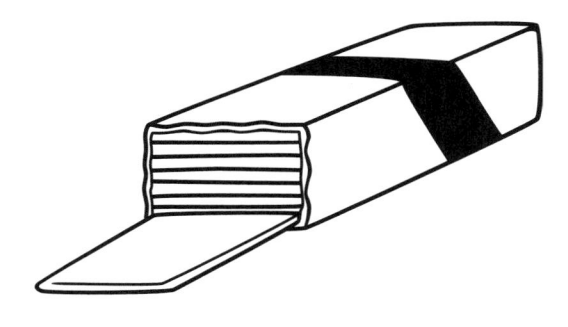

Final G Picture Cards

bag	bug
egg	frog
hug	jog

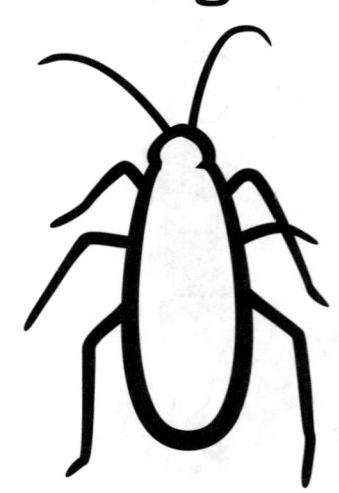

Final G Picture Cards

jug	leg
log	mug
pig	rug

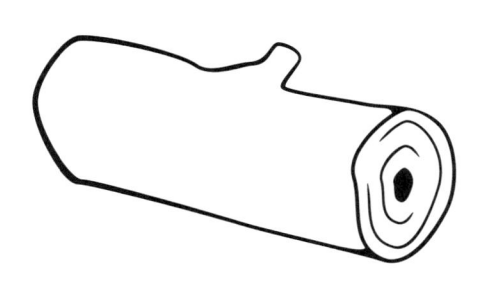

© 2008 Say It Right™ www.sayitright.org

Chapter 6 – K & G

Cub Puppet Pattern

128   The Entire World of Early Developing Sounds Instructional Workbook™   © 2008 Say It Right™   www.sayitright.org

K Activity Patterns

Cub Pattern

Chapter 6–K & G

Helmet Pattern

K Activity Patterns

Track Pattern

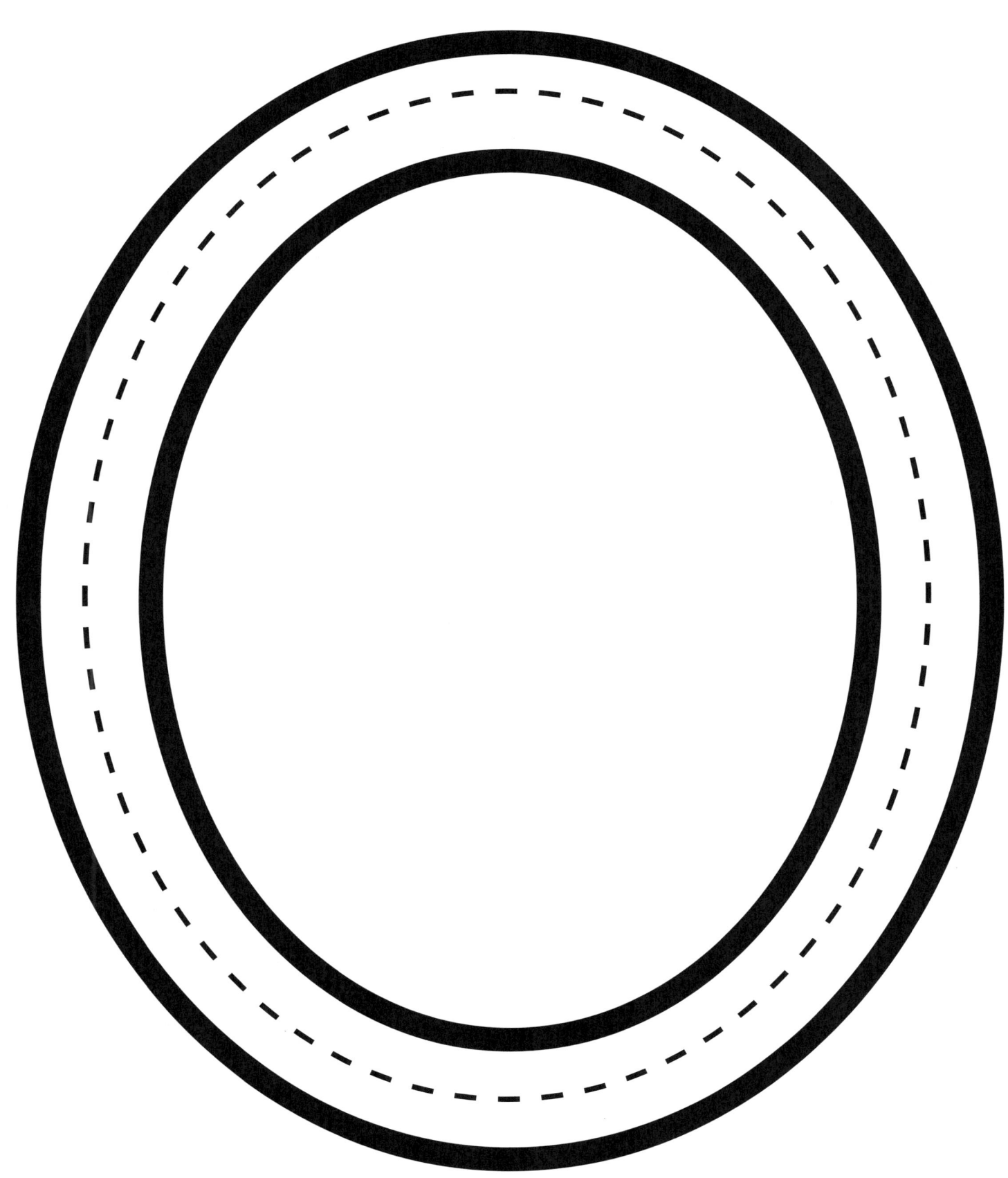

Chapter 6 – K & G

Bike Pattern

G Activity Patterns

Goose Pattern

Chapter 6 – K & G

Feather Pattern

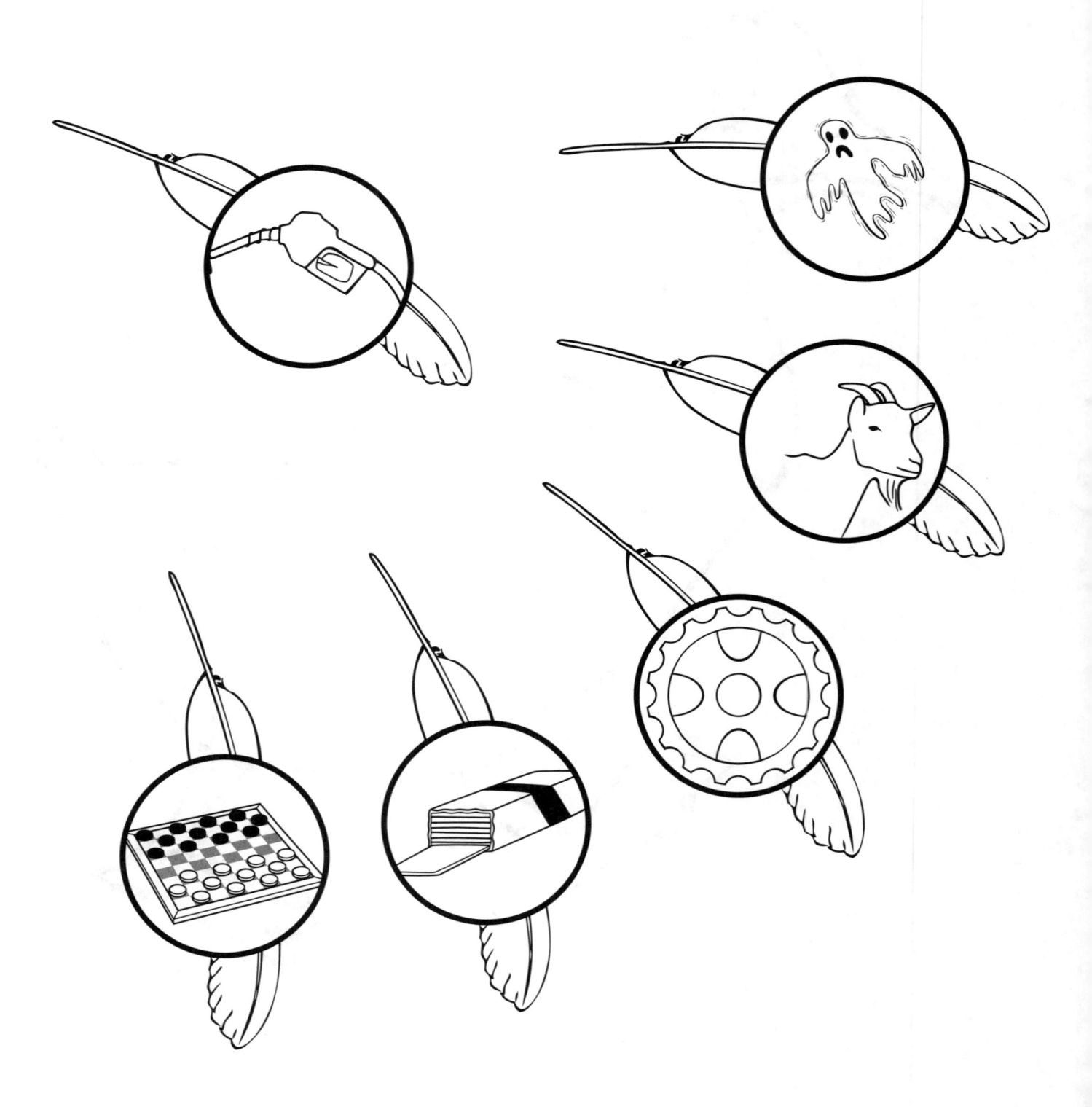

134 The Entire World of Early Developing Sounds Instructional Workbook™ © 2008 Say It Right™ www.sayitright.org

G Activity Patterns

Egg Pattern

135

Chapter 6 – K & G

The King's Cow

The king's cow has escaped. Can you help the king find his cow? Draw a line with your finger or a pencil until you find the cow.

K Homework

Cave

Child: Color or circle all the items in the cave that have a "K" sound in them.

Helper: While you interact with your child, bombard him or her with the questions, "What's in the cave?" Emphasize the word "cave" and the sound "K" as you ask the question.

Chapter 6–K & G

Hidden Pictures

Child: Find these pictures in the park scene: chick, bike, book, block, duck, lake, rake, sock, stick, snake. Circle the picture when you find it and then say the word.

Helper: Emphasize correct production of the "K" sound. Help your child say each word in this sentence, "I see a ___ in the park."

K Homework

Which One Doesn't Belong

Child: Three of the four pictures in each set belong together because they end with the "K" sound. Say each word in the set. Then, cross-out the one that does not end with a "K" sound.

Helper: Emphasize correct production of the "K" sound. Help your child read the words if he or she cannot read them. Put the words in a sentence and have your child repeat the sentence.

Chapter 6 – K & G

Gumballs!

Child: Name the pictures below. Color a gumball in the bubblegum machine each time you use a "G" sound correctly.

Helper: Help your child name the pictures then put them in a sentence. Emphasize correct production of the "G" sound."

140 The Entire World of Early Developing Sounds Instructional Workbook™   © 2008 Say It Right™   www.sayitright.org

G Homework

"G" Game

Child: Use a die and a game piece marker to play the "G" Game. Roll the die and move your game piece the number that is displayed. Say the name of the picture you landed on using a correct "G" sound.

Helper: Help your child name the pictures containing the "G" sound. For more advanced play, have your child say the "G" word the number of times shown on the die.

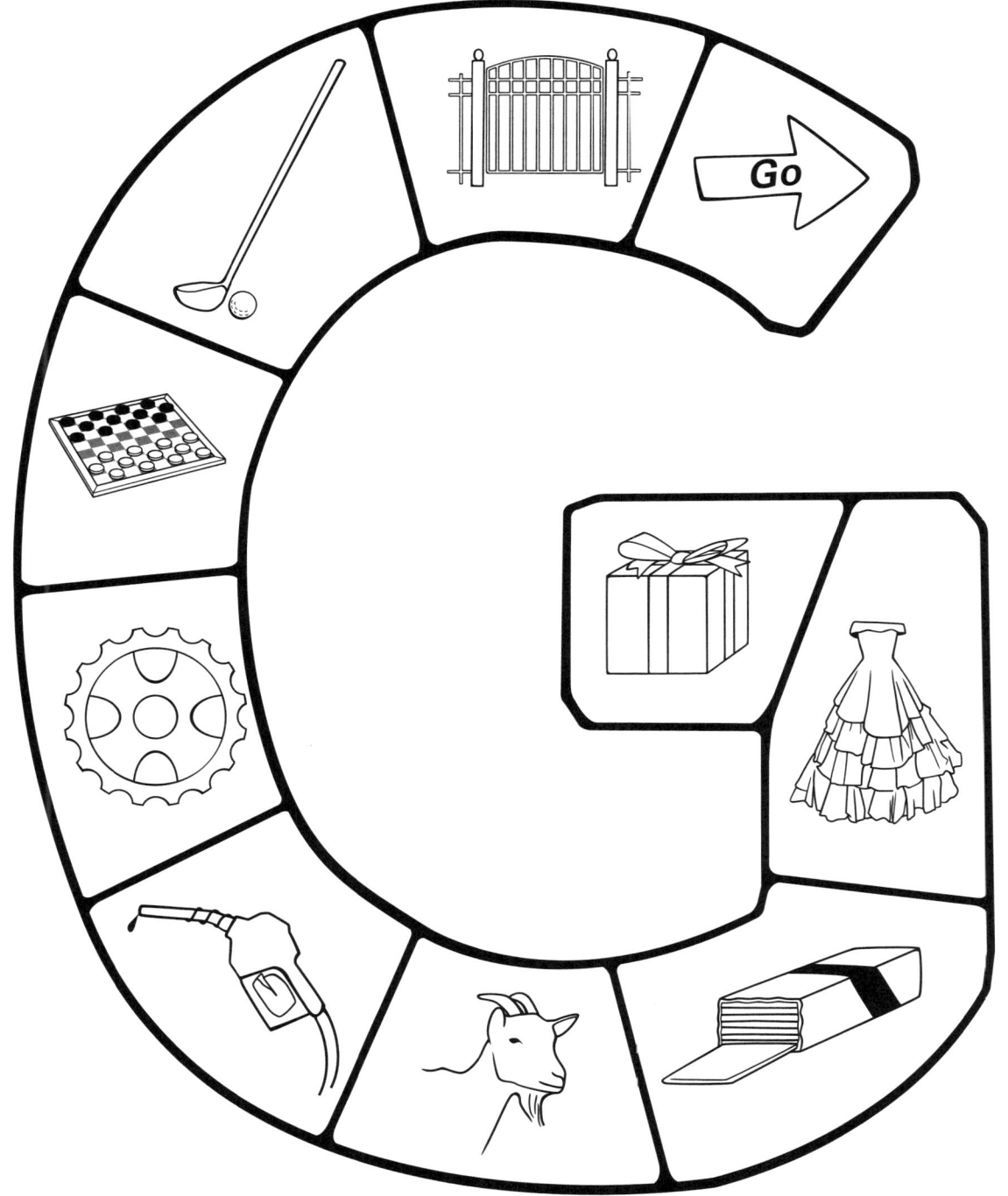

© 2008 Say It Right™   www.sayitright.org   The Entire World of Early Developing Sounds Instructional Workbook™

Chapter 6 – K & G

Create a Bug

Child: Cut apart the bug body and six legs. Tape the legs to the body. Name each part as you glue it on.

Helper: As your child assembles the bug, bombard him or her with the words "bug" and "leg." Put these words in a sentence too and emphasize correct production of "G."

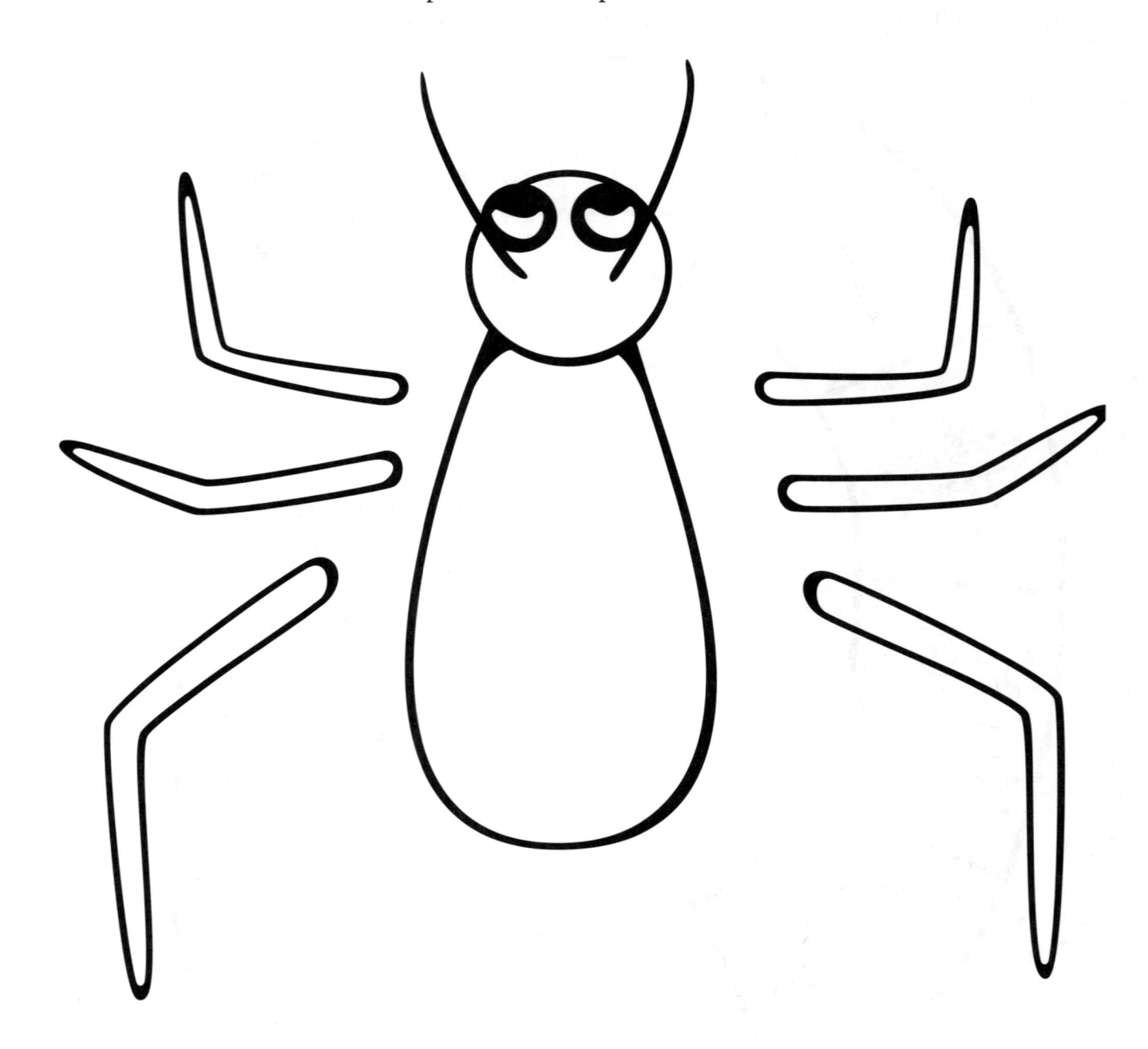

G Homework

Frog on a Log

Child: Cut apart the frog pictures and the log. Attach each frog to a picture on the log. Name each picture when you tape it on.

Helper: Say, "You are putting a frog on the log" each time your child tapes a frog on the log. Emphasize correct production of the words "frog" and "log." Help your child name the pictures and then put them in a sentence for your child to imitate.

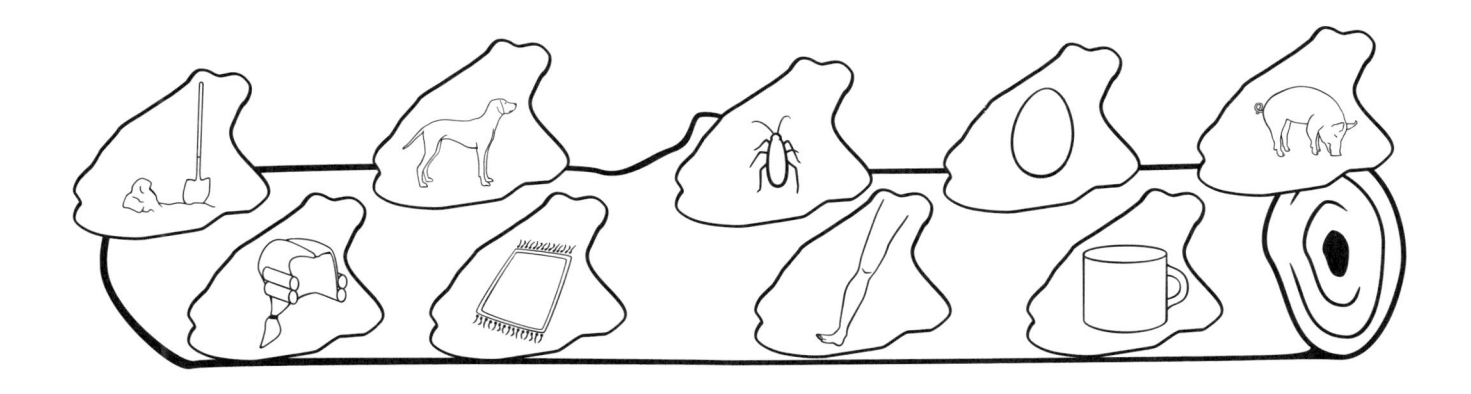

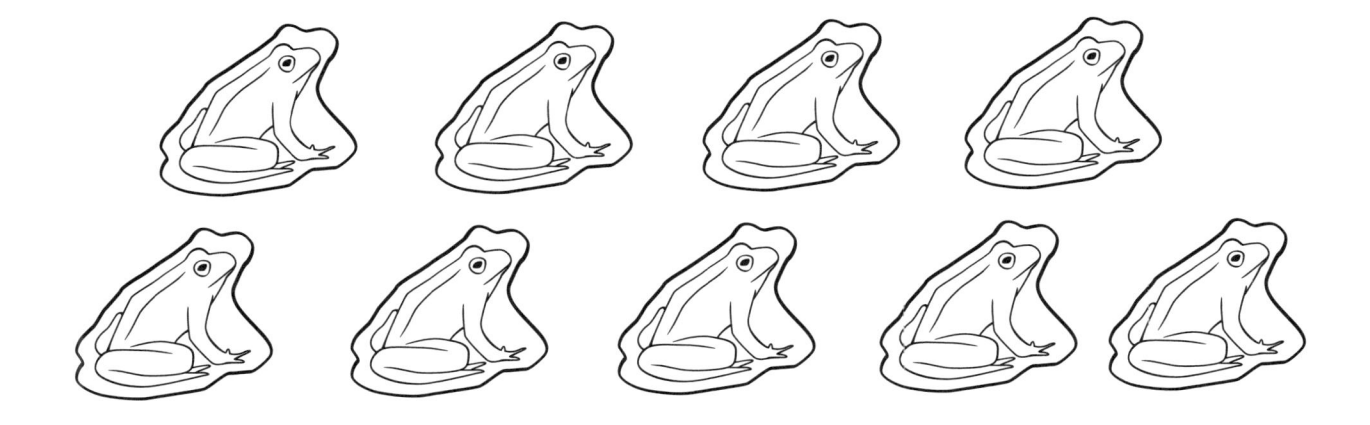

Chapter 7
Targeting T & D

- ➢ Screening Tool
- ➢ Teaching Tips
- ➢ Production Illustrations
- ➢ Target Lists
- ➢ Book Lists
- ➢ Activities
- ➢ Pictures
- ➢ Patterns
- ➢ Homework Pages

T & D Screening

Student Name_____ Date of Birth_____

Screening Date_____ Examiner_____

Use "+" or "—" to indicate the child's production of the phoneme at each level (in isolation, in a word, in a phrase, and in a sentence). Use imitation, delayed imitation, or pictures to elicit the child's productions.

Target–Initial /t/	Target–Final /t/	Target–Initial /d/	Target–Final /d/
SOUND IN ISOLATION: /t/		**SOUND IN ISOLATION:** /d/	
two	bat	deer	bed
number two	flying bat	running deer	make the bed
My sister is two years old	I saw a bat in the sky.	A deer ran through the field.	My shoes are under the bed.
tail	feet	dime	sad
wagging tail	two little feet	shiny dime	sad face
The horse has a long tail.	You wear socks on your feet.	I need a dime to buy a piece of candy.	She is feeling sad today.
toy	bite	doll	slide
a new toy	a big bite	old doll	slippery slide
Wrap the toy before the party.	The dentist said to bite down.	The girl wanted a doll for her birthday.	The child waited to use the slide.

DATA COLLECTION/SCREENING NOTES:

© 2008 Say It Right™ www.sayitright.org The Entire World of Early-Developing Sounds Instructional Workbook™

T & D Teaching Tips

Development Information

The consonant pair of /t/ and /d/ begins to develop early. Children will start to use /t/ and /d/ as early as 18 months of age. Mastery of the /t/ and /d/ sound pair occurs for most children between 3 and 4 years of age (Sander, 1972). The plosive energy and forward motion that combine to create these two sounds makes them salient and easy to produce, thus early development is possible.

Production of /t/ and /d/

This sound pair is alveolar or lingua-alveolar (i.e., made with contact between the tongue and alveolar ridge) and plosive (i.e., produced with a burst of air). The /t/ is unvoiced, thus the vocal folds are not set into vibration, while the /d/ is voiced. The teeth are held slightly apart and the velum is lifted to block air from escaping through the nasal cavity, thus allowing air pressure to build in the mouth and explode through the lips.

Stimulating Production of /t/ and /d/

- For children who struggle to produce /t/ and /d/, some work with the sound in isolation may be warranted. The following strategies may be useful when encouraging accurate production during treatment activities:

- Use an age-appropriate description of the processes for producing these sounds, in conjunction with the diagrams on page 148 as you assist children with their first attempts to produce these sounds.

- Use an age-appropriate description of the processes for producing these sounds.

- Sit side-by-side with the child in front of a mirror. Encourage the child to watch as you open your lips slightly and push your tongue to your alveolar ridge. Cue the child to match your model. Direct the child to imitate your productions of /t/ and /d/.

- Consider allowing the child to apply a small amount of peanut butter or other flavor on the alveolar ridge. Cue movement of the tongue to touch the peanut butter. Encourage production of /t/ or /d/ during this process.

- Use a tissue, cottonball, or small cracker placed on a flat surface. Have the child watch you release a burst of air to produce /t/ or /d/ as you make the item move across the surface. Encourage the child to do match your model.

- To encourage the voicing contrast, direct the child to apply light fingertip pressure to his/her throat or your throat as the /t/ and /d/ contrasts are produced. Talking about "turning on" the voice to make the buzzing associated with /d/.

Chapter 7 – T & D

T & D Production Illustrations

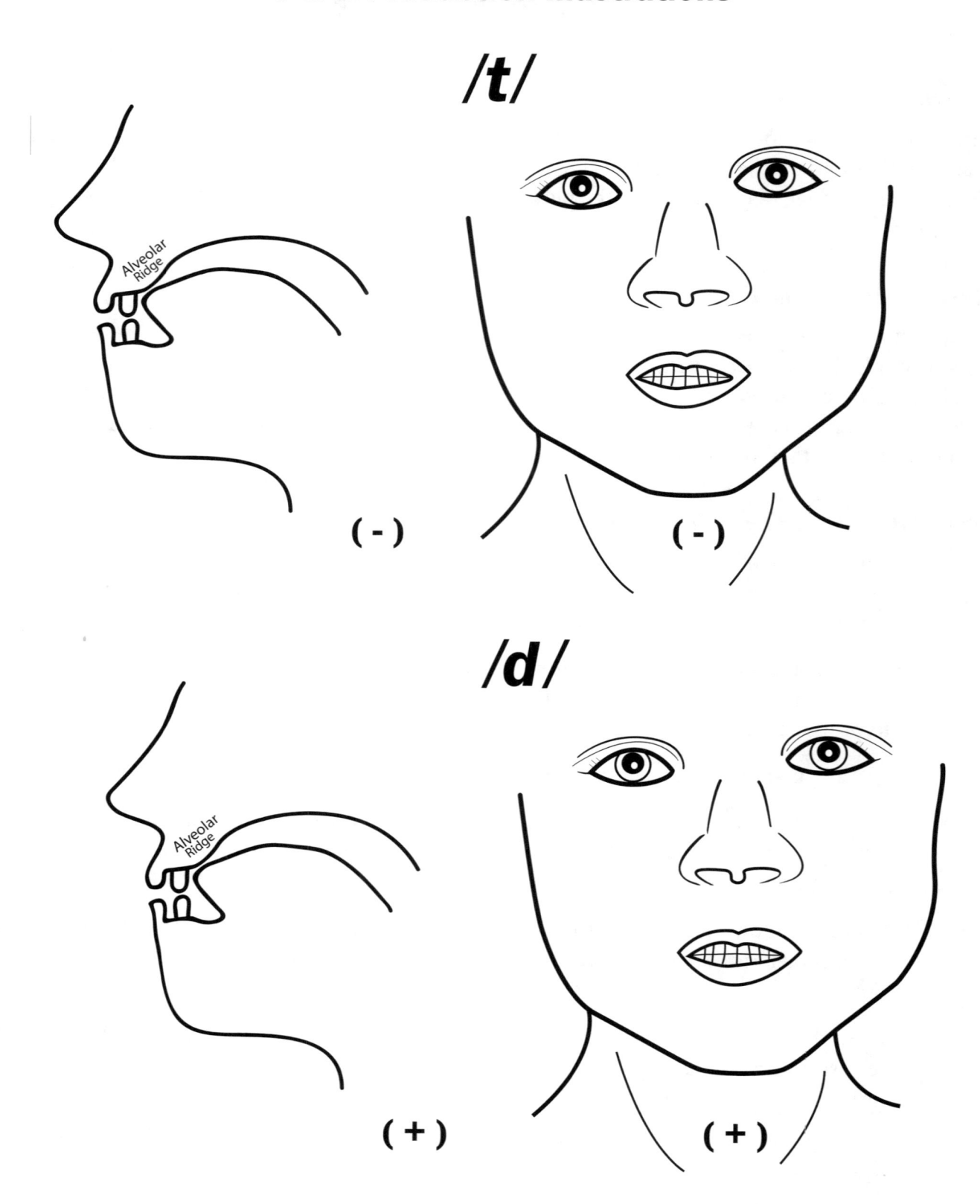

/t/

(-) (-)

/d/

(+) (+)

T & D Target Lists

Especially during early stages of practice, single-syllable words are most facilitative for accurate productions of target sounds. Consider the surrounding consonant and vowel sounds in a target word to control for other sounds the child may be lacking. For example, when first targeting initial /t/ with a child, avoid words that also contain medial and/or final /t/. Gradually, as a child becomes more successful with practice of a selected target, words of increasing length and complexity can be added to the production-practice activities.

The Entire World of Early Developing Sounds™ suggests using the target words listed for the early stages of practice with young children working on /t/ and /d/. Pages 160-167 provide representations of these words in picture form for use with production practice activities. Suggested target phrases and sentences are also provided. Phrases and sentences are most useful with older children who can read. *The Entire World of T & D Articulation Flip Book* (Ristuccia, 2007) is an excellent source for illustrated, interactive phrase and sentence practice.

When working with older children, the word, phrase, and sentence lists may be useful as stimulus items in mass production practice. If using the phrases and sentences with nonreaders, direct or delayed imitation will be necessary (i.e., saying the phrase or sentence as a model and then having the child repeat it with or without a delay). Ideally, production of phrases and sentences will be elicited naturally during structured and unstructured activities, thus it is possible that the phrase and sentence lists would not need to be used with younger children.

To target medial /t/ and /d/, use the target words in combination with another word (e.g., "my turn" to elicit medial /t/ or "my dog" for medial /d/). Medial /t/ and /d/ target words can be added once a child is ready for practice with multisyllabic words. As medial /t/ and /d/ words are selected, continue to control for facilitative contexts to ensure children successfully produce the new sound. In addition, use multisyllabic words that are meaningful to the child (e.g., duckling, bootie, etc.).

Chapter 7 – T & D

T & D Single Word Practice

Word–Initial /t/	Word–Final /t/	Word–Initial /d/	Word–Final /d/
tack	bat	date	bead
tail	bite	day	bed
tape	boat	deer	bud
tea	boot	dime	food
teeth	cat	dive	mud
ten	eat	dog	read
toad	feet	doll	rod
toe	hat	dome	road
top	kite	door	sad
toy	light	dot	seed
tub	pot	dough	sled
two	rat	dove	slide

T & D Phrase-Level Practice

Word–Initial /t/	Word–Final /t/	Word–Initial /d/	Word–Final /d/
a sharp **tack**	brown **bat**	save the **date**	string the **bead**
the dog's **tail**	take a **bite**	a new **day**	make the **bed**
sticky **tape**	a big **boat**	white **deer**	rose **bud**
green **tea**	a cowboy **boot**	shiny **dime**	too much **food**
brush **teeth**	a black **cat**	**dive** in	in the **mud**
ten years old	**eat** dinner	**dog** bone	**read** often
baby **toad**	four **feet**	tiny **doll**	fishing **rod**
a big **toe**	a small **hat**	the large **dome**	on the **road**
spinning **top**	fly a **kite**	open the **door**	**sad** day
a new **toy**	**light** bulb	color the **dot**	tiny **seed**
in the **tub**	cooking **pot**	cookie **dough**	new **sled**
two books	hungry **rat**	the baby **dove**	park **slide**

Chapter 7 – T & D

T & D Sentence-Level Practice

Word–Initial /t/	Word–Final /t/	Word–Initial /d/	Word–Final /d/
The **tack** held the paper.	She saw a **bat** fly in the sky.	She marked the **date** on her calendar.	I used a small **bead** for the necklace.
The dog's **tail** wagged.	The bug's **bite** stung her.	It was the first **day** of school.	She sleeps in a small **bed**.
The **tape** is sticky.	The big **boat** was in the water.	The **deer** ran in the forest.	The rose **bud** is red.
I will drink the **tea**.	His **boot** fell off.	I need one more **dime**.	There was a lot of **food**.
You will brush your **teeth**.	The **cat** climbed the tree.	The boy will **dive** into the pool.	The pig is in the **mud**.
She will be **ten** this year.	He will **eat** the sandwich.	The **dog** found the bone.	She will **read** the magazine.
The **toad** jumped high.	His **feet** are small.	Her **doll** is lost.	The **rod** is missing.
He bumped his big **toe**.	I wear a **hat** in the sun.	The **dome** on the train.	The **road** is under construction.
He has a **top** with his pants to go.	The yellow **kite** flew high.	She heard a knock on the **door**.	It was a **sad** movie.
The new **toy** is broken.	The **light** was turned off.	There was a **dot** on the paper.	Plant the **seed** in the garden.
The **tub** was filled with bubbles.	The **pot** is on the stove.	She ate the cookie **dough**.	Use a **sled** in winter.
She will be **two**-years-old.	The gray **rat** was big.	The **dove** flew away.	You can **slide** down fast.

T & D Book List

Reading a story is a natural and motivating activity for children. Children's stories are filled with opportunities to bombard the child with words containing the target sound and to elicit productions of the target. Consult the following list to select books that contain multiple opportunities for words that contain /t/ or /d/.

Title	Publication Information	Interest Level	Target Words
Initial /t/			
Tails	Matthew Van Fleet (2003) Red Wagon Books	2-5 years	tail, touch, tab
Ten Apples Up on Top!	Dr. Suess (1998) Random House	2-6 years	two, ten, top, topple, tumble
Teddy Bear, Teddy Bear	Steve Scott (1998) HarperFestival	2-5 years	teddy, turn, touch
A Toad for Tuesday	Russell E. Erickson (1998) HarperTrophy	4-8 years	toad, Tuesday, Toolia, two
Tub Toys	Terry Miller Shannon and Timothy Warner (2002) Tricycle Press	3-6 years	tub, toy, time
Ten Terrible Dinosaurs	Paul Strickland (1997) Dutton Juvenile	Baby-preschool	ten, terrible
Final /t/			
Who Took the Farmer's Hat?	Joan L. Nodset (1988) HarperTrophy	4-8 years	hat, it, fat, flowerpot, that
Geraldine's Blanket	Holly Keller (1988) HarperTrophy	Baby-preschool	blanket, left, part
Who Will Tuck Me in Tonight?	Carol Roth (2006) North-South Books	Baby-preschool	right, don't, tight, just, tonight
Tie Your Sock and Clap Your Feet	Lenny Hort (2000) Atheneum/Anne Schwartz Books	4-8 years	feet, seat

Chapter 7 – T & D

	INITIAL /d/		
TITLE	PUBLICATION INFORMATION	INTEREST LEVEL	TARGET WORDS
Barnyard Dance	Sandra Boynton (1993) Workman Publishing	1-6 years	*dance, do-si-do, done*
Dad's Day Dinosaur	Diane Dawson Hearn (1999) Aladdin Library	2-6 years	*Dad's, dinosaur, day, dinner*
No, David!	David Shannon (1998) Scholastic	3-7 years	*David, don't, dangerous, down*
Dinosaurs After Dark	Jonathan Emmett (2006) HarperCollins	3-7 years	*dinosaurs, dark*
Dear Daisy, Get Well Soon	Maggie Smith (2002) Dragonfly Books	Baby-preschool	*Daisy, dear, down, day, delivered*
Good Night, Gorilla	Peggy Rathman (1996) Putnam Juvenile	Baby-preschool	*night*

	FINAL /d/		
Bread, Bread, Bread	Ann Morris (1993) HarperCollins	4-8 years	*bread, food, knead*
Five Little Monkeys Jumping on the Bed	Eileen Christelow (1998) Clarion Books	1-6 years	*bed, head, said, bumped, called*
The Noisy Way to Bed	Ian Whybrow (2004) Macmillan Children's Books	4-8 years	*bed, tread*
Ten in a Bed	Penny Dale (2007) Candlewick	Baby-preschool	*bed, said, rolled*
What's on My Head?	Margaret Miller (1998) Little Simon	1-6 years	*head*

T & D Activity Pages

Regardless of your approach to treatment, a variety of activities should be used to bombard children with correct productions of the target sound and to elicit production practice. The activities in this unit include a range of sound-specific options for /t/ and /d/. They are designed to appeal to children between the ages of 2 and 7.

In addition, remember the following are available to support your teaching of the /t/ and /d/ sounds:

- **More Activity Ideas** that can be used to target any sound are included in Appendix A.

- Sound-specific **Pictures** to be used with activities are found on pages 160-167.

- A **Blank Card Pattern**, to include your own words, is found in Appendix D.

- **Book Lists** for selecting stories are included on pages 153-154.

- **Word, Phrase, and Sentence Lists** are provided on pages 149, to use with activities or with more traditional boards games (e.g., Sorry! Uno, and Kerplunk). To earn a turn, have the older student read or repeat words, phrases, or sentences containing the selected target phoneme. The goal is to encourage as many repetitions of the target sound as possible—be creative!

- **Homework Pages** (pages 176-183) provide activities that can be easily used by parents or other care providers to encourage successful practice in other settings. Be certain to direct children to return completed Homework Pages so that you can encourage self-evaluation and monitoring of their practice. Consider having students carry a "speech folder" to store these materials and facilitate communication with others on a regular basis.

- Appendix B provides a **Parent Memo** that can be used along with selected homework activity pages.

- Appendix E includes a blank **Lesson Plan**. Use the form to ensure that all essential lesson plan components are accounted for within each session. Be certain to probe for accuracy, provide instruction/bombardment for the target sounds, and plan for a sufficient amount of successful mass production practice.

- Appendix F provides a blank **Data Collection Form** to monitor progress and adjust treatment.

- Don't forget that **Suggestions for Conversation and Carryover** are provided in Appendix B. Plan for generalization from the start and incorporate these suggestions along the way.

Chapter 7 – T & D

Initial T Activities

Snack Ideas
- Tootsie Rolls
- Tiger in the grass (green frosting on a graham cracker; stand an animal cracker up in the icing)
- Tea, toad juice (green Kool-Aid® or juice)

Craft
- Tiger Mask—Cut eyes out of a paper plate. Add a nose, mouth and stripes. Tape or tie yarn to the sides to tie on for a mask.
- Tiger Tails—Cut out tail pattern found on page 169. Attach with a safety pin or tape.

Motor and Movement
- Growl Like A—Have the children act out the following animal movements to:

  Can you growl like a tiger?
  Can you slither like a snake?
  Can you hop like a frog?
  Can you fly like a bat?
  Can you climb like a monkey?
  Can you roar like a lion?
  Can you bark like a dog?
  Can you stre-ttt-ccchhhh like a cat?

Songs and Finger Play

Little Tiger
This little tiger is very wild, (thumb)
This little tiger is a loving child. (pointer)
This little tiger has a tail that's long, (middle)
This little tiger has a tail that's strong (ring)
This little tiger likes to prowl and smell, (pinkie)
But his teeth are too small to bite very well.

Tiger's Tail

Materials
- Initial /t/ book
- Tiger Pattern and Tiger Tail Pattern, pages 168-169
- Brads
- Crayons or markers
- Scissors

Procedure

1. Bombard the children with word-initial /t/ by introducing the sound with a story from the selected book list on page 153.

2. Duplicate copies of the Tiger and rotating Tail pattern for each child.

3. Cut out and color (optional) the Tiger and the Tiger Tail Patterns.

4. Attach the two pieces of paper together with a brad in the center of the circle.

5. Instruct children that they can rotate the tails to find the one that they want to go with the tiger.

6. Bombard with the target words, *tiger* and *tail,* or elicit production of each target, as the tails are selected. Bombard with and elicit productions of sentences and phrases such as "Wow! That makes a funny tiger tail!" or "That makes the right tiger tail."

T Activity Pages

Final T Activities

Float a Boat

Materials
- Final /t/ book
- Sail Pattern, page 170
- Word-final /t/ pictures, page 162
- Tape
- Straw or stick
- Egg carton
- Large pail or plastic bin

Procedure

1. Bombard the children with word-final /t/ by introducing the sound with a story selected from the book list on page 153.

2. Duplicate a Sail Pattern for each child. Duplicate the set of word-final /t/ pictures. Attach one picture to each side of the Sail Pattern.

3. Punch two or three holes along the longest side of the sail and weave a straw or stick through the sail. Attach the sail to the lid or bottom of an egg carton.

4. Have children stand around a large pail or bin filled with water and take turns floating their boats. Have them name the pictures on their sails as the boats are launched. If their boats float, have them say, "The boat can float!"

5. Bombard the children with word-initial /t/ words and elicit productions of sentences and phrases if appropriate.

Snack Ideas
- Dots candy
- Hot chocolate

Craft
- Paint a Boat—Provide each child with a Boat Pattern (page 171) and Bingo dobbers of various colors. Have them decorate the boat with dots.

Motor and Movement
- Sailing—Arrange chairs from your classroom in rows that look like a boat. Take turns being the captain of the boat. Pretend to row the boat.

Songs and Finger Play

Row, Row, Row Your Boat

Row, row, row your boat

Gently down the stream.

Merrily, merrily, merrily merrily,

life is but a dream.

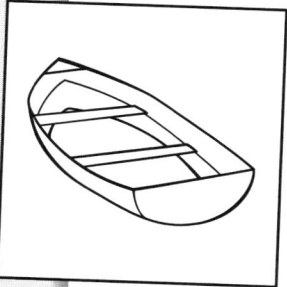

Chapter 7 – T & D

Initial D Activities

Snack Ideas
- Danish, donut, dog treats (puppy chow recipe)

Craft
- Dog Ear Headband—Make a paper headband for the child. Using the ear pattern found on page 174, color and cut out the ears and attach to the headband.

Motor and Movement
- Simon Says—Play Simon Says. Give your children directions that include actions a dog would complete (e.g., shake your tail, bark like a dog, chase your tail, shake, beg for a bone, dig for a bone).

Songs and Finger Plays

Old Mother Hubbard

Old Mother Hubbard went to the cupboard,

To fetch her poor dog a bone;

When she got there, the cupboard was bare,

And so the poor dog had none.

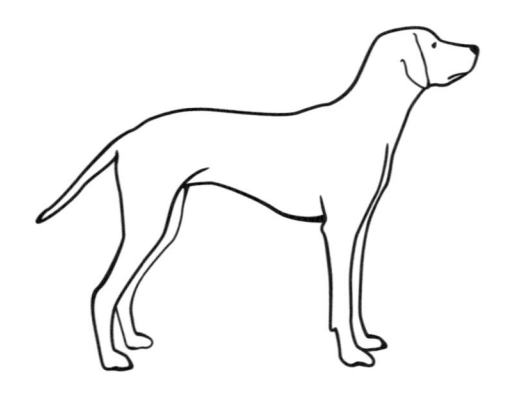

Diggin' Dog

Materials
- Dog pattern on page 172
- Bone pattern on page 173
- Word-initial /d/ pictures, page 164
- Craft or popsicle stick
- Glue or tape
- Crayons or markers

Procedure

1. Bombard the children with word-initial /d/ by introducing the sound with a story from the selected book list.

2. Duplicate one Dog pattern and several Bone patterns with word-initial /d/ pictures glued to each bone.

3. Color the dog and glue it to a Popsicle stick. Each child can complete one or make one as the "class dog." The dog can "bury" bones in the classroom.

4. Instruct the children that they are to gather the buried bones. When they find a bone they name the picture on the bone and bring it to the circle.

5. Bombard with the words "dog," "dig" and "dug" and, as appropriate, elicit productions based on each child's skill level as they count and label the bones the dog dug up.

D Activity Pages

Final D Activities

Hide the Toad

Materials
- Final /d/ book
- One Toad Pattern, page 175
- Word-final /d/ pictures, page 166
- Glue or tape
- Crayons or markers

Procedure

1. Bombard the children with word-final /d/ by introducing the sound with a story selected from the book list on page 154.

2. Duplicate word-final /d/ pictures. Duplicate one Toad Pattern for each child.

3. Bombard the children with the word "toad" as they color their toads and glue or tape one picture on their toads.

4. Help each child hide their toad in the classroom while the other children close their eyes and count to ten. Then have the children look for the toad. Once a toad is found, the child who finds it tells what picture is on it.

5. As appropriate, elicit phrase and sentence productions based on each child's skill level.

Snack Ideas
- Toad in the grass (green frosting or cream cheese spread on a cracker with a gummy toad placed on top)
- Lemonade

Craft
- Stuffed Toad—Duplicate two Toad Patterns (page 175) for each child. Have the children color or paint both toads. Put the non-colored sides of the toads back-to-back and staple or tape the edges. Leave enough room to stuff with cotton or paper.

Motor and Movement
- Hide-n-Seek
- Lily Pad Hop—Duplicate numerous Lily Pad Patterns (page 176) and place them around the room. Encourage children to jump from one lily pad to another saying "lily pad" as they jump. A variation can include adding a final /d/ picture to the lily pad and having the child name the picture he or she jumps on.

Songs and Finger Plays

Five Little Toads

Five little toads sitting on a well.

One looked up and down he fell.

...Continue with four, three, two, and one.

Initial T Picture Cards

tack	tail
top	tape
tea	teeth

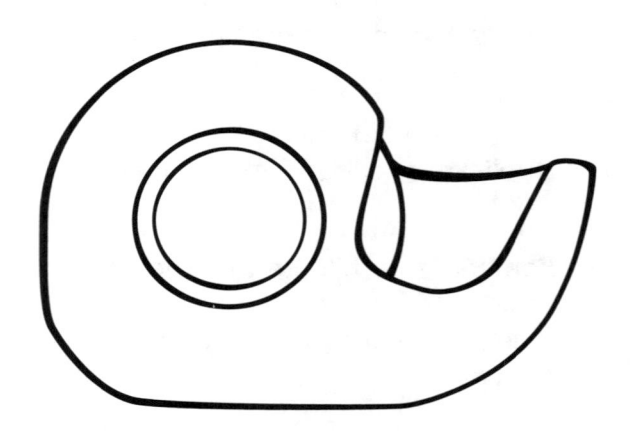

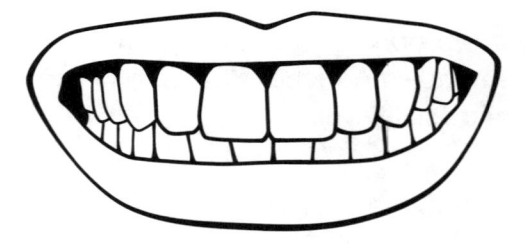

160 The Entire World of Early Developing Sounds Instructional Workbook™ © 2008 Say It Right™ www.sayitright.org

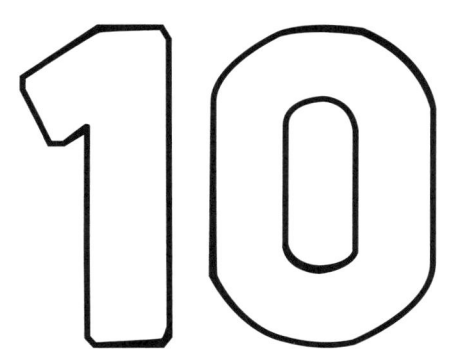

Initial T Picture Cards

ten	toad
toe	toy
tub	two

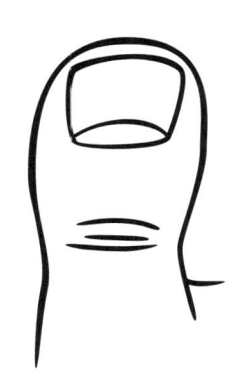

Final T Picture Cards

bat

cat

bite

boat

boot

pot

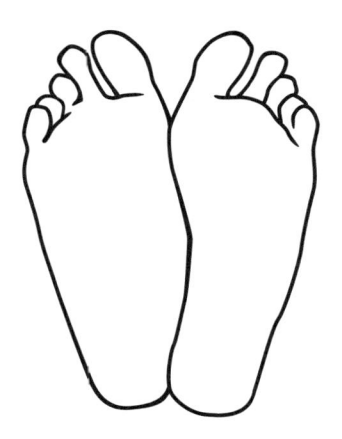

Final T Picture Cards

feet	hat
eat	kite
light	rat

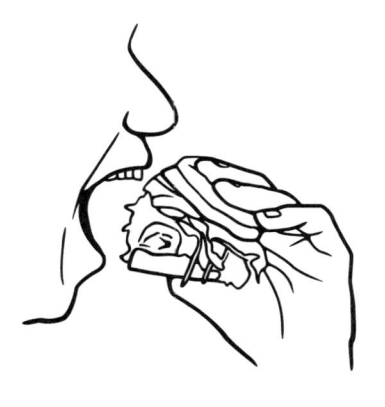

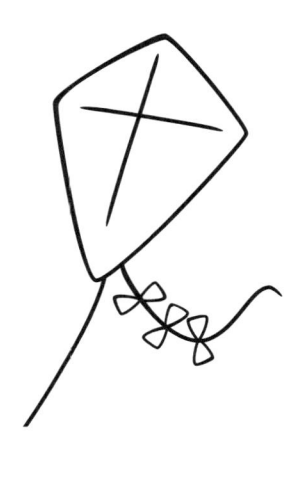

163

Initial D Picture Cards

day	date
dime	deer
dog	dive

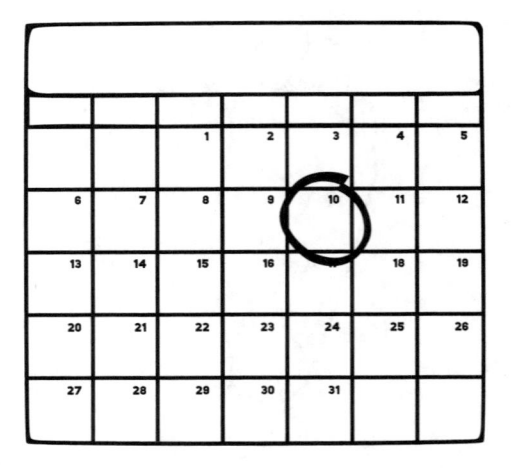

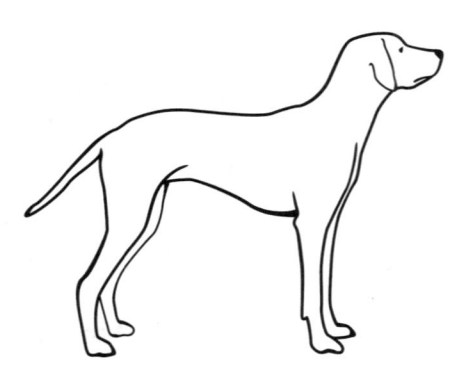

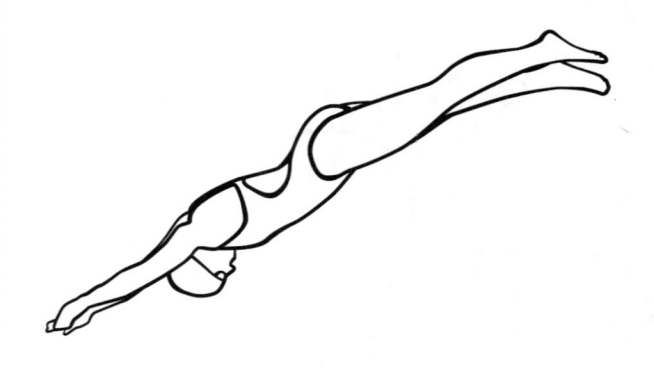

164 The Entire World of Early Developing Sounds Instructional Workbook™   © 2008 Say It Right™   www.sayitright.org

Initial D Picture Cards

dove	doll
dot	door
dough	dome

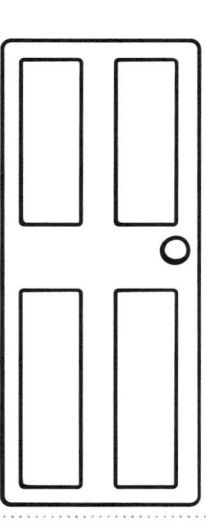

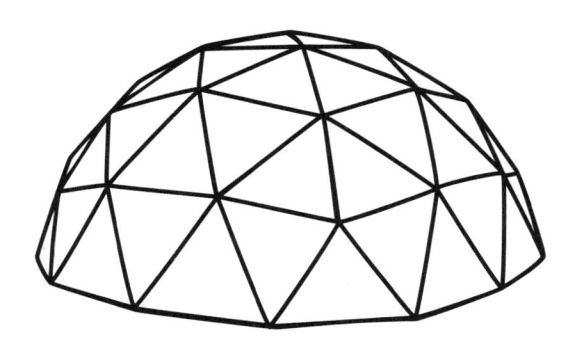

Final D Picture Cards

bed

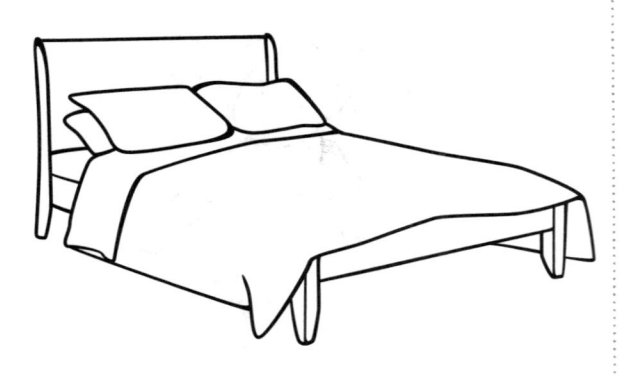

bud

sled

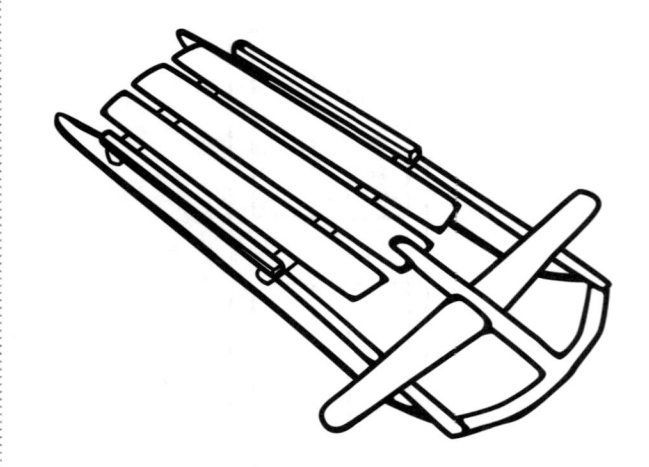

rod

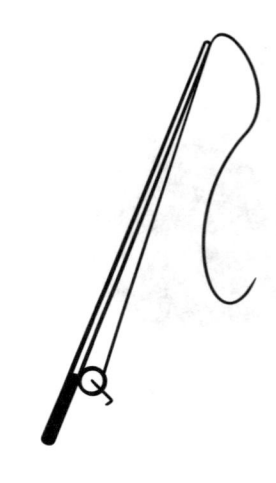

slide

bead

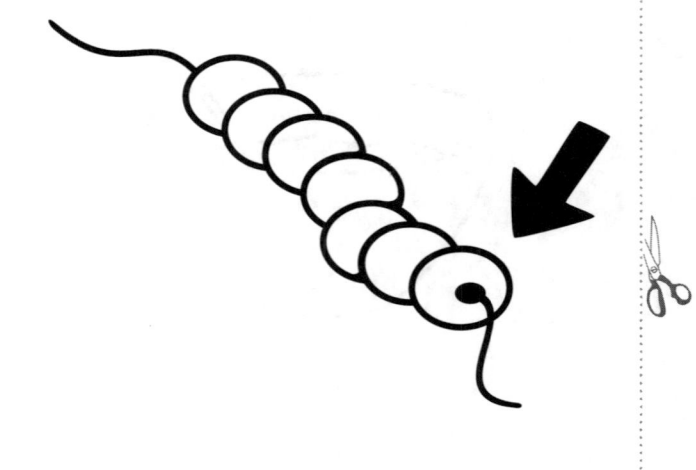

166 The Entire World of Early Developing Sounds Instructional Workbook™ © 2008 Say It Right™ www.sayitright.org

Final D Picture Cards

read	**mud**
road	**sad**
seed	**food**

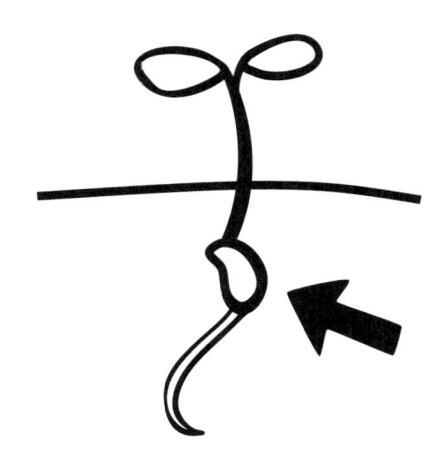

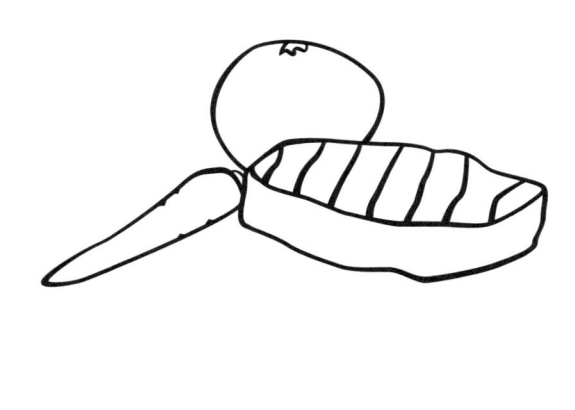

167

Chapter 7 – T & D

Tiger Pattern

Tiger's Tail

Cut out wedge
openning.

T Activity Patterns

Tiger Tail Pattern

169

© 2008 Say It Right™ www.sayitright.org The Entire World of Early Developing Sounds Instructional Workbook™

Chapter 7 – T & D

Sail Pattern

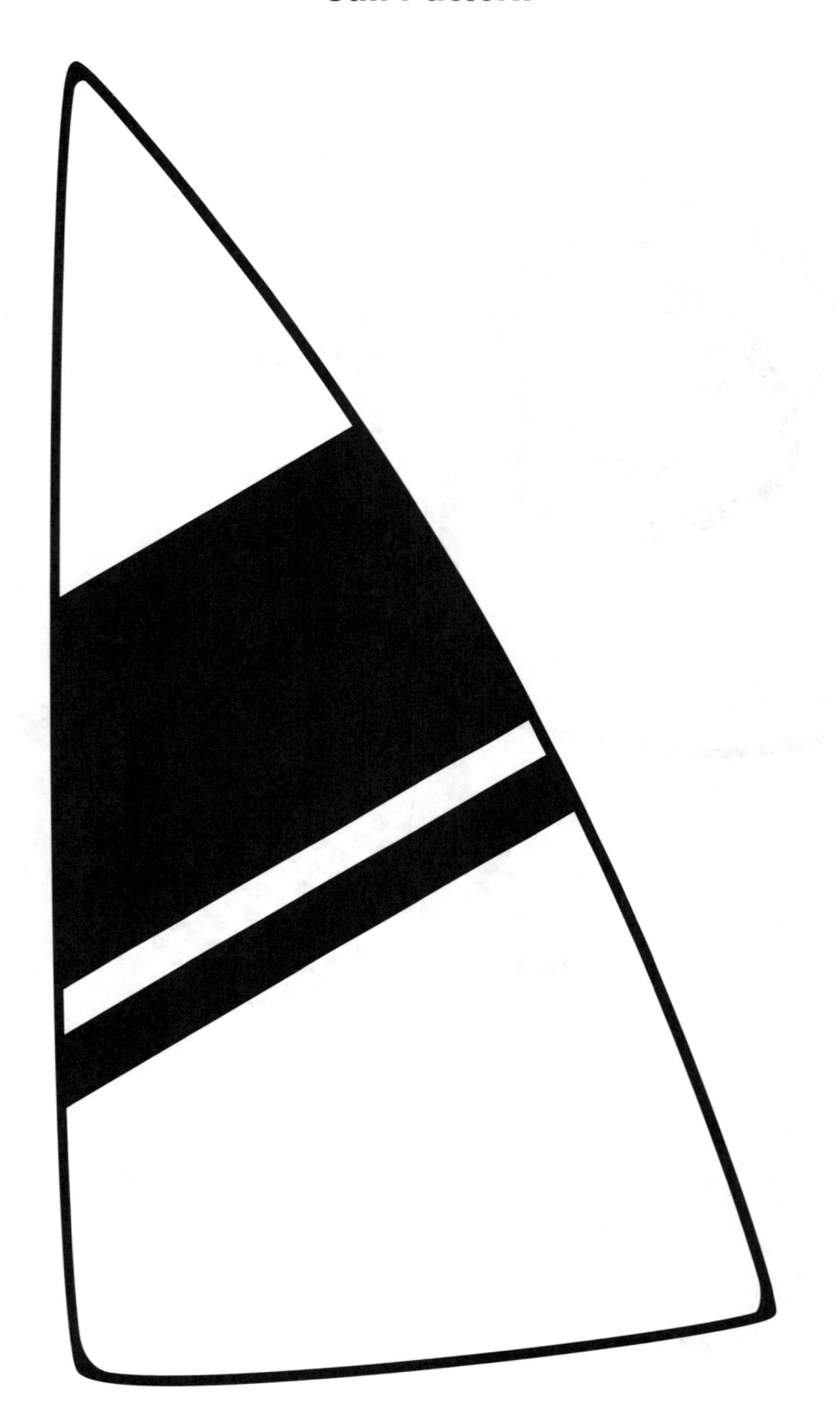

T Activity Patterns

Boat Pattern

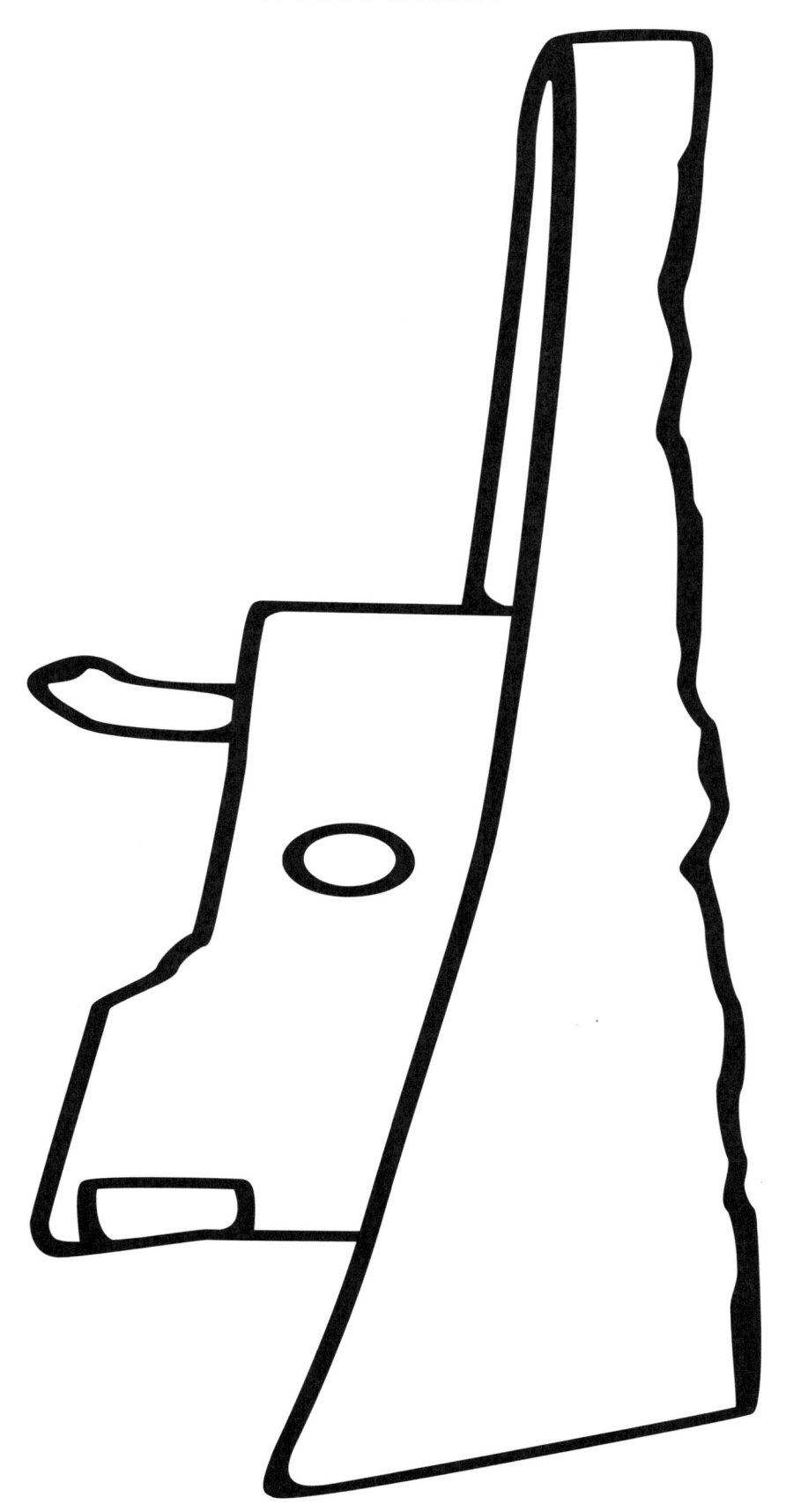

Chapter 7 – T & D

Dog Pattern

Bone Pattern

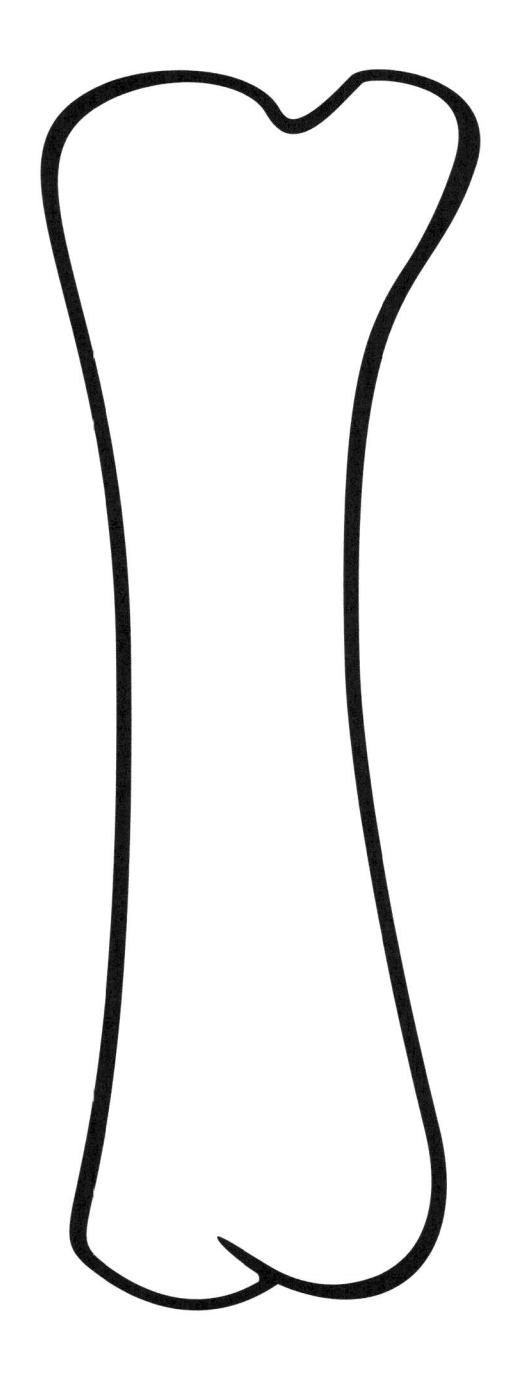

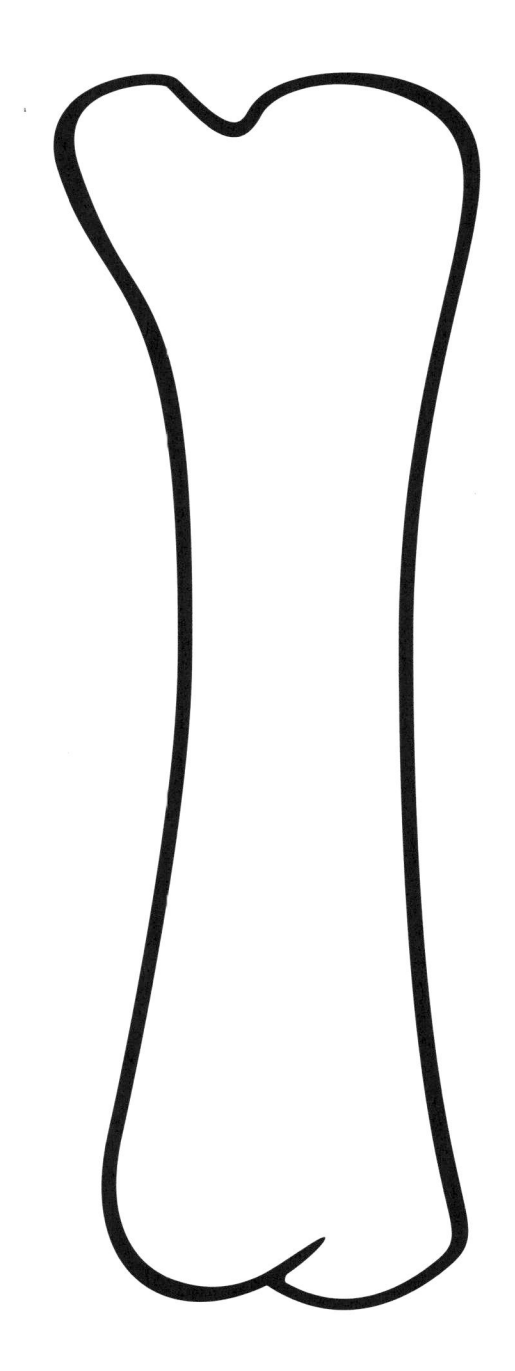

D Activity Patterns

Chapter 7 – T & D

Dog Ear Pattern

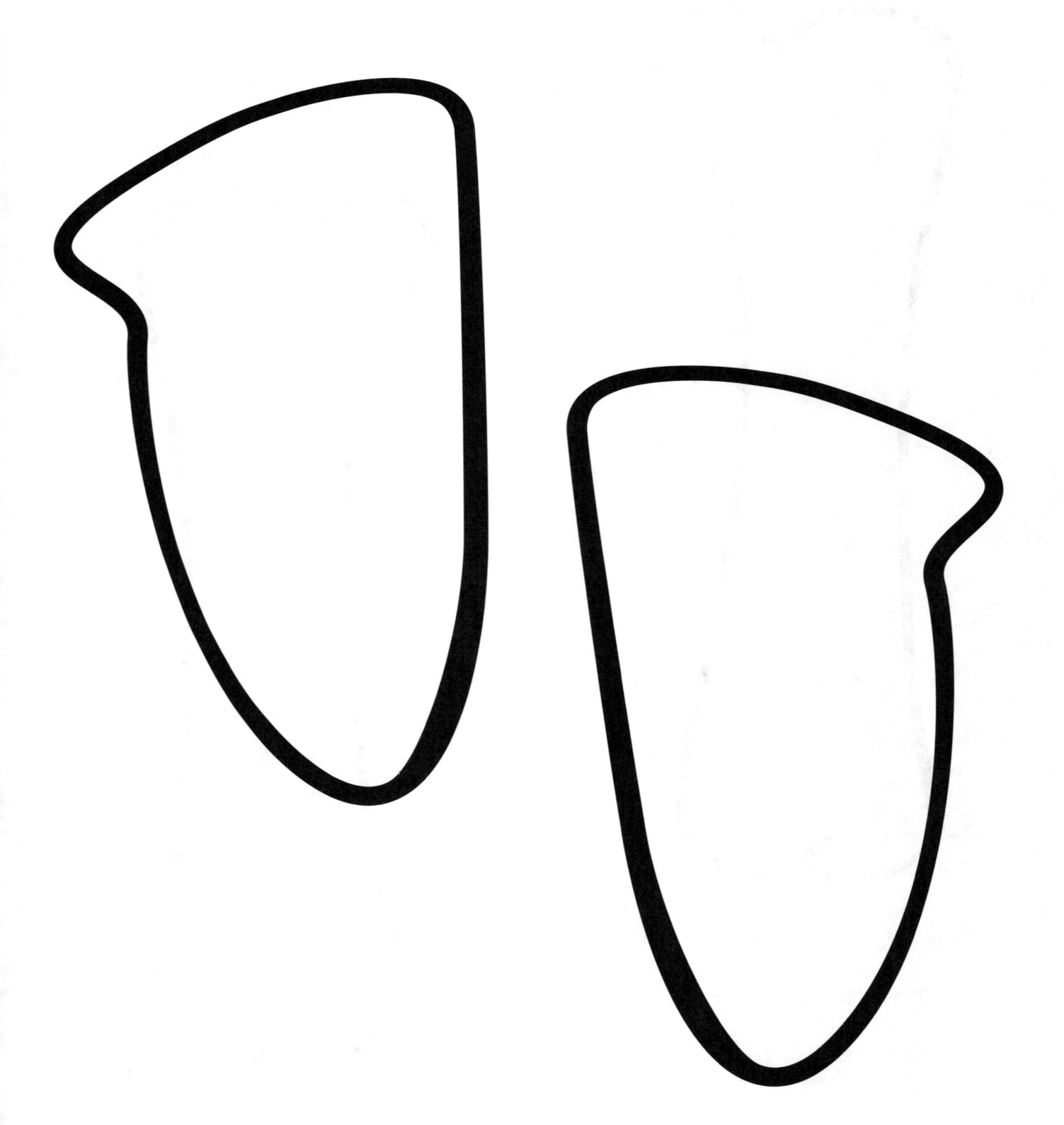

174   The Entire World of Early Developing Sounds Instructional Workbook™   © 2008 Say It Right™   www.sayitright.org

D Activity Patterns

Toad Pattern

Chapter 7 – T & D

Lily Pad Pattern

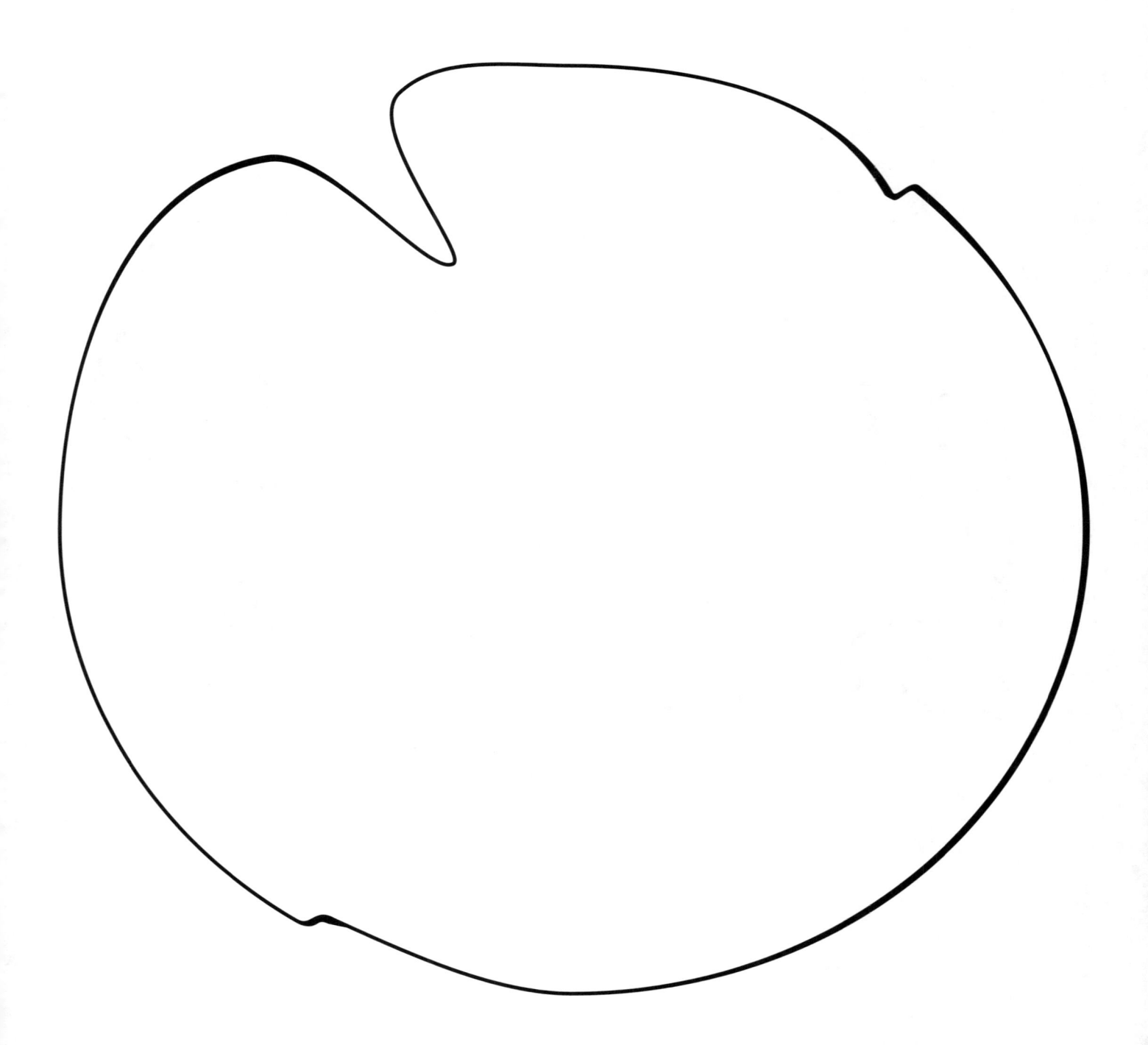

T Homework

The T-Team

Child: Ted, Tom, Tim, and Todd are the T-Team. Help them find the words that begins with the "T" sound. Draw a line from each person to a picture that starts with the "T" sound. Name the pictures as you find them.

Helper: Help your child name the pictures. Emphasize the "T" sounds.

Ted **Tom** **Tim** **Todd**

177

Chapter 7 – T & D

Tic-Tac-Toe

Child: Cut out the numbers 10 and 2 to use as tic-tac-toe markers. Place the numbers on the tic-tac-toe board. Take turns to get three in a row to win. Say the numbers "10" and "2" as you place markers on the board.

Helper: While you interact with your child, emphasize the "Ts" in Tic-Tac-Toe.

T Homework

Eight is Great!

Child: Find and circle the number 8s you see. Each time you circle an eight, say "eight."

Helper: Focus on correct production of the final "T" sound.

Chapter 7 – T & D

The Hat

Child: Circle all the pictures that rhyme with the word "hat." Say a correct "T" sound when you say the words.

Helper: Name each picture and have your child repeat it. Help them decide if it ends with the "T" sound.

D Homework

What's on Dan's Desk?

Child: What's on Dan's desk? Name each item you see.

Helper: Name each picture and have your child repeat it. Help your child decide if it starts with the "D" sound.

Chapter 7–T & D

Digging Dog

The dog dug up many things in the yard. Help him find all the things that start with /d/. Color in the things that start with the /d/ sound and say the name of the item aloud as you color.

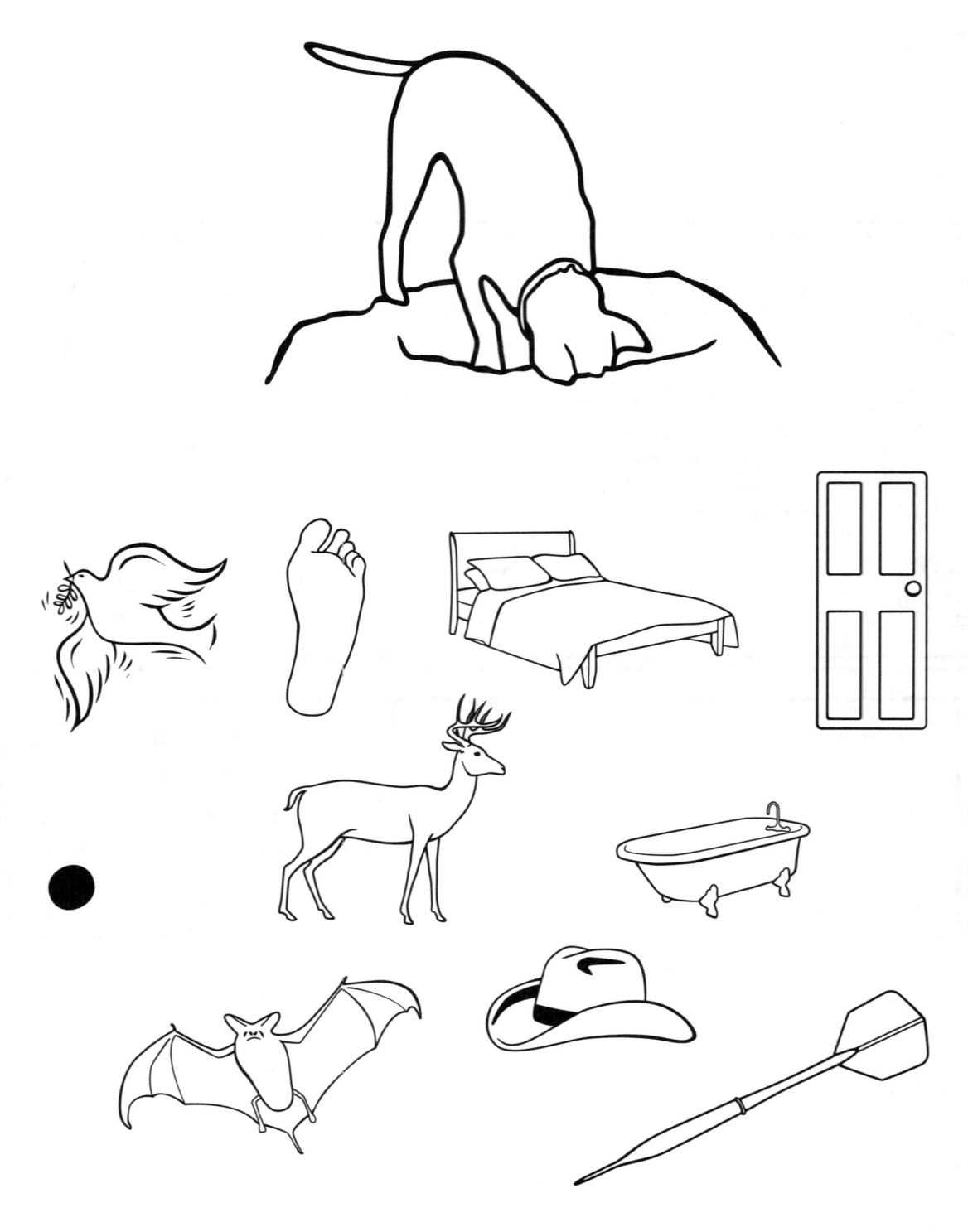

182 The Entire World of Early Developing Sounds Instructional Workbook™

D Homework

Feed The Toad

Child: The toad likes to eat flies. Name the pictures on the flies. If the picture ends with a "D" sound, color it. The toad gets to eat all the flies that are colored. How many flies does he get to eat?

Helper: Name each picture and have your child repeat it. Help your child decide if it ends with the "D" sound.

Chapter 7 – T & D

Ride on a Road

Child: Someone left a mess. The road is full of things. Name all the that you see. Draw a line to the trash can for the items that do not belong there.

184 The Entire World of Early Developing Sounds Instructional Workbook™ © 2008 Say It Right™ www.sayitright.org

Chapter 8
Targeting F & V

- Screening Tool
- Teaching Tips
- Production Illustrations
- Target Lists
- Book Lists
- Activities
- Pictures
- Patterns
- Homework Pages

F & V Screening

Student Name_____ Date of Birth_____

Screening Date_____ Examiner_____

Use "+" or "—" to indicate the child's production of the phoneme at each level (in isolation, in a word, in a phrase, and in a sentence). Use imitation, delayed imitation, or pictures to elicit the child's productions.

Target–Initial /f/	Target–Final /f/	Target–Initial /v/	Target–Final /v/
SOUND IN ISOLATION: /f/		**SOUND IN ISOLATION:** /v/	
face	calf	van	cave
wash your face	running calf	red van	dark cave
She had a smile on her face.	The calf eats grass.	The boys sits in the van.	The bear is in the cave.
fan	cough	view	drive
the small fan	cover your cough	nice view	drive slow
The fan is blowing air.	The little girl has a cough.	The room had a nice view of the ocean.	The police car will drive fast.
five	leaf	vest	hive
five years old	yellow leaf	the man's vest	hive of bees
There are five frogs in the pond.	There is only one leaf on the tree.	The man wore a vest.	The hive of bees was under the porch.

DATA COLLECTION/SCREENING NOTES:

F & V Teaching Tips

Development Information

The consonant pair of /f/ and /v/ usually begin to appear during the second year of life. Typically developing children will start to experiment with /f/ and /v/ through mouth noises. Mastery of the /f/ and /v/ sound pair occurs for most children between 2½ and 4 years of age (Sander, 1972).

Production of /f/ and /v/

This sound pair is labial-dental (i.e., made with contact between the top teeth and bottom lip) and continuant or strident in manner (i.e., produced with a steady and continuous sustained airstream). The /f/ is unvoiced, thus the vocal folds are not set into vibration, while the /v/ is voiced. The tongue lies flat in the mouth, but an accurate /f/ and /v/ can be produced with a variety of tongue placements. The teeth are held slightly apart and the velum is lifted to block air from escaping through the nasal cavity, thus allowing air to be focused through the slightly open teeth and lips.

Stimulating Production of /f/ and /v/

For children who struggle to produce the /f/ and /v/ sounds, some work with the sound in isolation may be warranted. Due to the visual and sustained nature of these sounds, the following strategies may be useful when encouraging accurate production during treatment activities:

- Use an age-appropriate description of the processes for producing these sounds.

- Use the illustrations on page 188 to provide additional instruction for placement of /f/ and /v/. As needed, keep these images displayed during practice with these target sounds.

- Sit side-by-side with the child in front of a mirror. Encourage the child to watch as you gently bite your bottom lip with your top teeth. Cue the child to match your model. Direct the child to imitate your productions of /f/ and /v/.

- Consider allowing the child to apply a small amount of peanut butter or sticky candy as a reinforcer onto the bottom lip. Encourage the child to gently bite the flavor off the bottom lip with the top teeth. Model production of /f/ or /v/ during this moment.

- Use a tissue, cottonball, or small cracker placed on a flat surface. Have the child watch you release a visible and continuous airstream as you produce /f/ or /v/, making the item move across the surface. Encourage the child to match your model.

- To encourage the voicing contrast, direct the child to apply light fingertip pressure to his/her throat or your throat as the /f/ and /v/ contrasts are produced. Talking about "turning on" the voice to make the buzzing associated with /v/.

Chapter 8 – F & V

F & V Production Illustrations

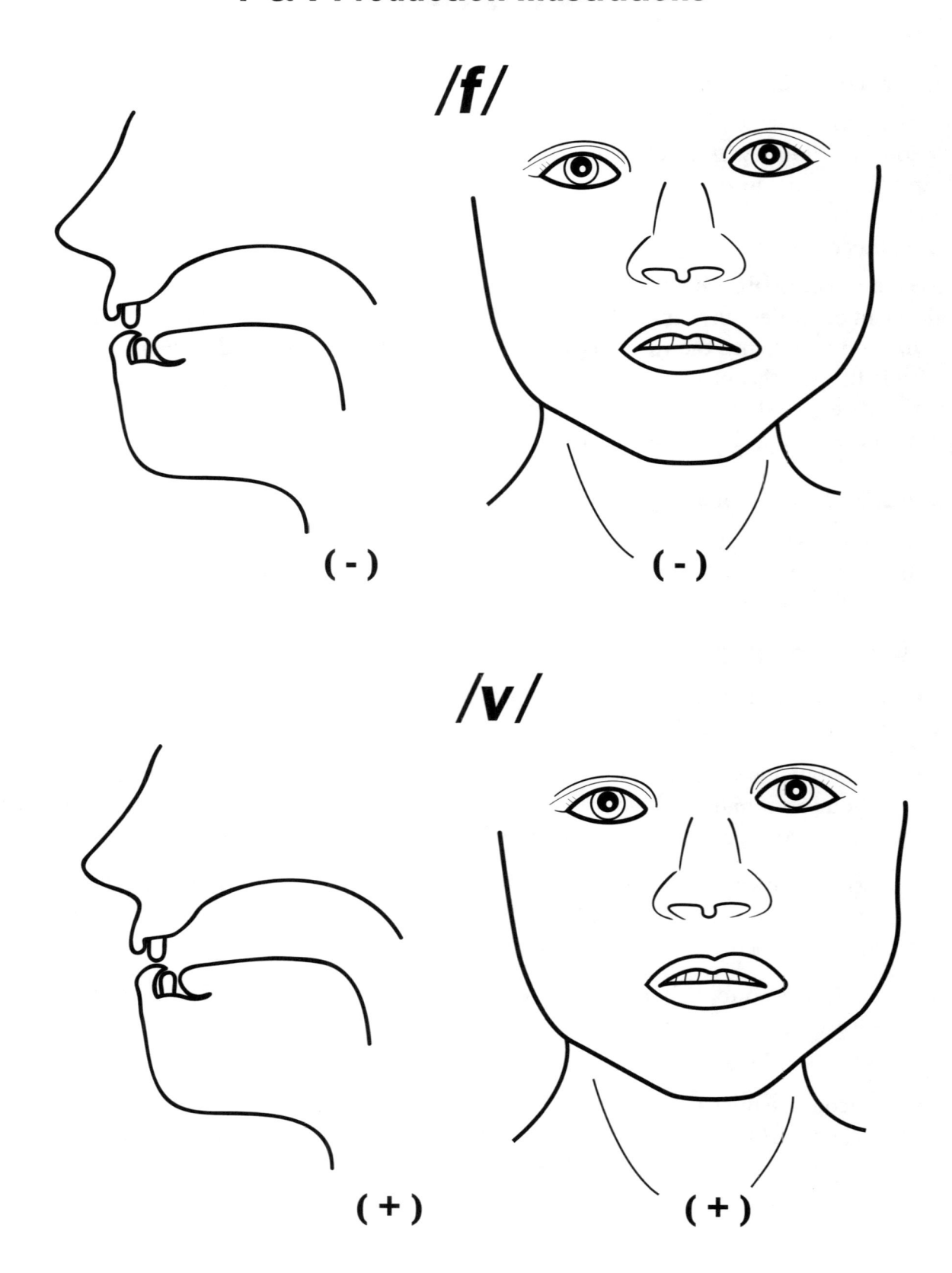

/f/

(-) (-)

/v/

(+) (+)

F & V Target Lists

Especially during early stages of practice, single-syllable words are most facilitative for accurate productions of target sounds. Consider the surrounding consonant and vowel sounds in a target word to control for other sounds the child may be lacking. For example, when first targeting initial /f/ with a child, avoid words that also contain medial and/or final /v/. Gradually, as a child becomes more successful with practice of a target sound, words of increasing length and complexity can be added to the production-practice activities.

The Entire World of Early Developing Sounds™ suggests using the target words listed for the early stages of practice with young children working on /f/ and /v/. Pages 200-207 provide representations of these words in picture form for use with production practice activities. Suggested target phrases and sentences are also provided. Phrases and sentences are most useful with older children who can read. *The Entire World of TH, F &V Articulation Flip Book* (Ristuccia, 2004) is an excellent source for illustrated, interactive phrase and sentence practice.

When working with older children, the word, phrase, and sentence lists may be useful as stimulus items in mass production practice. If using the phrases and sentences with nonreaders, direct or delayed imitation will be necessary (i.e., saying the phrase or sentence as a model and then having the child repeat it with or without a delay). Ideally, production of phrases and sentences will be elicited naturally during structured and unstructured activities, thus it is possible that the phrase and sentence lists would not need to be used with younger children.

To target medial /f/ and /v/, use the target words in combination with another word (e.g., "campfire" to elicit medial /f/ or "blue van" for medial /v/). Medial /f/ and /v/ target words can be added once a child is ready for practice with multisyllabic words. As medial /f/ and /v/ words are selected, continue to control for facilitative contexts to ensure children successfully produce the new sound. In addition, use multisyllabic words that are meaningful to the child (e.g., feather, vacuum, etc.).

Chapter 8 – F & V

F & V Single Word Practice

Word-Initial /f/	Word-Final /f/	Word-Initial /v/	Word-Final /v/
face	calf	van	cave
fall	chef	vase	dive
fan	cough	veil	drive
farm	knife	vein	dove
feet	leaf	view	glove
fence	loaf	vest	five
fin	reef	vet	hive
fish	roof	vine	love
five	safe	vise	move
food	thief	voice	shave
foot	wife	vote	stove
four	wolf	vow	wave

F & V Phrase-Level Practice

Word–Initial /f/	Word–Final /f/	Word–Initial /v/	Word–Final /v/
her **face**	little **calf**	red **van**	dark **cave**
leaves **fall**	happy **chef**	glass **vase**	**dive** in
a big **fan**	nasty **cough**	see the **veil**	**drive** in
a big **farm**	sharp **knife**	see my **vein**	the white **dove**
big **feet**	a yellow **leaf**	a nice **view**	one **glove**
wood **fence**	**loaf** of bread	a blue **vest**	I'm **five**
a sharp **fin**	the coral **reef**	a **vet**	a big **beehive**
time to **fish**	on the **roof**	grape **vine**	**love** letter
just **five**	**safe** to open	in the **vise**	time to **move**
more **food** please	not a **thief**	hear his **voice**	**shave** the dog
my **foot**	my **wife**	**vote** tomorrow	the new **stove**
four years old	big **wolf**	take a **vow**	**wave** good-bye

Chapter 8 – F & V

F & V Sentence-Level Practice

Word–Initial /f/	Word–Final /f/	Word–Initial /v/	Word–Final /v/
She has a smile on her **face**.	The **calf** ate the grass.	He will park the **van**.	The **cave** is dark and cold.
Someone may **fall** on those stairs.	He is a good **chef**.	Put the flowers in the **vase**.	She will **dive** in the deep end of the pool.
Turn on the **fan**.	She has a bad **cough**.	She wore a **veil**.	I can **drive** to the store.
I live on a **farm**.	The **knife** is sharp.	She could see the small **vein**.	The **dove** made a nest in the tree.
His **feet** hurt.	The tree had a red **leaf**.	They had a great **view** of the lake.	He wore one **glove**.
You need to paint the **fence**.	It is a **loaf** of wheat bread.	His **vest** is too tight.	She will turn **five** next week.
The shark has a **fin**.	She swam in the coral **reef**.	He is a good **vet**.	The **hive** of bees is in the tree.
The **fish** swim in the water.	The **roof** needs repair.	The **vine** had thorns.	He is in **love** with her.
She has **five** pieces of candy.	The bank has a big **safe**.	Use a **vise** to hold the wood.	I need to **move** the car.
All the **food** was tasty.	The **thief** came through the window.	She has a beautiful **voice**.	He will **shave** in the morning.
His **foot** is stuck.	His **wife** is pretty.	You need to **vote** on Tuesday.	The **stove** is hot.
He will turn **four** tomorrow.	The **wolf** howled.	She made a **vow**.	I can **wave** hello.

F & V Book List

Reading a story is a natural and motivating activity for children. Children's stories are filled with opportunities to bombard the child with words containing the target sound and to elicit productions of the target. Consult the following list to select books that contain multiple opportunities for words that contain /f/ or /v/.

\	INITIAL /f/		
TITLE	PUBLICATION INFORMATION	INTEREST LEVEL	TARGET WORDS
Fall Leaves Fall!	Zoe Hall (2000) Scholastic	4-8 years	fall
Five Little Ducks	Raffi (1999) Crown Books	1-6 years	five, four, far
Fuzzy Yellow Ducklings	Matthew Van Feet (1995) Dial Books	2-8 years	fuzzy, furry, feel, fold, fun, feet, frogs
Touch and Feel Farm	Dorling Kindersley Publishing (1998) Author	1-5 years	farm, feel, fuzzy, furry, farmer, fun, fur
I Am Fire	Jean Marzollo (1996) Scholastic	3-7 years	fire, fireworks
The Foot Book	Dr. Suess (1968) Random House	2-7 years	foot, feet, fun, four, front, fur, fuzzy
Farm Flu	Teresa Bateman (2004) Albert and Whitman Co	4-8 years	farm
The Mitten	Jan Brett (1989) Putnam Publishing	4-8 years	mitten, mole, mouse, my, made, move
\	FINAL /f/		
The Dog Who Cried Woof	Bob Barkly (2001) Scholastic	4-8 years	woof
Who Says Woof?	John Butler (2003) Viking Books	2-5 years	woof, ruff
What's the Time Grandma Wolf?	Ken Brown (2001) Peachtree Publishing	Baby-preschool	wolf
Dandelion Puffs	Debbie Powell (1989) Rigby	2-5 years	puff

Chapter 8 – F & V

FINAL / f /			
Title	**Publication Information**	**Interest Level**	**Target Words**
Three Billy Goats Gruff	Mary Finch (2001) Barefoot Books	Baby-preschool	*gruff*
Huff and Puff Go to School	Jean Warren (1994) Totline Publications	Baby-preschool	*Huff, Puff*

INITIAL /v/			
Title	**Publication Information**	**Interest Level**	**Target Words**
The Very Busy Spider	Eric Carle (1985) Philomel Books	Baby-preschool	*very*
The Very Hungry Caterpillar	Eric Carle (1981) Philomel Books	4-8 years	*very, vegetables*
Noah's Very Big Boat	Susan Isbell ((1997) Abingdon Press	4-8 years	*very*
Growing Vegetable Soup	Lois Ehlert (1990) Voyager Books	4-8 years	*vegetables*
Vegetable Glue	Susan Chandler (1997) Meadowside Children's Book	4-8 years	*vegetables*
Arthur's Great Big Valentine	Lillian Hoban (1991) HarperTrohpy	4-8 years	*valentine*

FINAL / v /			
Does a Kangaroo Have a Mother Too?	Eric Carle (2000) HarperCollins	4-8 years	*have*
I Love You Stinky Face	Lisa McCourt (2004) Scholastic	4-8 years	*love*
Wave Hello Thomas!	W. Rev Awdry (1993) Random House	2-6 years	*wave*
Can I Have a Stegosaurus, Mom? Can I? Please!?	Lois Grambing (1998) Troll Communications	4-8 years	*have*
Can I Have a Tyrannosaurus, Dad? Can I? Please!?	Lois Grambling (2000) Troll Communications	4-8 years	*have*

F & V Activity Pages

Regardless of your approach to treatment, a variety of activities should be used to bombard children with correct productions of the target sound and to elicit production practice. The activities in this unit include a range of sound-specific options for /f/ and /v/. They are designed to appeal to children between the ages of 2 and 7.

In addition, the following are available to support your teaching of the /p/ and /b/ sounds:

- **More Activity Ideas** that can be used to target any sound are included in Appendix A.

- Sound-specific **Pictures** to be used with activities are found on pages 200-207.

- A **Blank Card Pattern**, to include your own words, is found in Appendix D.

- **Book Lists** for selecting stories are included on pages 193-194.

- **Word, Phrase, and Sentence Lists** are provided on pages 189-192, to use with activities or with more traditional boards games (e.g., Sorry! Uno, and Kerplunk). To earn a turn, have the older student read or repeat words, phrases, or sentences containing the selected target phoneme. The goal is to encourage as many repetitions of the target sound as possible—be creative!

- **Homework Pages** (pages 214-221) provide activities that can be easily used by parents or other care providers to encourage successful practice in other settings. Be certain to direct children to return completed Homework Pages so you can encourage self-evaluation and monitoring of their practice. Consider having students carry a "speech folder" to store these materials and facilitate communication with others on a regular basis.

- Appendix B provides a **Parent Memo** that can be used along with selected homework activity pages.

- Appendix E includes a blank **Lesson Plan**. Use the form to ensure that all essential lesson plan components are accounted for within each session. Be certain to probe for accuracy, provide instruction/bombardment for the target sounds, and plan for a sufficient amount of successful mass production practice.

- Appendix F provides a blank **Data Collection Form** to monitor progress and adjust treatment.

- Don't forget that **Suggestions for Conversation and Carryover** are provided in Appendix B. Plan for generalization from the start and incorporate these suggestions along the way.

Chapter 8 – F & V

Initial F Activities

Snack Ideas
- Fruit snacks, fruit, frozen yogurt or popsicles
- Fruit juice

Craft
- Footprint Tracing—Trace each child's foot. Color them in or decorate them and create characters.

Motor and Movement
- Follow the Leader—Have children follow the leader through various places in the classroom. Allow each child to be the leader if he or she is comfortable.

Songs and Finger Play

Two Little Feet

Two little feet go tap, tap, tap.
Two little hands go clap, clap, clap.
One little body turns around.
One little body sits quietly down.

Follow the Feet

Materials
- Initial /f/ book
- Foot Pattern, page 208
- Word-initial /f/ pictures, page 200
- Bucket or basket
- Scissors
- Glue or tape

Procedure

1. Bombard the child with word-initial /f/ by introducing the sound with a story selected from the book list.
2. Place the bucket or basket on the floor somewhere in the room.
3. Duplicate 4 to 12 copies of the Foot Pattern. Cut the feet out and place them on the floor in footprint fashion to lead from one spot in the room to the bucket or basket.
4. Duplicate the set of word-initial /f/ pictures and cut them apart. Place the /f/ pictures in the bucket or basket.
5. Have children follow the footprints to the bucket. Have the children take turns "following the footprints" as you bombard them with /f/ words in the phrase, "Follow the footprints. What did you find?"
6. Have the child draw a card from the bucket or basket and name the picture. Bombard with /f/ words and elicit productions of sentences and phrases such as, "Fun! You found a fish!"
7. Consider variations such as attaching the /f/ pictures to a foot and having the children each step on one of the feet and name the picture on the foot they are on.

F Activity Pages

Final F Activities

Where's My Other Half?

Materials
- Final /f/ book
- Leaf Pattern, page 209

Procedure

1. Bombard the child with word-final /f/ by introducing the sound with a story selected from the book list.

2. Duplicate several Leaf Patterns and cut them in half. Give each child a leaf half and tell then to find the other half of their leaf. One child at a time can ask each classmate, "Do you have my leaf half?" or use an appropriate level of production based on his or her skill.

3. Bombard the children with the words "leaf" and "half" and, as appropriate, elicit productions based on each child's skill level as they search for the other half of their leaf.

4. This can also be completed as an individual activity.

Snack Ideas
- Half and apple or an orange, loaf of bread, leaf-shaped cookies in a variety of colors

Craft
- Leaf on the Tree—Duplicate the Leaf and Tree Patterns (page 209-210). Cut out the leaves. Color them and add them to the tree.

Motor and Movement
- Leaf Jump—Duplicate the Leaf Pattern. Place one leaf in front of each child. Give children directions to follow emphasizing final /f/, such as, "jump off the leaf" and "jump over the leaf." Emphasize the final /f/ sound in the words used.

Songs and Finger Play

Leaf Colors

Red leaf, gold leaf,

Yellow leaf too.

A basket full of leaves just for you!

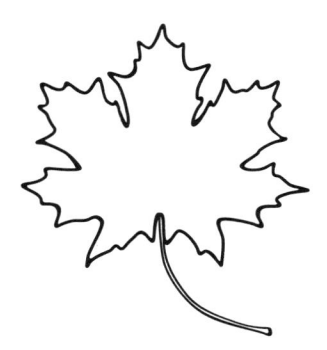

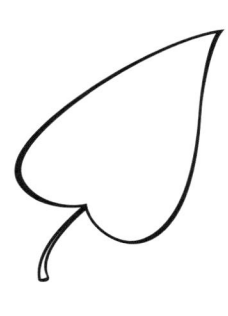

Chapter 8—F & V

Initial V Activities

Snack Ideas
- Vegetables
- Vet juice (Kool-Aid or juice)

Craft
- Animal Puppets—Duplicate the Animal Puppet Patterns found on page 212. Cut out, color, and add a popsicle stick to create a puppet. Bombard the child with the word "vet" as you create the animal you would find at the vet.

Motor and Movement
- Vet Picks a Pet (sung to the tune of *The Farmer and the Dell*)—the children stand in a circle around the child designated as "the vet." Sing verses similar to *the Farmer and the Dell* starting with, "The vet picks a pet, the vet picks a pet. Hi-ho the derry-oh, the vet picks a pet." Use the animal puppets the children created for the craft activity. Then have each child act as a pet the vet picks.

Songs and Finger Plays

The People in Your Neighborhood

Oh, who are the people in your neighborhood
In your neighborhood
In your neighborhood.
Oh, who are the people in your neighborhood,
The people that you meet each day.
*Oh, the **VET** is a person in your neighborhood,*
In your neighborhood, in your neighborhood.
*The **VET** is a person in your neighborhood,*
A person that you meet each day.

The Vet's Van

Materials
- Van Pattern and Animals, page 211
- Initial /v/ book
- Glue or tape
- Crayons or markers
- Scissors

Procedure

1. Bombard the child with word-initial /v/ by introducing the sound with a story selected from the book list on page 194.

2. Duplicate one Van Pattern and Animals for each child.

3. Tell the children to add the animal pictures to the "vet's van."

4. Bombard them with the words "van" and "vet" and, as appropriate, elicit productions based on each child's skill level as they color the van and glue or tape animals in the van windows. Use phrases and sentences such as, "The dog goes in the "(vet's van)" pausing to see if the child will use the appropriate word to fill in the blank.

5. Variations include using the word-initial /v/ pictures and adding them to the van rather than the animals.

⇐Add verses with other people in the neighborhood: grocer, mail carrier, etc..

V Activity Pages

Final V Activities

I Have Five

Materials
- Initial /v/ book
- Hand Pattern, page 213
- Word-final /v/ pictures, page 206
- Tape or Velcro®

Procedure

1. Bombard the child with word-final /v/ by introducing the sound with a story selected from the book list on page 195.

2. Duplicate the Hand Pattern and the word-final /v/ pictures. Choose five pictures. Have the child tape or Velcro the pictures to the Hand Pattern. Help each child name all five cards.

3. Bombard the child with phrases such as, "Great! Give me five for naming all the pictures." Elicit sentence or phrase productions based on each child's skill level.

4. A glove can be used as a variation to using the Hand Pattern.

Snack Ideas
- Five crackers or five small cookies
- Five Alive juice

Craft
- Shaving Cream Finger Paint—Spray shaving cream on a desk or table and add food coloring. Have the children make handprints by spreading the shaving cream around and blotting their hands on a piece of paper. Help the child count all five fingers and emphasize the word "five."

Motor and Movement
- Number Grid—Create a game "mat" by taping off a 4' x 3' grid on the floor. In each square place pieces of colored tape similar to the dots on a die. Include two of each number (e.g., 2-ones, 2-twos). Give each child a turn to roll a die and then move to the amount they rolled. Once on their spot, have them count the dots and say the number. When there are two children occupying one square, the child who was there first rolls again. Emphasize the words, "five" and "move" as the game progresses.

Songs and Finger Plays

Five Fingers

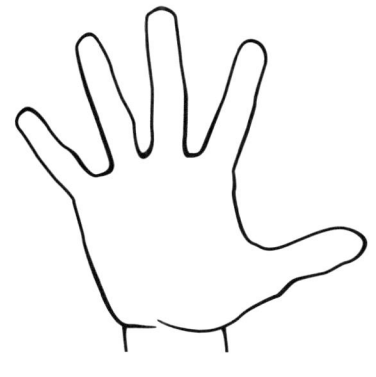

I have five fingers on each hand.   [Show each hand.]
I like to put them in the sand.   [Wiggle all fingers.]
When I hide my thumb just so,   [Bend thumbs back.]
There's only four that I can show.   [Show four fingers on each hand.]

Initial F Picture Cards

face	fall
fan	farm
feet	fence

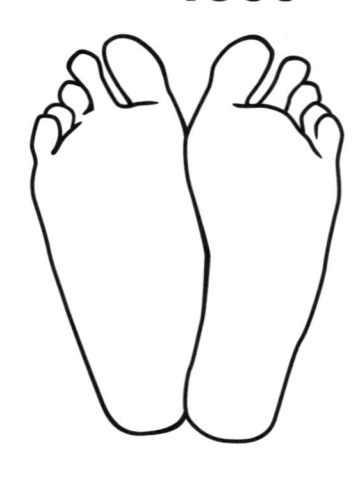

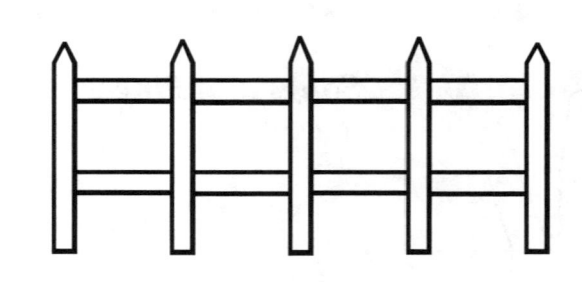

200 The Entire World of Early Developing Sounds Instructional Workbook™   © 2008 Say It Right™ www.sayitright.org

Initial F Picture Cards

fin	fish
five	food
foot	four

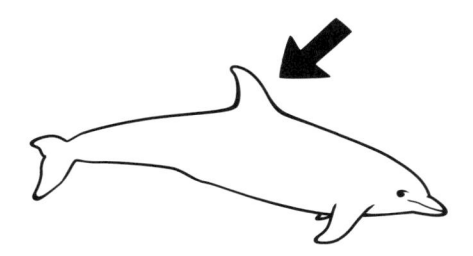

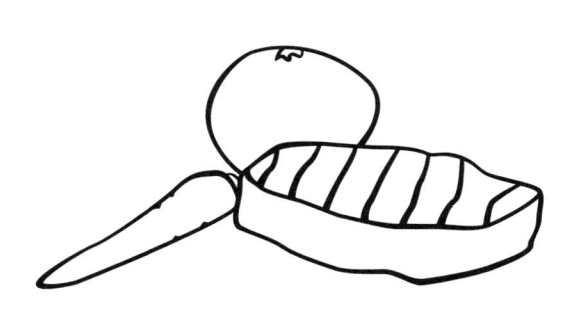

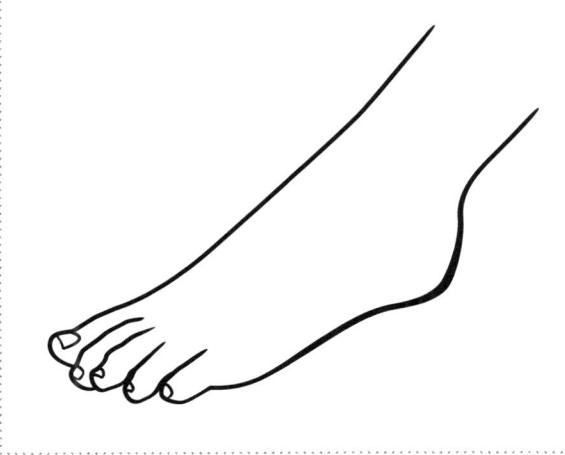

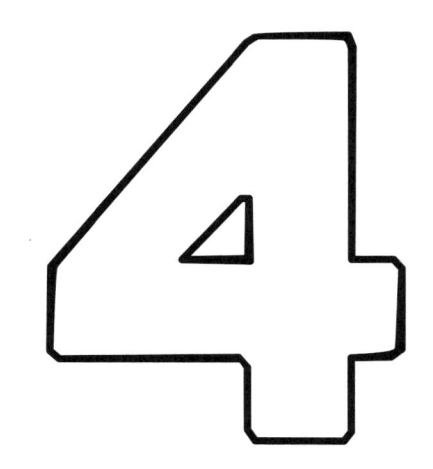

Final F Picture Cards

calf	chef
cough	knife
leaf	loaf

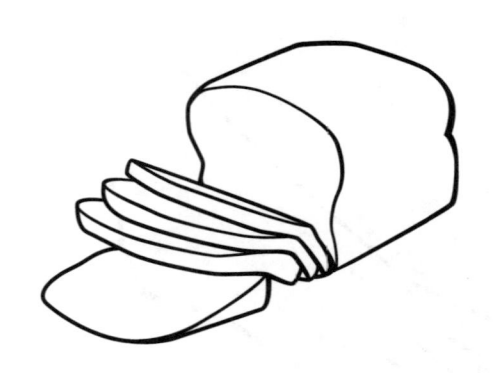

Final F Picture Cards

reef	roof
safe	thief
wife	wolf

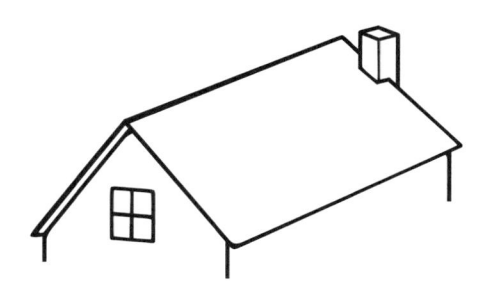

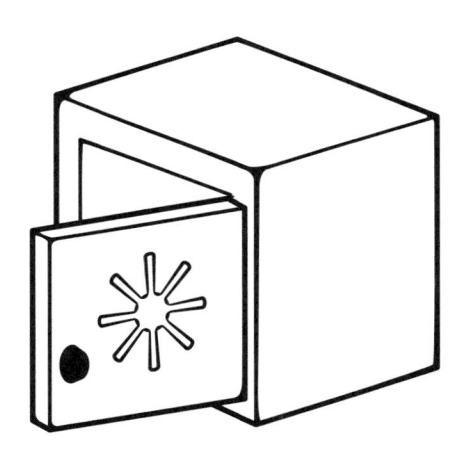

Initial V Picture Cards

van	vase
vet	vein
view	vest

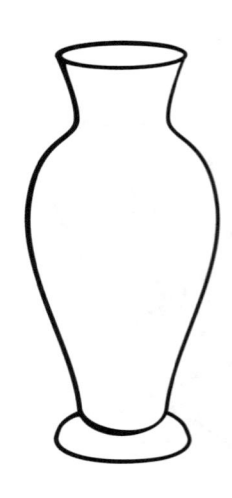

Initial V Picture Cards

veil	vise
vine	voice
vote	vow

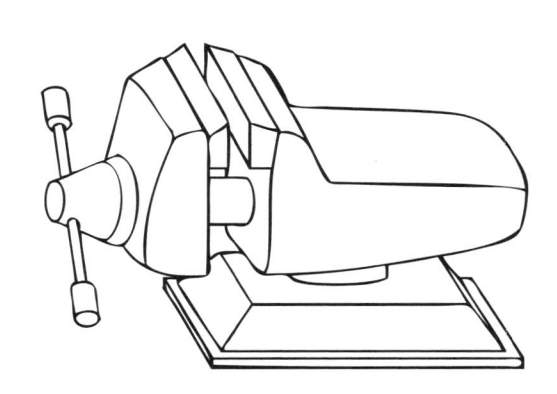

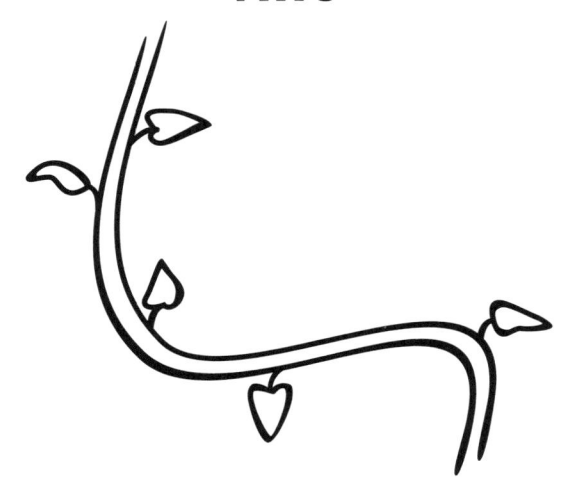

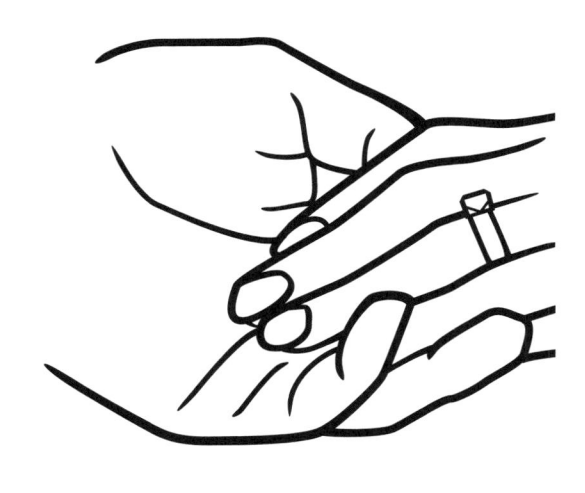

205

Final V Picture Cards

cave	dive
drive	dove
glove	five

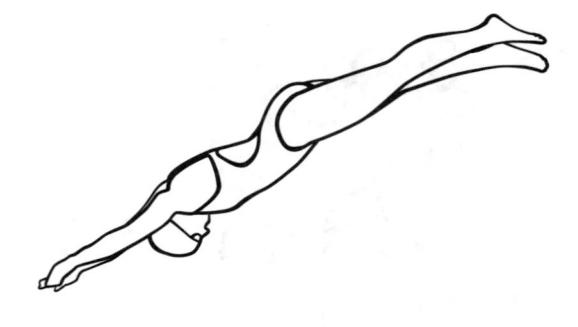

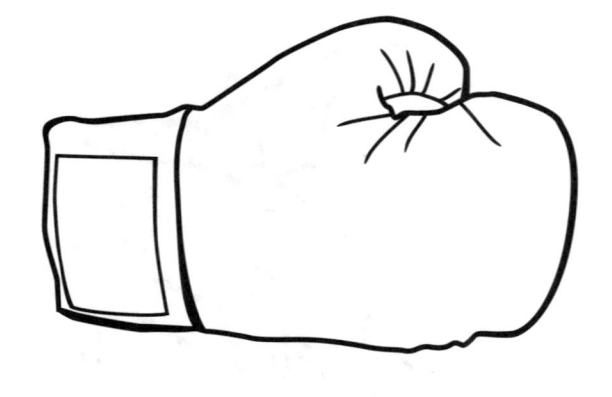

206 The Entire World of Early Developing Sounds Instructional Workbook™ © 2008 Say It Right™ www.sayitright.org

Final V Picture Cards

hive	love
move	shave
stove	wave

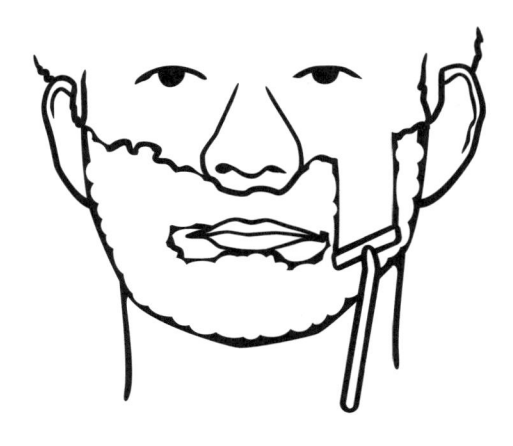

Chapter 8 – F & V

Foot Pattern

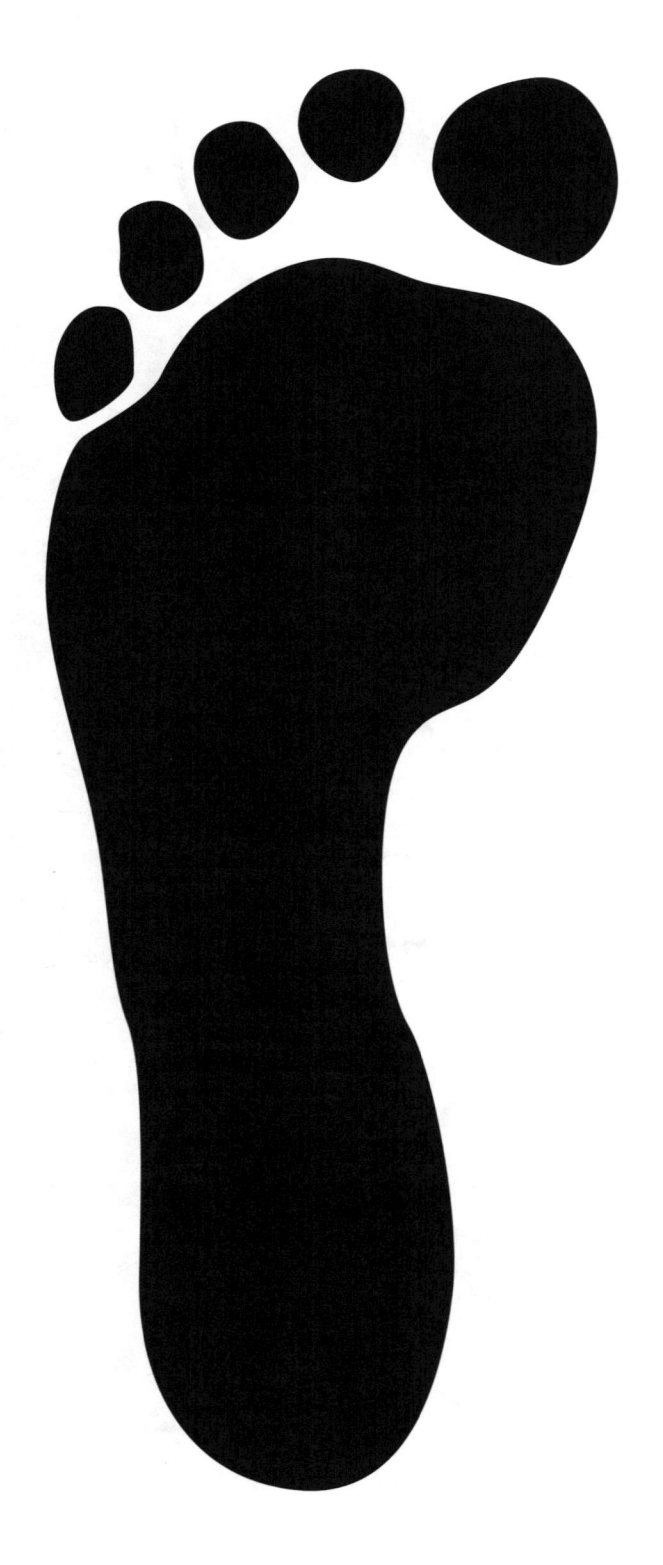

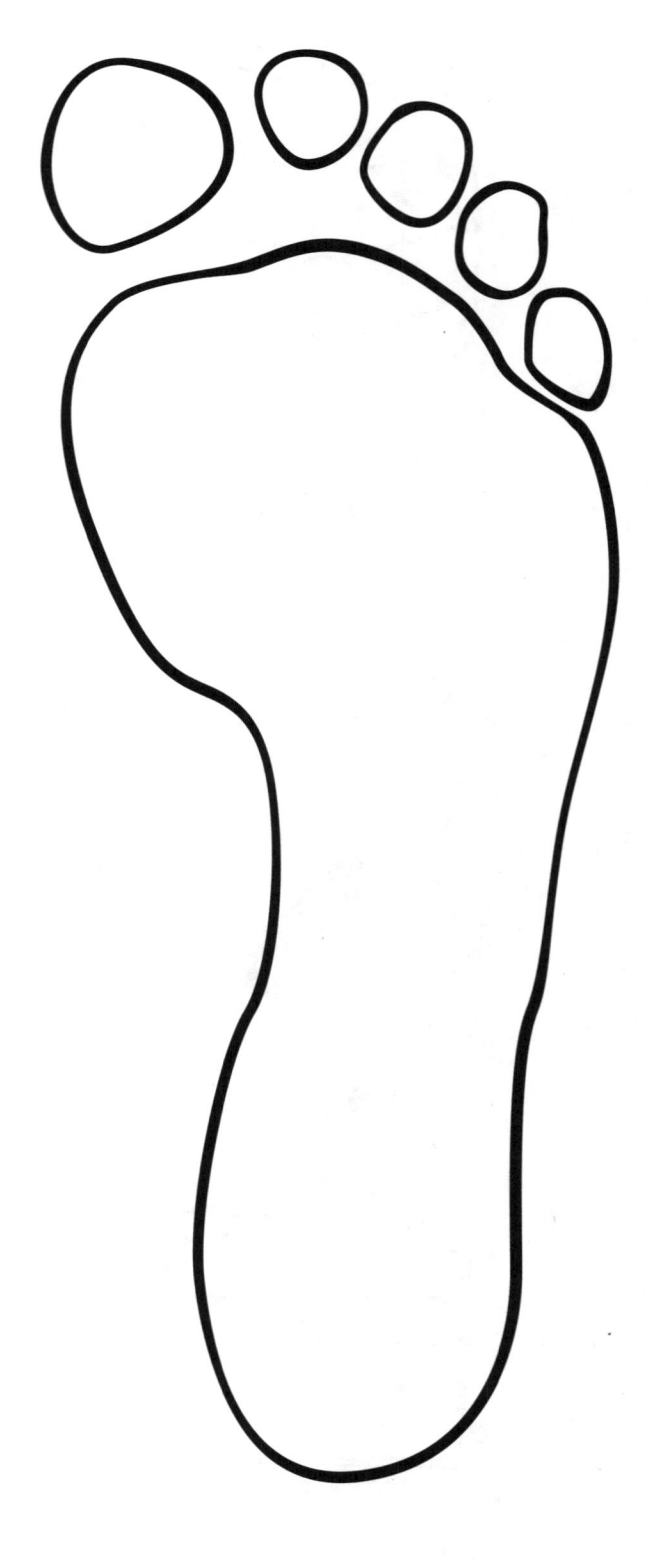

F Activity Patterns

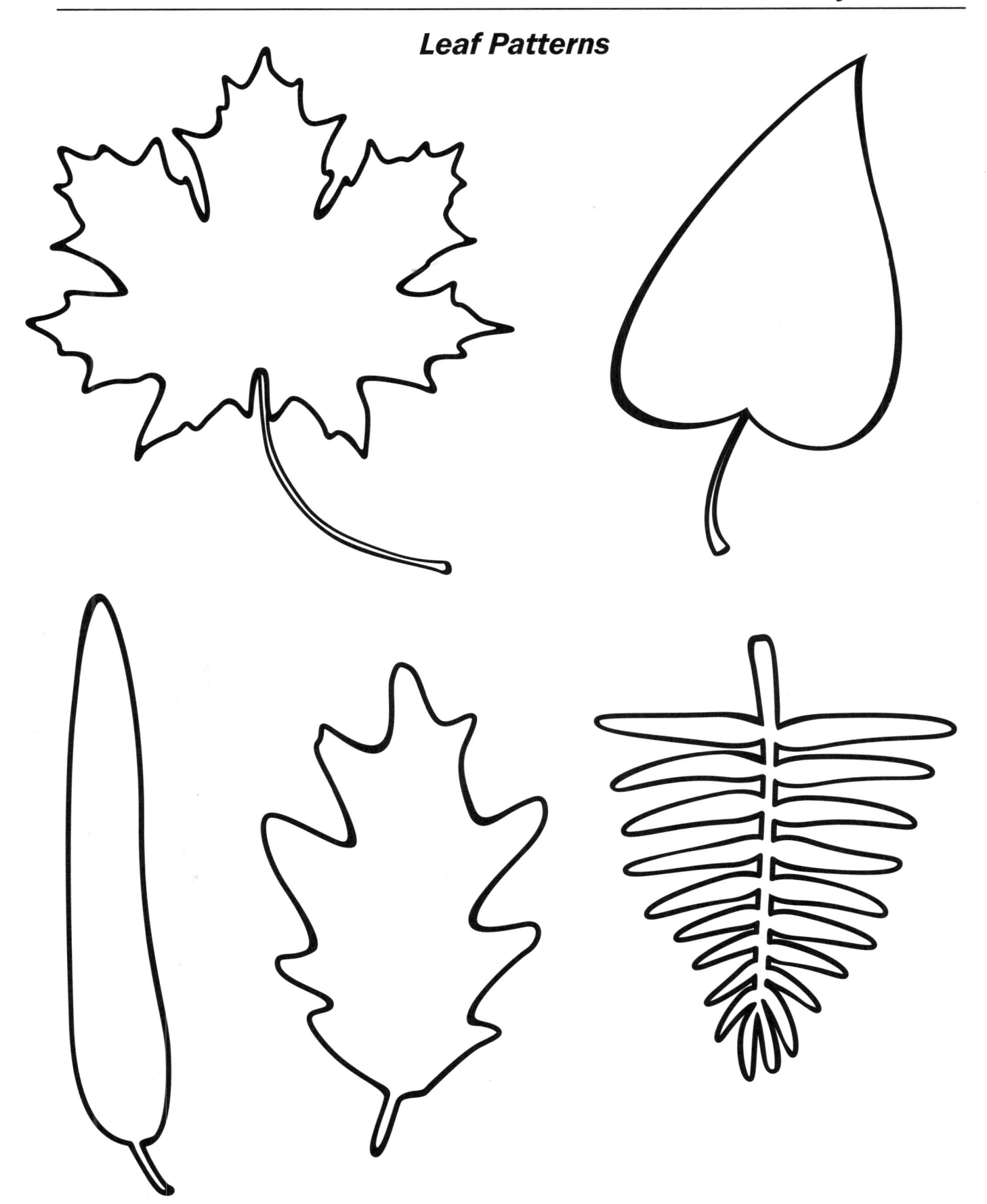

Leaf Patterns

Chapter 8 – F & V

Tree Pattern

V Activity Patterns

Van Patterns

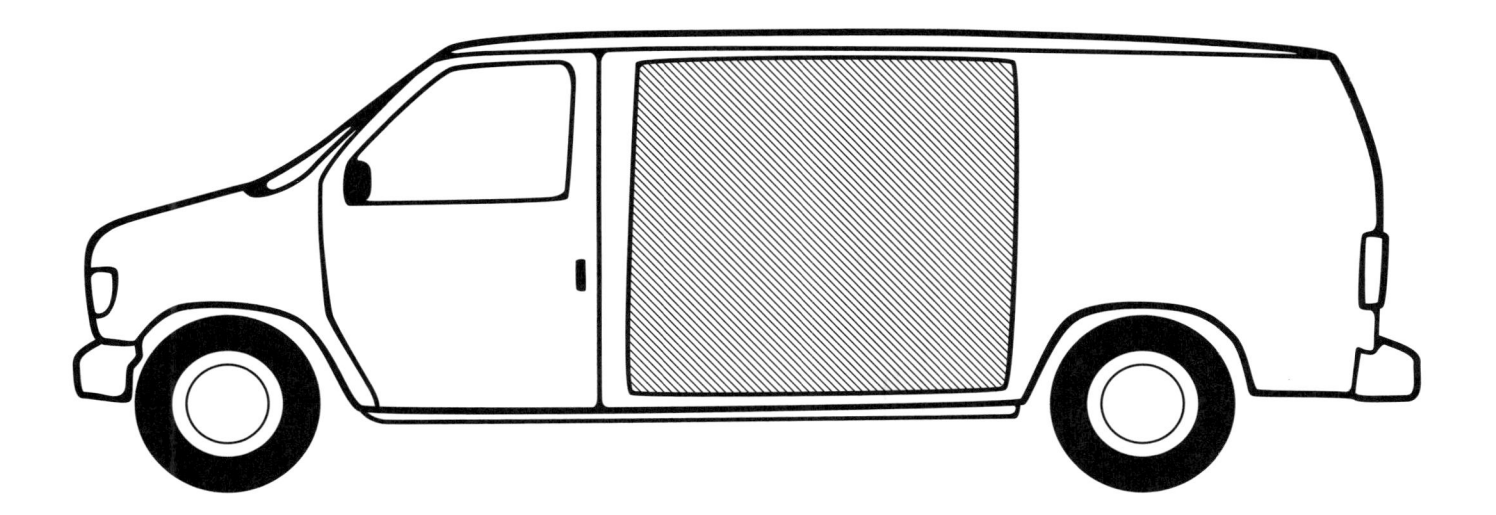

Chapter 8–F & V

Animal Puppet Patterns

V Activity Patterns

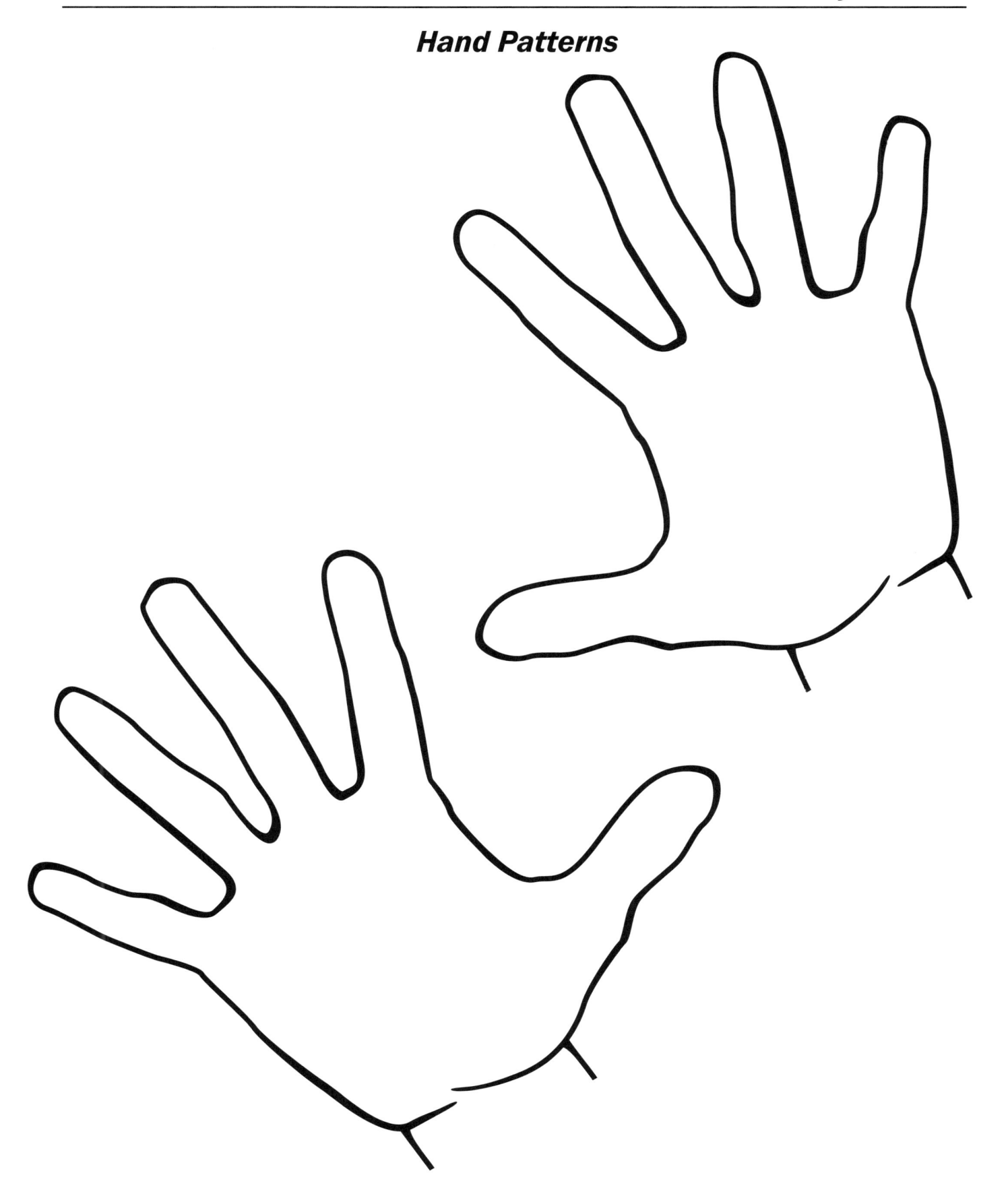

Hand Patterns

Chapter 8– F & V

Find the Fish

Child: Find five fish that match the one at the top of the page.

Helper: Focus on helping the child correctly say the "F" sound in the words "fish," "find," and "five."

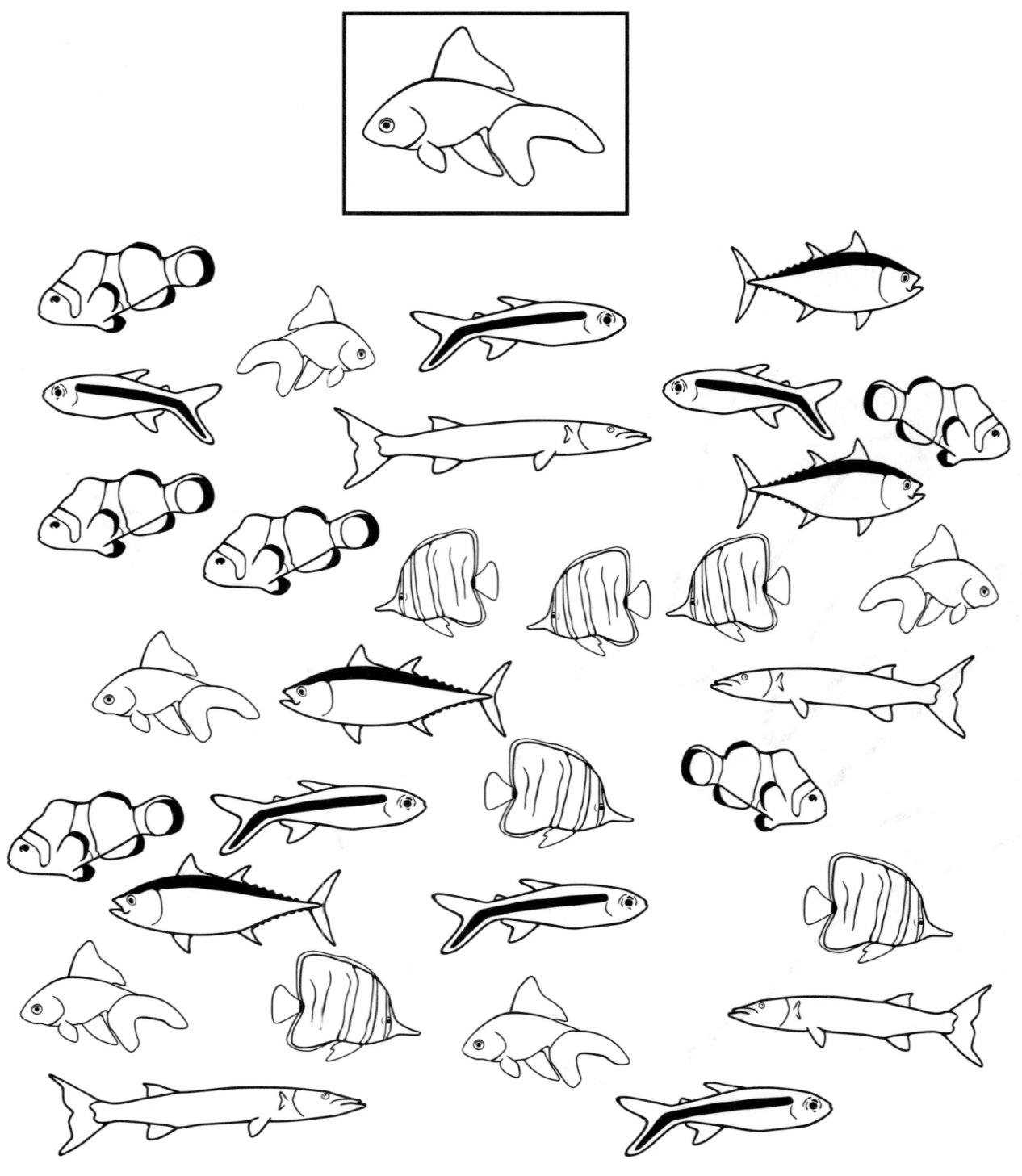

F Homework

Find the Food

Child: Circle all the foods you see. For each picture, say "____ is food" or "____ is not food."

Helper: Focus on helping the child correctly say the "F" sound in the word "food."

215

Chapter 8—F & V

Jeff the Chef

Child: Jeff is a chef who made a loaf of bread. Retell the story after you hear it.

Helper: Read the story aloud. Emphasize a correct "F" sound. Encourage the child to retell the story using the correct production of "F." For more practice, cut out the pictures and have the child put them in the correct order.

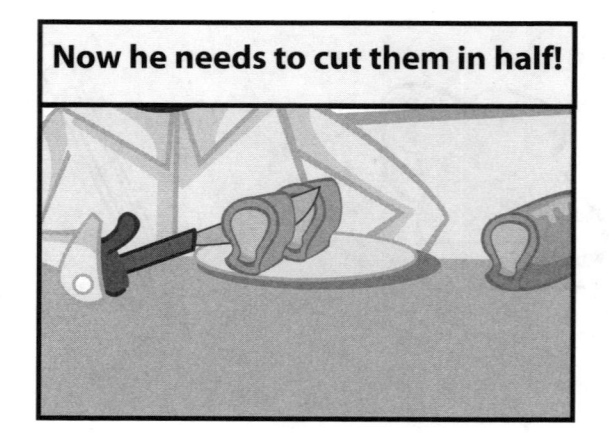

Jeff the chef needs to make a loaf of bread.

With a poof and a puff and a little bit of fluff,

Jeff is sure he's made enough.

His wife comes in to take a loaf.

When he realizes that she had invited her staff!

Now he needs to cut them in half!

F Homework

Coral Reef

Child: Hidden in the coral reef are pictures that end with the "F" sound. Find the pictures and name each one. Color the picture if you use the "F" sound correctly.

Helper: Focus on helping the child correctly say the "F" sound at the end of the words.

Chapter 8 – F & V

The Growing Vine

Child: The vine is full of leaves. On the leaves are pictures of words that start with the "V" sound. Name each picture. Color the picture when you use the "V" sound correctly.

Helper: Focus on helping the child correctly say the "V" sound in the words.

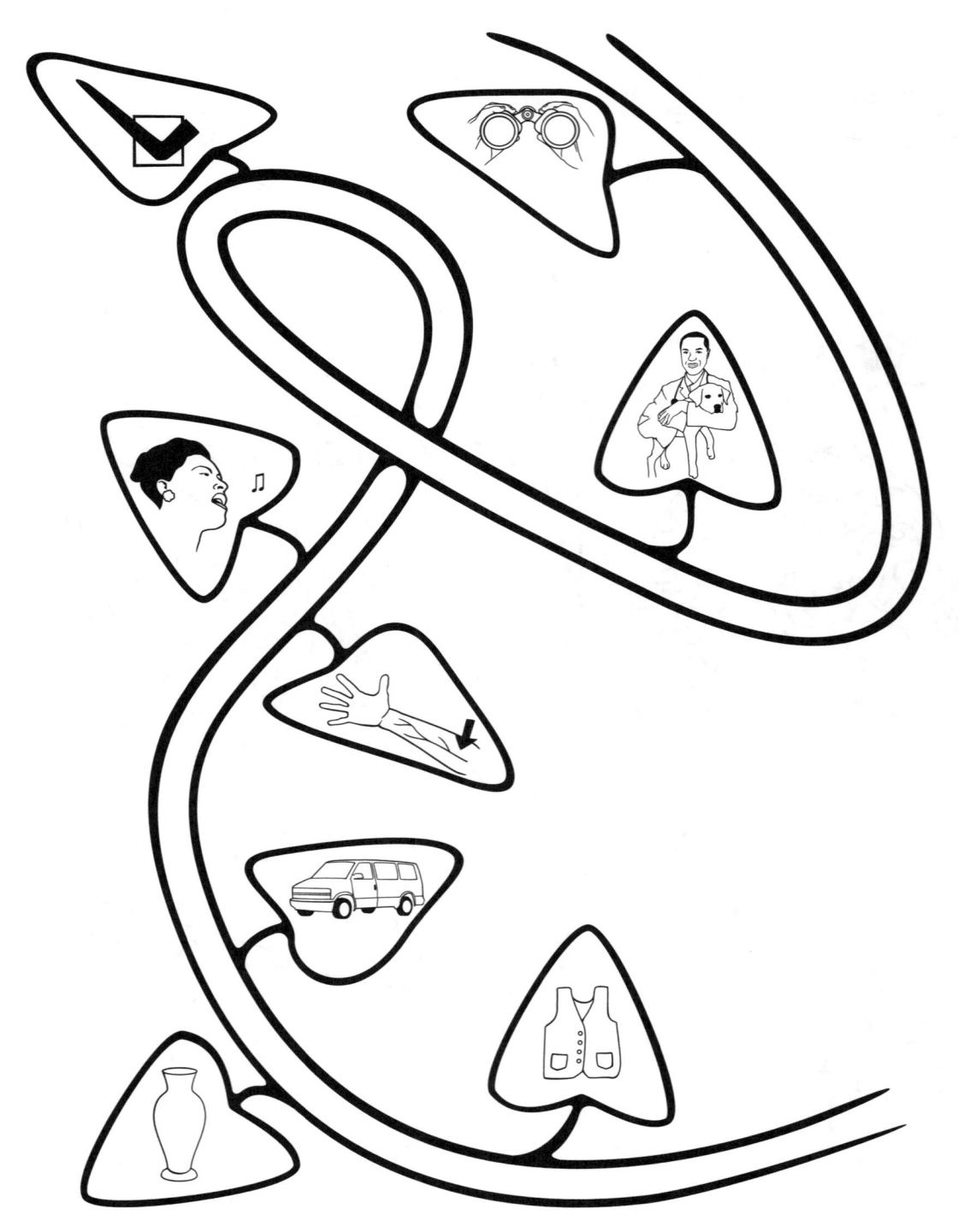

V Homework

Vic's Vest

Child: Help Vic design his vest. Color the four pictures. Cut them out and paste them on the pockets of the vest. Wherever you see the letter "v," color it, and make the "V" sound.

Helper: Focus on helping the child correctly say the "V" sound at the beginning of the words

Chapter 8 – F & V

Brave Dave Enters the Cave

Child: Dave was brave to enter the cave. Retell the story after you hear it.

Helper: Read the story aloud. Emphasize a correct "V" sound. Encourage the child to retell the story using the correct production of "V." For more practice, cut out the pictures and have the child put them in the correct order.

- Brave Dave sees a cave.
- He wonders what is in the cave?
- He wants to prove that he is brave.
- He moves closer to the cave.
- It is dark, but he is brave.
- Look what he found, a glove in the cave!
- He put it on and gave a wave.
- Dave was brave to enter the cave.

V Homework

Save It Up

Child: The piggy bank needs coins. Color the coins that rhyme with "save" and cut them out. Glue them onto the bank. Name each picture as you glue it to the bank.

Helper: Help the child correctly say the "V" sound.

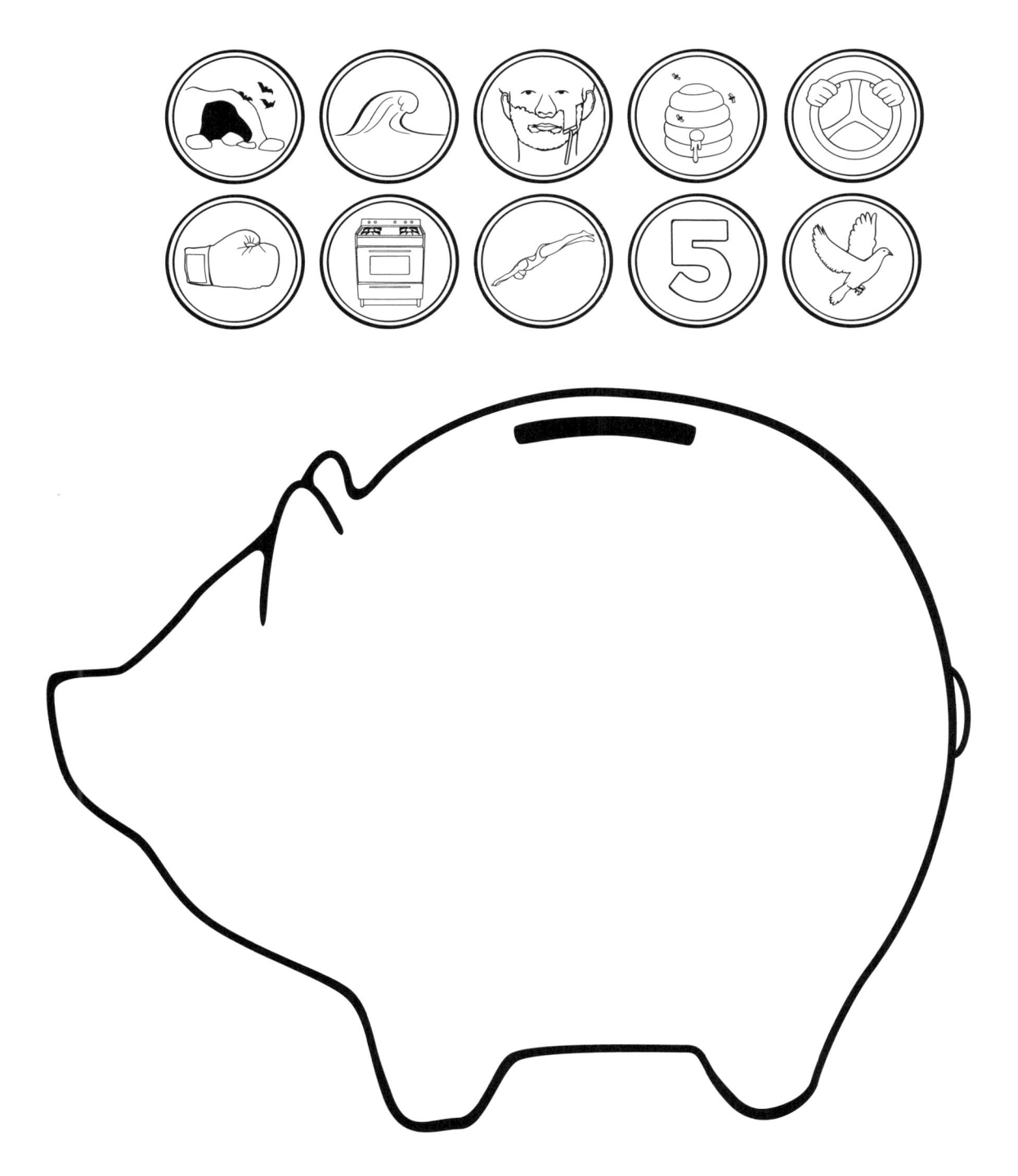

Chapter 8
Targeting W & H

- Screening Tool
- Teaching Tips
- Production Illustrations
- Target Lists
- Book Lists
- Activities
- Pictures
- Patterns
- Homework Pages

W & H Screening

Student Name_____ Date of Birth_____

Screening Date_____ Examiner_____

Use "+" or "—" to indicate the child's production of the phoneme at each level (in isolation, in a word, |in a phrase, and in a sentence). Use imitation, delayed imitation, or pictures to elicit the child's productions.

Target–/w/	Target–/h/
SOUND IN ISOLATION: /w/	**SOUND IN ISOLATION:** /h/
one	house
number one	my house
I have one sister and two brothers.	My house is white and brown.
web	hat
spider web	funny hat
The spider made a web.	The clown dropped the hat in the mud.
wet	hen
all wet	mother hen
The dog is all wet from the rain.	The hen sat on a pile of eggs.

DATA COLLECTION/SCREENING NOTES:

W & H Teaching Tips

Development Information

Both /w/ and /h/ begin to develop early. Children will start to use both of these sounds as early as 12 months of age. Mastery of /w/ and /h/ occurs for most children between 2 and 3 years of age (Sander, 1972). The open airway makes these two sounds easy to produce, thus early development is possible. Furthermore, /w/ is a visual sound and adds to it's salience.

Production of /w/ and /h/

Both /w/ and /h/ are made on a continuous stream of air and with a relatively open airway. However, /w/ is a *bilabial* sound as both lips come together in a gentle manner to shape the airstream. For /h/, the glottis gently shapes the resonance of the airstream at the back of the pharynx. Both sounds are voiced, thus the vocal folds are set into motion during production. For /w/, the teeth are held slightly apart and the velum is lifted to block air from escaping through the nasal cavity, thus allowing the resonating airstream to come only out of the mouth.

Stimulating Production of /w/ and /h/

For children who struggle to produce /w/ and /h/, some work with the sound in isolation may be warranted. The following strategies may be useful when encouraging accurate production during treatment activities:

- Use the illustrations on page 226 to provide additional instruction for placement of /w/ and /h/. As needed, keep these images displayed during practice with these target sounds.
- Use an age-appropriate description of the processes for producing these.
- Sit side-by-side with the child in front of a mirror. Encourage the child to watch as you open your lips slightly and produce /h/ and/or /w/. Direct the child to imitate your productions of /w/ and /h/.
- For production of /w/, consider allowing the child to apply a small amount of flavored lip balm as a reinforcer to encourage pressing of the lips together.
- Use a tissue, cottonball, or small cracker placed on a flat surface. Have the child watch you release a burst of air to produce /w/ or /h/ and make the item move across the surface. Encourage the child to match your model.
- To encourage voicing, direct the child to apply light fingertip pressure to his/her throat or your throat as the /w/ and /h/ contrasts are produced. Talking about "turning on" the voice to make the buzzing associated with both sounds.

Chapter 9 – W & H

W & H Production Illustrations

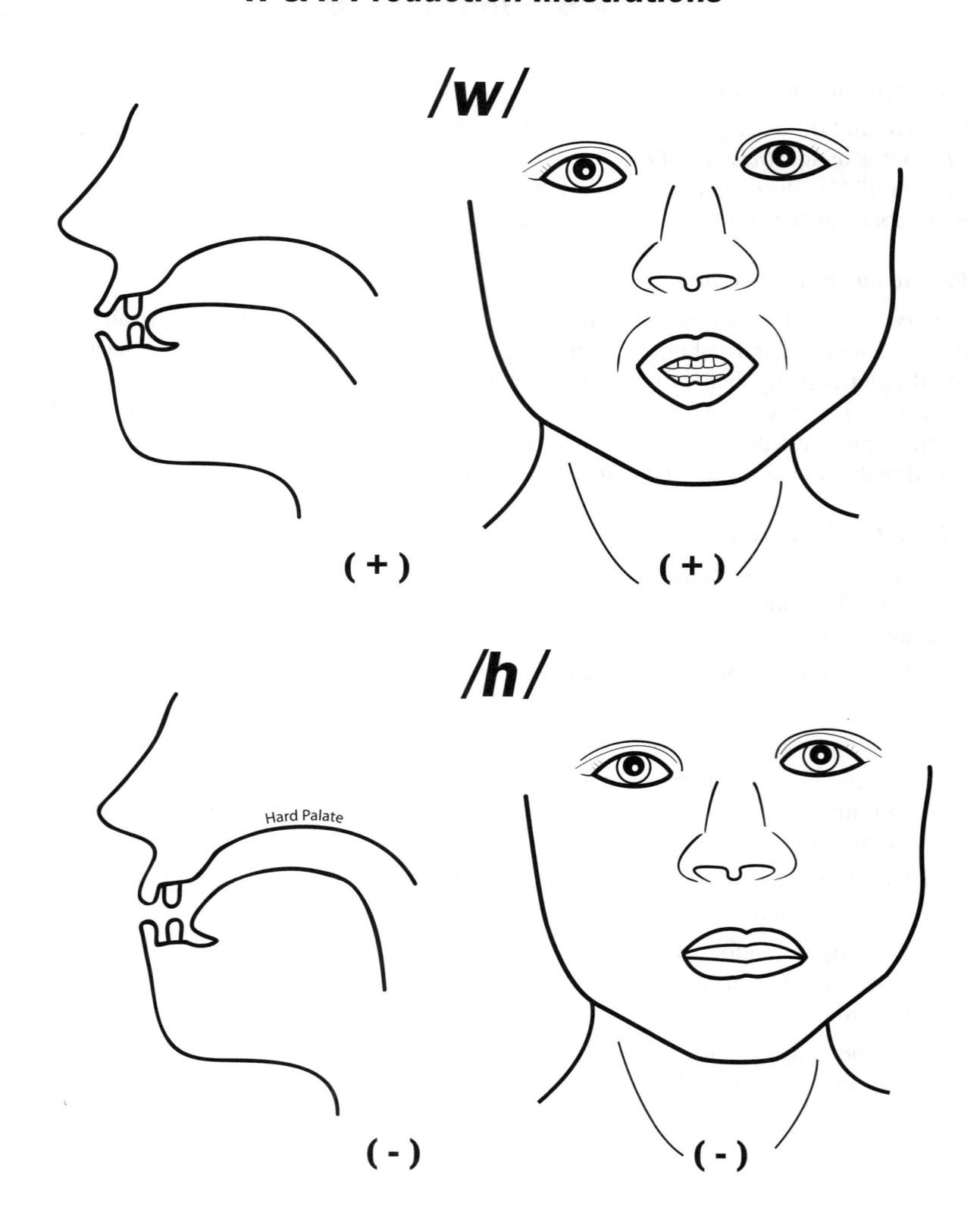

/w/

(+)　　　(+)

/h/

Hard Palate

(-)　　　(-)

226　The Entire World of Early Developing Sounds Instructional Workbook™　　© 2008 Say It Right™　www.sayitright.org

W & H Target Lists

Especially during early stages of practice, single-syllable words are most facilitative for accurate productions of target sounds. Consider the surrounding consonant and vowel sounds in a target word to control for other sounds the child may be lacking. For example, when first targeting initial /w/ with a child, avoid words that also contain medial and/or final /w/. Gradually, as a child becomes more successful with practice of a selected sound, words of increasing length and complexity can be added to the production-practice activities.

The Entire World of Early Developing Sounds™ suggests using the target words listed for the early stages of practice with young children working on /w/ and /h/. Pages 236-239 provide representations of these words in picture form for use with production practice activities. Suggested target phrases and sentences are also provided. Phrases and sentences are most useful with older children who can read. *The Entire World of W, H & L Articulation Flip Book* (Ristuccia, 2007) is an excellent source for illustrated, interactive phrase and sentence practice.

When working with older children, the word, phrase, and sentence lists may be useful as stimulus items in mass production practice. If using the phrases and sentences with nonreaders, direct or delayed imitation will be necessary (i.e., saying the phrase or sentence as a model and then having the child repeat it with or without a delay). Ideally, production of phrases and sentences will be elicited naturally during structured and unstructured activities, thus it is possible that the phrase and sentence lists would not need to be used with younger children.

To target medial /w/ and /h/, use the target words in combination with another word (e.g., "spider-web" to elicit medial /w/ or "doghouse" for medial /h/). Medial /w/ and /h/ target words can be added once a child is ready for practice with multisyllabic words. As medial /w/ and /h/ words are selected, continue to control for facilitative contexts to ensure children successfully produce the new sound. In addition, use multisyllabic words that are meaningful to the child (e.g., *washing machine, webkin,* etc.).

Chapter 9 – W & H

W & H Single Word Practice

Word–Initial /w/	Word–Initial /h/
one	hat
walk	he
wall	head
wash	hen
wave	hide
web	high
well	hike
wet	home
whale	hook
wig	hop
win	hot
wood	house

W & H Phrase-Level Practice

Word–Initial /w/	Word–Initial /h/
one time	big blue **hat**
a long **walk**	**he** is sad
over the **wall**	my **head**
wash the clothes	mother **hen**
wave hands	go **hide**
a spider's **web**	up **high**
a deep **well**	**hike** down the path
wet dog	our **home**
the big **whale**	sharp **hook**
a clown's **wig**	bunny **hop**
win a ribbon	**hot** pepper
paint the **wood**	the blue **house**

Chapter 9 – W & H

W & H Sentence-Level Practice

Word–Initial /w/	Word–Initial /h/
I need **one** more apple.	She wore a new **hat**.
Let's go for a **walk**.	**He** is going to read the book.
The **wall** is painted.	The dog's **head** is big.
He needs to **wash** the clothes.	The **hen** laid an egg.
The girl can **wave**.	They played **hide** and seek.
The spider spins a **web**.	The kite flies **high** in the sky.
The **well** is deep.	She will **hike** up the mountain.
She got **wet** in the pool.	It is time to go **home**.
The **whale** swam in the ocean.	It is a sharp **hook**.
The clown has a colorful **wig**.	The frog will **hop** over the log.
She is going to **win** the race.	The cookies are **hot**.
The **wood** is in the workshop.	The boy's **house** is big.

W & H Book List

Reading a story is a natural and motivating activity for children. Children's stories are filled with opportunities to bombard the child with words containing the target sound and to elicit productions of the target. Consult the following list to select books that contain multiple opportunities for words that contain /w/ or /h/.

	INITIAL /w/		
TITLE	PUBLICATION INFORMATION	INTEREST LEVEL	TARGET WORDS
I Went Walking	Sue Williams (1996) Red Wagon Books	2-5 years	went, walking, what
Who Says Woof?	John Butler (2003) Viking Books	2-5 years	woof
Who Wants One?	Mary Serfozo (1989) Margaret K. McElderry	4-8 years	wants, won't want, whale
Wheels!	Annie Cobb (1996) Random House Books	4-8 years	wheels, wheel, wide, were, would
Wait, Skates!	Mildred D. Johnson (2000) Children's Press	4-8 years	wait
Wake Up, Wake Up!	Brian Wildsmith (1993) Harcourt	2-4 years	wake
Wave Hello to Thomas!	W. Rev Awdry (1993) Random House	2-6 years	wave
The Wheels on the Bus	Paul D. Zelinsky (1990) Dutton Children's Books	2-7 years	wheels, wipers, wah

Chapter 9 – W & H

	INITIAL /h/		
TITLE	PUBLICATION INFORMATION	INTEREST LEVEL	TARGET WORDS
Happy Hiding Hippos	Bobette McCarty (1994) Simon and Schuster	2-5 years	happy, hiding, hippos, herd, home, hats, hide
Hot-Air Henry	Mary Calhoun (1984) Harper Trophy	2-4 years	hot, Henry, hopped, happy, hill, honk, hear
Harriet's Horrible Hair Day	Dawn Lesley Stewart (2000) Peachtree Publishers	4-8 years	Harriet, horrible, hair, head, hat, how
Harold and Chester in Hot Fudge	James Howe and Leslie Morrill (1990) William Morrow	4-8 years	Harold, hot
A House Is a House for Me	Mary Ann Hoberman (1999) Sagebrush	3-8 years	house, home, how, have, head, hat, hum, ham, hand, hut, hangar, hippos, hutches, hill, hive, hole
Hippo-NOT-amus	Tony and Jan Payne (2005) Scholastic	4-8 years	hippo, he, home
Goldfish Hide and Seek	Satoshi Kitamura (2000) Random House	2-5 years	hide

W & H Activity Pages

Regardless of your approach to treatment, a variety of activities should be used to bombard children with correct productions of the target sound and to elicit production practice. The activities in this unit include a range of sound-specific options for /w/ and /h/. They are designed to appeal to children between the ages of 2 and 7.

In addition, remember the following are available to support your teaching of the /w/ and /h/ sounds:

- **More Activity Ideas** that can be used to target any sound are included in Appendix A.
- Sound-specific **Pictures** to be used with activities are found on pages 236-239.
- A **Blank Card Pattern**, to include your own words, is found in Appendix D.
- **Book List**s for selecting stories on page 231-232.
- **Word, Phrase,** and **Sentence Lists** are provided on pages 227-230, to use with activities or with more traditional boards games (e.g., Sorry!, Uno, and Kerplunk). To earn a turn, have the older student read or repeat words, phrases, or sentences containing the selected target phoneme. The goal is to encourage as many repetitions of the target sound as possible—be creative!
- **Homework Pages** (pages 242-245) provide activities that can be easily used by parents or other care providers to encourage successful practice in other settings. Be certain to direct children to return completed Homework Pages so you can encourage self-evaluation and monitoring of their practice. Consider having students carry a "speech folder" to store these materials and facilitate communication with others on a regular basis.
- Appendix B provides a **Parent Memo** that can be used along with selected homework activity pages.
- Appendix E includes a blank **Lesson Plan**. Use the form to ensure that all essential lesson plan components are accounted for within each session. Be certain to probe for accuracy, provide instruction/bombardment for the target sounds, and plan for a sufficient amount of successful mass production practice.
- Appendix F provides a blank **Data Collection Form** to monitor progress and adjust treatment.
- Don't forget that **Suggestions for Conversation and Carryover** are provided in Appendix B. Plan for generalization from the start and incorporate these suggestions along the way.

Chapter 9 – W & H

Initial W Activities

Snack Ideas
- Watermelon, waffles, wheat crackers
- Water, watermelon-flavored Kool-Aid

Craft
- Wishing Wells—Collect one small milk carton for each child prior to this activity. Cut a small opening on one side of each carton to give the appearance of a well. Leave the top and bottom of the carton intact. Give the children pre-cut brown or red construction paper to glue onto the remaining three sides of the well (small rocks glued to the sides also works). Have the child name three wishes. Write them down on small strips of paper, and have each child put the wishes into the well.

Motor and Movement
- Wishing Wand—Pick one child to hold a "wishing wand," while the other children dance to music. Play music for several seconds and then turn it off. When the music stops, the child holding the wand waves it over the head of a dancer and asks him or her to make a wish. Continue the process until each child has had a chance to wave the wand.

Songs and Finger Play

Wiggle Fingers
Wiggle finger, wiggle go [wiggle fingers]
Wiggle high [raise hands high, wiggle fingers]
Wiggle low [lower hands and wiggle finger]
Wiggle left [wiggle fingers to the left]
Wiggle right [wiggle fingers to the right]
Wiggle fingers out of sight [wiggle fingers behind back].

Wishing Well

Materials
- Initial /w/ book
- Large pail or basket
- Word-initial /w/ pictures, pages 236
- Paper clips

Procedure

1. Bombard the child with word-initial /w/ by introducing the sound using a story selected from the book list on page 231.

2. Duplicate the set of word-initial /w/ pictures and cut them apart. Attach a large paper clip to each picture for weight and place the pictures in the large pail or basket.

3. Have children circle the large container—the wishing well. Tell the children to take turns "pulling wishes out of the well." Bombard them with the phrase, "What is your wish?" and have them respond by naming the picture they pull out.

4. Have children listen as you bombard them with initial /w/ words like "wish," "want," "well," and "wishing." Also bombard them with phrases and sentences, such as "Wow! That is a great wish!" Have them repeat the phrases and sentences if appropriate for the child.

H Activity Pages

Initial H Activities

Whose Hat?

Materials
- Initial /h/ book
- Hats and Occupations Patterns, page 240 and 241
- Scissors
- Glue or tape
- Markers or crayons

Procedure
1. Bombard the child with word-initial /h/ by introducing the sound with a story selected from the book list on page 232.
2. Duplicate one Hats and Occupations Pattern for each child. Color each hat. Cut the patterns out.
3. Give each child a person relating to an occupation. Hold up a hat and ask, "Whose hat is this?" Encourage the children to find who it belongs to by matching the hat to the occupation.
4. Bombard the children with the words "whose" and "hat" as she determines who the hats belongs to. Elicit productions based on each child's skill level.

Snack Ideas
- Create a hat snack with round crackers and peanut butter or icing. Add a Hershey's Kiss to the top to form a hat.
- Hot chocolate

Craft
- Paper Hats—Duplicate one Create-a-Hat Pattern (page 242) for each child. Decorate the hats and have a hat parade to display the hat each child created.

Motor and Movement
- Pass the Hat—Have children sit in a circle. Explain that you will play music and pass a hat around the circle. When the music stops, the child holding the hat can put it on and say, "I have the hat" or "hat."
- Hide the Hat—Show the children a hat that you will be hiding. Have them close their eyes while you hide the hat. Have the children look for the hat while you say, "The hat is hiding." Give clues such as, "You're getting hot" or "You're cold" depending on how close or far away they are from the hiding place.

Songs and Finger Play

My Hat

*My **hat**, it has three corners,*
*Three corners has my **hat***
*And **had** it not three corners,*
*It would not be my **hat**.*

Initial W Picture Cards

one	walk
wall	wash
wave	web

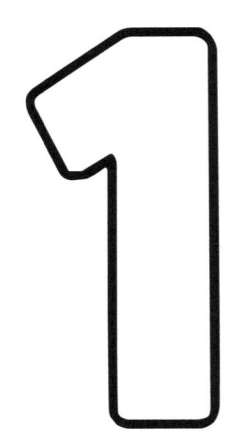

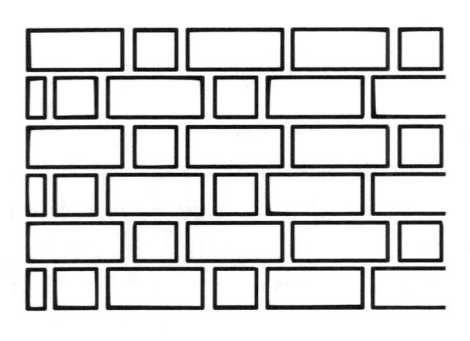

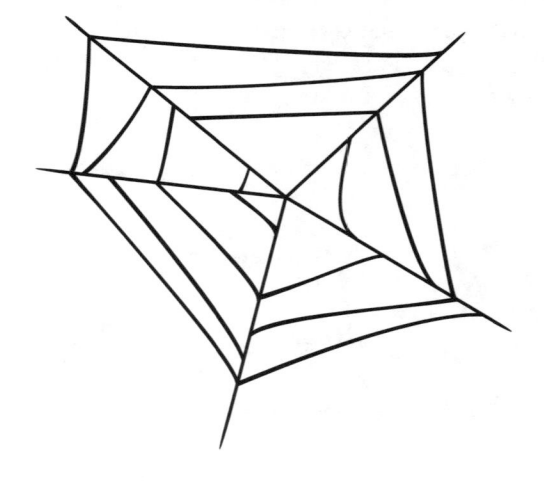

236 The Entire World of Early Developing Sounds Instructional Workbook™ © 2008 Say It Right™ www.sayitright.org

Initial W Picture Cards

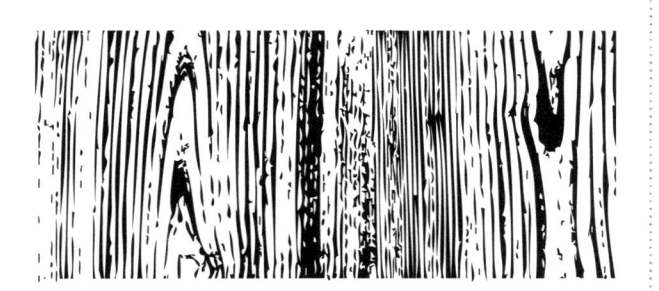

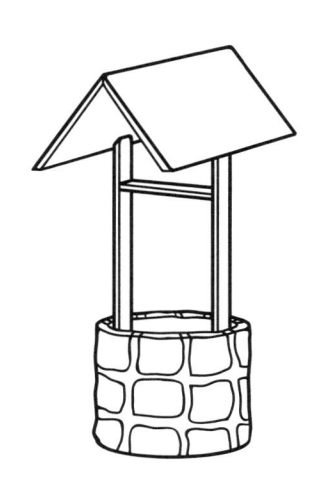

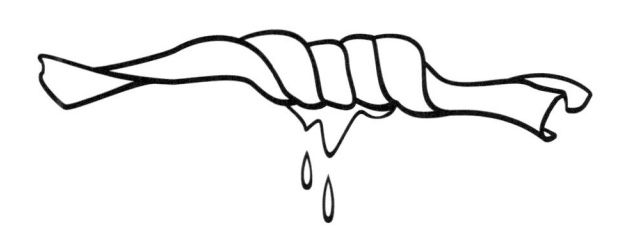

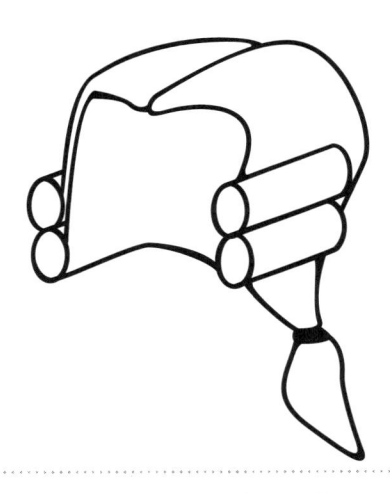

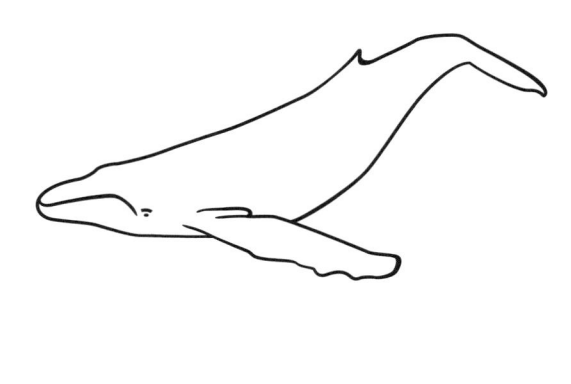

wood	well
wet	wig
win	whale

237

Initial H Picture Cards

hat

head

hen

hide

he

hill

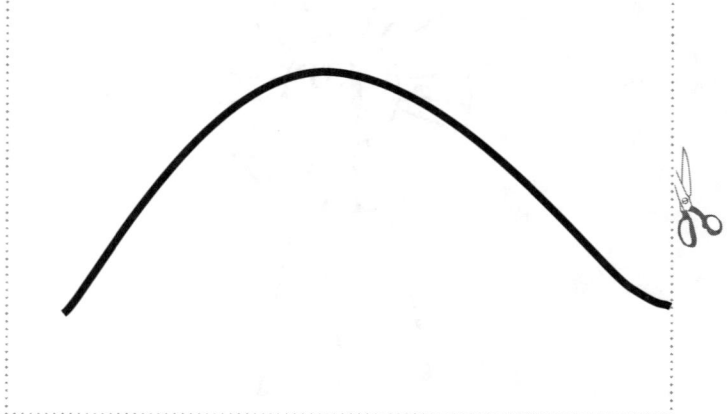

238 The Entire World of Early Developing Sounds Instructional Workbook™

© 2008 Say It Right™ www.sayitright.org

Initial H Picture Cards

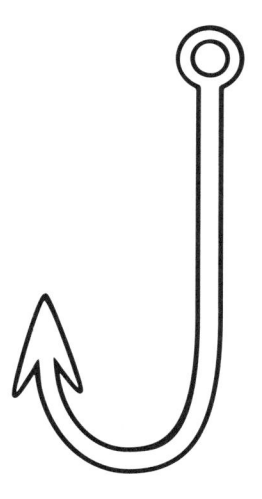

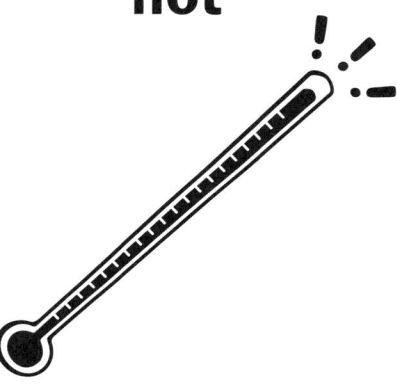

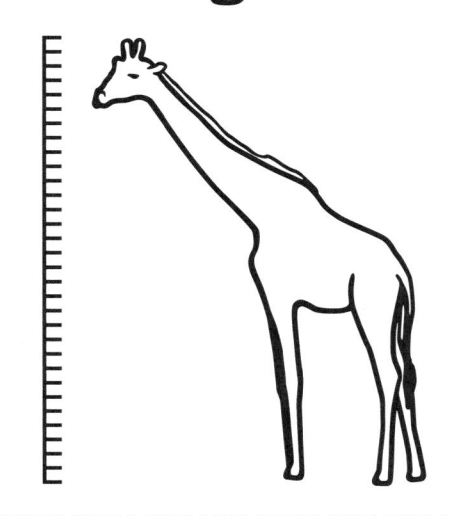

hook	hop
hot	house
high	hawk

Chapter 9 – W & H

Hats Pattern

240   The Entire World of Early Developing Sounds Instructional Workbook™   © 2008 Say It Right™   www.sayitright.org

H Activity Patterns

Occupations Pattern

Chapter 9 – W & H

Create-a-Hat Pattern

Cut out along dotted lines all the way to the edge. Color in curved front headpiece. Attach back band with tape or staples. Adjust to size.

W Homework

W—Wall

Child: Name each picture on the wall. If you've used a good "W" sound, color in the brick on the wall.

Helper: If your child says the "W" sound correctly in the word, make up a phrase or sentence using the word and have your child repeat it.

Chapter 9 – W & H

Wagon Wheel

Child: Cut out the four pictures. Name each picture and then stick it on the wagon wheel.

Helper: Emphasize correct production of the "W" sound at the beginning of the words. Then make up a phrase or sentence using the pictures and the words "wagon wheel." Have your child repeat it.

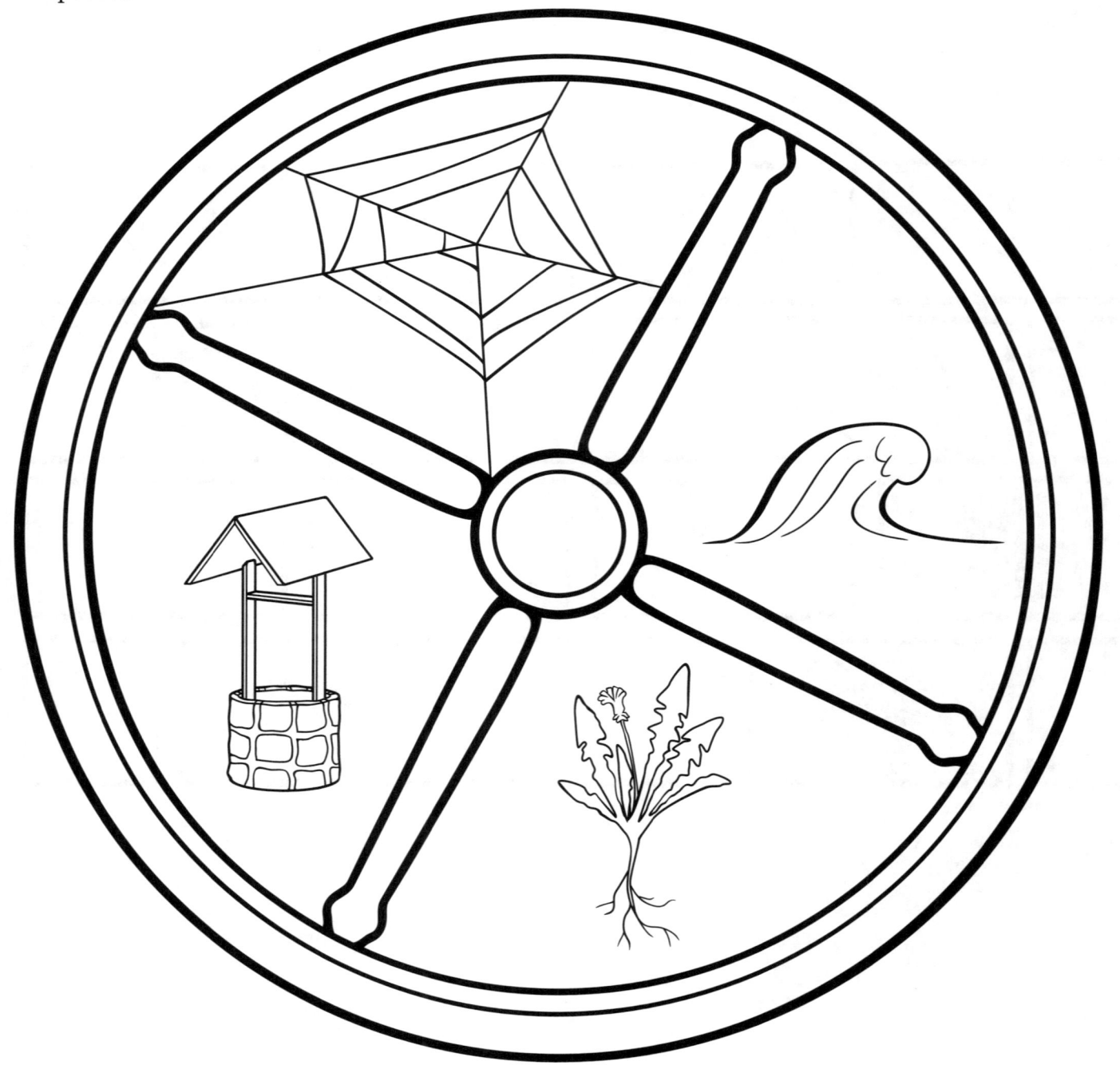

H Homework

Hold It in Your Hand

Child: Cut out the pictures then name each one. Place each picture on the hand and say, I have (a) ____ in the hand.

Helper: Emphasize the "H" sound at the beginning of the words. Help your child say the sentence.

Chapter 9 – W & H

Whose House?

Child: Who belongs in which house? Draw a line from the house to the person or animal that lives there. Before drawing the line, say, "Who's house?" Then, answer the question with: "It's the _____'s house."

Helper: Emphasize production of the "H" sound at the beginning of the words.

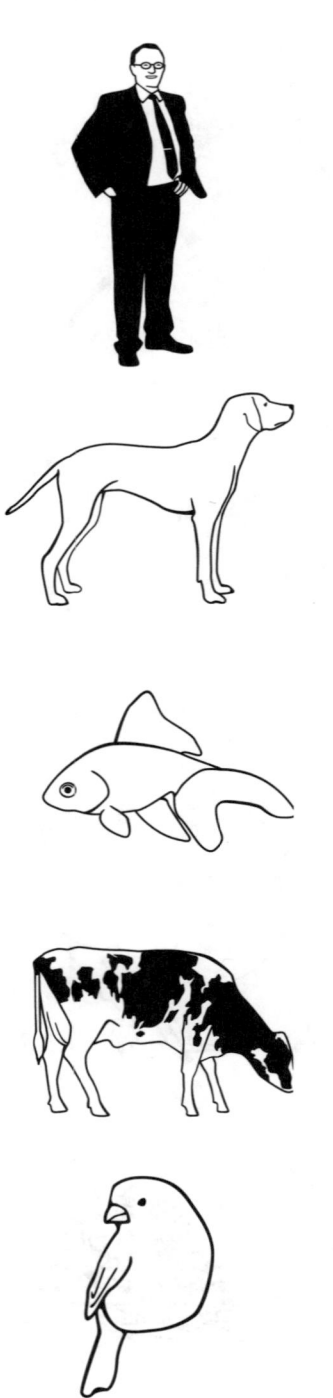

246 The Entire World of Early Developing Sounds Instructional Workbook™ © 2008 Say It Right™ www.sayitright.org

Appendix

Appendix A: General Activity Ideas

Appendix B: Parent Memo

Appendix C: Suggestions for Conversation and Carryover

Appendix D: Blank Card Pattern

Appendix E: Lesson Plan Format

Appendix F: Data Collection Form

Appendix A

General Activity Ideas

▸ *Flashlight Game*
Select pictures for a specific target sound and attach them to locations and items around the room. Have the child find and name the pictures by shining the flashlight on each one. This can be done with or without the lights on, depending on the child's comfort level. As each item is found, bombard the child with the word and/or encourage the child's accurate productions of the words or phrases (e.g., for "pig," "I found a pig").

▸ *Hallway Hunt*
Select pictures for a specific target sound and attach them throughout the hallway or child's home. Provide the child with a fun container to collect pictures in (e.g., a "pail" when working on initial /p/ or a "bag" if working on initial /b/). As items are located, bombard the child with the word (e.g., for "pen," "Look! A pen. Put the pen in the pail"). Encourage the child's accurate productions of the words and phrases.

▸ *Laundry Line*
String a length of yarn or light rope between two chairs or across the room. Have a small laundry basket or laundry bag filled with items such as socks, T-shirts, and shorts, but also include a set of target word picture cards among the clothing. Provide a set of clothespins in a small container. Encourage the child to select items from the bag and hang them on the line. As target words are selected, help the child produce the words.

▸ *Mail Time*
Use a decorated box or image on a poster board with slits to represent a mailbox. Select pictures (or use picture cards) for the target sound. As the child practices productions of the targets, allow him or her to place the cards into envelopes and send them through the mail slot.

▸ *Surprise Bucket*
Place a covering with a hole over the top of a bucket or box. Place selected pictures or objects for a specific target sound in the bucket. Encourage the child to reach into the bucket, remove cards, and practice his or her production of the targets.

▸ *Bean Bag Toss*
Set selected target word cards in a tic-tac-toe grid pattern on the floor. Encourage the child to toss a beanbag toward the cards. Bombard the child with the target sound, for example for /b/, "The bean bag bopped onto the ball." Encourage the child's accurate productions of the target words.

Appendix A

▸ *Magnetic Darts*
Attach target word cards to a magnetic cookie sheet, chalkboard, or dry erase board. Have the child toss a magnetic dart at the picture cards. Facilitate the child's productions of the target words as he or she tells or talks about the picture hit with the dart. (Note: Inexpensive magnetic darts can be found in the toy section of dollar stores and discount chains.)

▸ *Memory Match*
Select and duplicate a matched set of target word pictures. Use the cards in a traditional game of "Concentration" to make matches. Use only six or eight cards at a time for children under 3 years of age.

▸ *Go Fish*
Select and duplicate a matched set of target word pictures. Use the cards in a traditional game of "Go Fish" to collect matches by asking, "Do you have…?" Use only six or eight cards at a time for children under 3 years of age.

▸ *Fishing*
Create a simple fishing pole by attaching a two-foot length of string to a three-foot dowel. Attach a magnet or paperclip to the end of the fishing line. Select pictures of target words and attach a paperclip to each. Spread the picture cards, facedown, on the floor. Sit the child in a chair ("the boat") near the pictures. Allow the child to "fish" for the cards. As each fish is snagged, bombard the child with the target words and/or encourage the child's accurate productions.

▸ *Roll a Sound*
Create a large die using a cardboard cube. Attach selected target word cards to each side of the die. Have the child roll the die across the table or floor and practice productions of the target words. For a twist, create two dice and see if the child can get a match.

▸ *Rice/Bean Bucket*
Select target word pictures or objects containing the target sound and hide them in a medium-sized tub filled with dry, uncooked, rice or beans. As target words are revealed, encourage the child to name each.

▸ *ZAP!*
Select target words. Purchase 50 or more small craft sticks. On one end of 10 of the sticks, write the word "ZAP!" with a permanent marker. On the other sticks, write random "point value" numbers (such as 25, 50, 10, etc.). Determine a winning amount of points (e.g., 100) before starting play. Each child takes a turn producing the target words singly or in phrases or phrase, or sentences; then chooses a stick. Each child collects the sticks as "practice points." Each time a child pulls a "ZAP!" stick, the "practice points" should be returned to the collection. The winner is the player obtaining the predetermined number of points.

Appendix B

Parent Memo

To: Parents or guardians of _____

Subject: **Speech Homework**

Attached you will find practice activities that can be completed at home with your child. Additional support at home will encourage your child's use of newly learned speech skills in new situations. This can increase gains and the rate of change.

Most recently we have been working on _____

_____

_____

Follow the directions provided for each home activity page. Keep the activity low-pressure to encourage use of the newly learned skills. When your child is producing the target words successfully, use the activities to encourage lots of accurate practice. If your child is struggling to use the sound correctly, provide a model and have him or her try again. Additional specific tips and suggestions for work with your child includes: _____

_____

_____

_____

Please have your child return the homework on _____. If you have any questions, please contact me at _____.

Sincerely,

_____

Your Child's Speech-Language Pathologist

Appendix C

Suggestions for Conversation and Carryover

Since generalization into conversational speech is the ultimate goal of remediation, conversational-level practice to encourage carryover of the new sound is critical. Ertmer and Ertmer (1998) provide a framework for facilitating carryover when providing phonological intervention to children. The diagram below illustrates this plan.

- Increase motivation level
- Increase understanding of barriers to carryover
- Increase awareness of resources/aids for carryover
- develop strategies
- Increase self-monitoring using rehearsal
- Increase self-evaluation
- Revisit goals

Source: Ertmer & Ertmer (1998)

From this framework, develop specific plans and strategies for ensuring generalization. Consider the following suggestions. While these strategies are most applicable to children over five years of age, there is something for young children too.

1. Use **authentic targets** and tasks during structured intervention time. Include target words from the child's home and school activities during practice activities. For example, for a preschool child working on generalization of /p/ and /b/, talk about fruits and vegetables containing initial /p/ and /b/ words (peach, pear, plum, pea, pumpkin, broccoli, beans, etc.). Talk explicitly about how these words start with the "special practice sounds." Consider incorporating this work with a vocabulary classification activity where the child sorts /p/

Appendix C

and /b/ words based on food groups. For an older child, use science and social studies vocabulary terms for speech practice. Obtain access to the child's classroom resources to select target words to use during treatment activities. For children of all ages, use classic stories, jokes, word games, and commercially available games that contain representations of the target sound(s). Draw explicit and frequent attention to correct and incorrect productions of the target sound(s) while using these authentic materials.

2. Keep attention to a ***child's motivation*** for carryover. Make subtle adjustments to services to heighten a child's level of motivation for improved speech. For example, use authentic and age-appropriate verbal praise to draw the child's attention to his or her improved or "new way" of making target sounds. Work with a child to keep a list of words that he or she has successfully carried over into conversation. As children watch this list grow, motivation and satisfaction can grow too.

3. Talk periodically with children regarding ***barriers to carryover***. Identify variables such as level of excitement, rate of speech, talking partners, level of fatigue, etc. that affect accurate use of target sounds. Consider having an older child start a "speech journal" where he or she is encouraged to reflect on carryover of targets on a regular basis.

4. Work with children to ***develop strategies to trigger their memory*** for using targets outside of the speech sessions and/or in conversational contexts. Role-play scenarios to practice selected strategies for real-world situations. Strategies should be based on a specific understanding of each individual child. Examples include, but are not limited to:

   - Have the child decorate and wear a "Speech Bracelet" that serves as a reminder for accurate use of a "special sound." Inexpensive materials for creating "speech bracelets" can be found at local craft supply shops.

   - Direct the child to invent and illustrate a "Superhero for Super Speech." Name the character and decide that the new superhero will be a reminder for correct use of speech sounds. Encourage the child to visualize the superhero during speaking situations.

5. Make the intervention room ***variables as similar to the real-world*** as possible to heighten carryover. Allow children to bring "non-speech" friends to sessions to practice skills at a conversational level. Furthermore, use materials and stimulus items from the home and classroom environments.

Appendix D Blank Card Pattern

Appendix E - Lesson Plan Format

Lesson Plan

Name _____ Date _____

Target Pattern/Sound _____

Component	Activity/Procedure/Materials
Introduction (Greeting • Warm-Up • Probe)	
Instructional Strategies	
Production-Practice Activities	❶ ❷ ❸
Closure (Data Probe • Review • Foreshadow)	

Appendix F - Data Collection Form

Data Collection Form

Practice Level →				

Children's Names and Date

References

American Speech-Language-Hearing Association. (2008). *Website information related to terminology*. Retrieved 5/1/08 from http://www.asha.org/public/speech/disorders/SpeechSoundDisorders.htm

Bankson, N., & Byrne, M. (1972). The effect of a timed correct sound production task on carryover. *Journal of Speech and Hearing Research, 15,* 160-168.

Broen, P., Doyle, S., & Bacon, C. (1993). The velopharyngeally inadequate child: Phonologic change with intervention. *Cleft Palate-Craniofacial Journal, 30,* 500-507.

Coplan, J., & Gleason, J.R. (1988). Unclear speech: Recognition and significance of unintelligible speech in preschool children. *Pediatrics, 82,* 447-452.

Eimas, P., Siqueland, E., Jusczyk, P., & Vigorito, J. (1971). Speech perception in infants. *Science, 171,* 303-306.

Elbert, M., Dinnsen, D., & Powell, T. (1984). On the prediction of phonologic generalization learning patterns. *Journal of Speech and Hearing Disorders, 49,* 309-317.

Ertmer, D., & Ertmer, P. (1998). Constructivist strategies in phonological intervention: Facilitating self-regulation for carryover. *Language, Speech, and Hearing Services in Schools, 29,* 67-75.

Fairbanks, G. (1960). *Voice and articulation drillbook* (2nd ed.). New York: Harper Brothers.

Gierut, J. (1989). Maximal opposition approach to phonological treatment. *Journal of Speech and Hearing Disorders, 54,* 9-19.

Grunwell, P. (1987). *Clinical phonology*. Gaithersburg, MD: Aspen.

Hodson, B. (2007). *Evaluating and enhancing children's phonological systems*. Eau Claire, WI: Thinking Publications.

Hodson, B. (1997). Disordered phonologies: What have we learned about assessment and treatment? In B. Hodson & M. Edwards (Eds.), *Perspectives in applied phonology* (pp. 197-224). Gaithersburg, MD: Aspen.

Hoffman, P. (1992). Synergistic development of phonetic skill. *Language, Speech, and Hearing Services in Schools, 23,* 254-260.

References

Kent, R. (1982). Contextual facilitation of correct sound production. *Language, Speech, and Hearing Services in Schools, 13*, 66-76.

McReynolds, L. (1987). A perspective on articulation generalization. *Seminars in Speech and Hearing, 8*, 217-239.

Montgomery, J. (1992, February). Books, books, books. *Clinically Speaking, 9* (1), 1-2.

Norris, J., & Hoffman, P. (1993). *Whole language intervention for school-age children.* San Diego, CA: Singular.

Ristuccia, C. L. (2007) *The entire world of early developing sounds articulation flip books.* Tybee Island, GA: Say It Right.

Rvachew, S., Rafaat, S., & Martin, M. (1999). Stimulability, speech perception skills, and the treatment of phonological disorders. *American Journal of Speech-Language Pathology, 8*, 33-43.

Sander, E. (1972). Do we know when speech sounds are learned? *Journal of Speech and Hearing Disorders, 37*, 55-63.

Shelton, R., Johnson, A., & Arndt, W. (1972). Monitoring and reinforcement by parents as a means of automating articulatory responses. *Perceptual and Motor Skills, 35*, 759-767.

Shriberg, L., & Kwiatkowski, J. (1990). Self-monitoring and generalization in preschool speech-delayed children. *Language, Speech, and Hearing Services in Schools, 21*, 157-169.

Stoel-Gammon, C., & Dunn, C. (1985). *Normal and disordered phonology in children.* Austin, TX: Pro-Ed.

Van Riper, C. (1939). *Speech correction: Principles and methods.* Englewood Cliffs, NJ: Prentice Hall.

Watson, M., Murthy, S.N. Jayaram, and Wadhwa, N. (2003). *Phonological analysis practice* [Software]. Eau Claire, WI: Thinking Publications.

Williams, A.L. (2003). *Speech disorders resource guide for preschool children.* Clifton, NY: Delmar Thomson Learning.

Flip Then Say™
Articulation Flip Books

Common articulation error sounds [S, Z, SH, CH, J, ZH, K, G, TH, F and V] are found in four colorful change-a-story flipbooks in the set. Each book contains three "flip-able" panels that allow students to change one or all three sections of amusing and fun sentence stories. Each panel is divided and color-coded by sound and word position (initial, medial, final) for quick and easy identification.

You'll love the convenience, ease of use, and versatility for receptive and expressive language practice. Your students will love practicing their sounds as they make endless sentence story combinations— over 200,000!

Set contains four flip books and a convenient carry-bag. Each book is also available for individual purchase. Ages 4 and up.

EWS-005	Flip Then Say™ Articulation Flip Book Set	$79.99
EWS-006	The Entire World of S & Z Flip Book (41 pages)	$25.00
EWS-007	The Entire World of SH & CH Flip Book (43 pages)	$25.00
EWS-008	The Entire World of K & G Flip Book (28 pages)	$25.00
EWS-009	The Entire World of TH, F & V Flip Book (36 pages)	$25.00

Never run out of practice sentences. Over 200,000 sentence combinations!

Educational Classroom Book of the Year

Early Developing Sounds Articulation Flip Books

Over 250,000 possible sentence story combinations!

All the common early developing sounds: [P & B], [T & D], [W, H & L], [M & N], and [R, S & L] Blends are covered in this adorable set of five flip books.

Each book contains three "flip-able" panels that allow students to change one or all three sections of amusing and fun sentence stories. Each panel is divided and color-coded by sound and word position (initial, medial, final) for quick and easy identification.

All sentence stories, designed for younger, non-reading children, show colorful yet concise concepts to practice. Over 250,000 sentence story combinations possible in all!

Set contains five flip books and a convenient carry-bag. Each book is also available for individual purchase. Ages 3 and up.

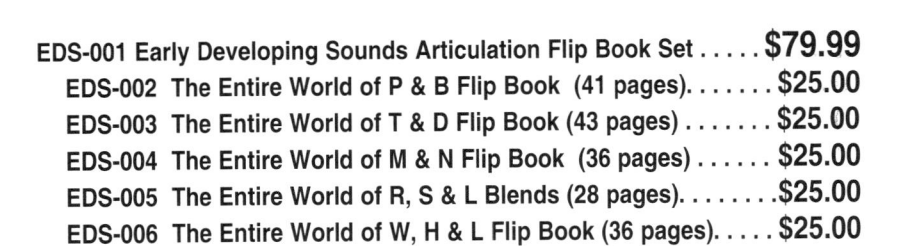

Award Winner — Creative Child Magazine 2007 Book of the Year Award — Flip Book for Kids

The rabbit   flew a kite   by the hotel.
                              by the corvette.

EDS-001	Early Developing Sounds Articulation Flip Book Set	$79.99
EDS-002	The Entire World of P & B Flip Book (41 pages)	$25.00
EDS-003	The Entire World of T & D Flip Book (43 pages)	$25.00
EDS-004	The Entire World of M & N Flip Book (36 pages)	$25.00
EDS-005	The Entire World of R, S & L Blends (28 pages)	$25.00
EDS-006	The Entire World of W, H & L Flip Book (36 pages)	$25.00

Ordering

How to Order

On-line
www.sayitright.org

FAX
912-480-4214

Phone
888-811-0759